Bhagavad Gita Essentials

Bhakti Marga's English translation of *Saṅskṛt* is based on *Śrīmad Bhagavad Gītā* with *Gītā-bhāṣya* of Bhagavad Rāmānujācārya, 2013, by U.Ve. Sri Rama Rāmānuja Achari. (Used and modified with permission.)

Publisher: Bhakti Marga Publications
English, Third Edition
ISBN: 978-3-96343-083-1

Bhakti Marga Publications
Am Geisberg, 1-8
65321, Heidenrod-Springen
Germany
publications@bhaktimarga.org
Bhaktimarga.org/publications

Bhagavad Gītā
Essentials

TABLE OF CONTENTS

Foreword 1
The Seeker's Journey 3
About Paramahamsa Vishwananda 5
About this Book 7
Introduction 9

Chapter One
Arjuna-viṣāda-yoga: The Lamentation of Arjuna 15

Chapter Two
Sāṅkhya-yoga: The Eternal Nature of the Soul 27

Chapter Three
Karma-yoga: Understanding Karma-yoga 43

Chapter Four
Jñāna-vibhāga-yoga: The Path of Knowledge 55

Chapter Five
Karma-sannyāsa-yoga: True Renunciation 69

Chapter Six
Dhyāna-yoga: Kṛṣṇa Describes Meditation 79

Chapter Seven
Jñāna-vijñāna-yoga: Knowledge of Kṛṣṇa 91

Chapter Eight
Akṣara-brahma-yoga: The Eternal Abode 101

Chapter Nine
Rāja-vidyā-guhya-yoga: The Secret of Devotion 111

Chapter Ten
Vibhūti-yoga: The Glories of Kṛṣṇa 125

Chapter Eleven
Viśvarūpa-darśana-yoga: The Cosmic Form 137

Chapter Twelve
Bhakti-yoga: The Yoga of Love 153

Chapter Thirteen
Kṣetra-kṣetrajña-yoga: Matter and Spirit 161

Chapter Fourteen
Guṇatraya-vibhāga-yoga: The Three Modes of Nature 173

Chapter Fifteen
Puruṣottama-yoga: Knowing the Supreme Person 181

Chapter Sixteen
Daivāsura-sampad-vibhāga-yoga:
The Divine and Demonic Qualities 189

Chapter Seventeen
Śraddhātraya-vibhāga-yoga: The Three Divisions of Faith 197

Chapter Eighteen
Mokṣa-sannyāsa-yoga: The Path to Liberation 209

List of Key Terms 231
References 239
Bibliography 243

FOREWORD

Thousands of years ago, in the middle of chaos, uncertainty, and fear on an enormous battlefield, supreme knowledge was given to humanity. We know it now as the *Bhagavad Gītā*.

The *Gītā* is a narrative between God and a conflicted warrior named Arjuna. The Supreme Lord, in the form of Kṛṣṇa, plays the humble role of a charioteer who masterfully instructs Arjuna about the profound mysteries of life.

The truth is, the world we are living in today is the same battlefield Arjuna found himself on. The only difference is that the battle each one of us faces is not on the outside, but on the inside.

In the face of these trials, we need a source of greater wisdom to help us overcome the devastating impact on our thinking, emotions and reactions. Fortunately for us, Kṛṣṇa's instructions have stood the test of time and provide the knowledge to help us triumph over the obstacles we face.

Paramahamsa Vishwananda's commentary on Kṛṣṇa's teachings opens up and applies the wisdom of the *Bhagavad Gītā* to our lives today. Ultimately, it helps us understand that we have a relationship with God, and that the goal of life is to become fully aware of that divine connection.

If we can integrate the teachings of the *Bhagavad Gītā* and Paramahamsa Vishwananda's commentary this way, we will begin a uniquely personal journey that takes us from the mind to the heart. And, despite the challenges along the way, it is the guidance of the *guru* that can help us to walk it with trust and courage.

--RC

THE SEEKER'S JOURNEY

There are some who think that life is totally random or must be explainable by science to be valid. There are others who sense there is something more, something with divine meaning and purpose. Ultimately however, everyone just wants to be loved and to experience lasting happiness.

To do this, most of us try to maximise pleasures and minimise discomforts through the material world. Many seek fulfilment in relationships or careers. Others turn to sex, drugs, food, shopping, or thrill-seeking to feel alive. The problem is, these desires naturally fuel a drive to accumulate more and more, attempting to fill the void felt inside.

Unfortunately, even the hard-earned happiness gained from these endeavours fades with time. Despite one's best efforts, the results often leave people feeling empty, disillusioned and even depressed. Others simply find themselves questioning if this is really all there is to life.

Realising that the empty promises of the material world cannot satisfy all their needs, many embark on a spiritual journey in search of the only source of real unconditional love: a relationship with God.

However, the spiritual path is by no means easy. Material desires can tempt us back into old unproductive patterns. Friends, books, movies, workshops, or religion don't always provide reliable answers, and even mystical experiences may not be enough to create lasting effects. Without a map, we can end up feeling lost and alone.

The *Bhagavad Gītā,* delivered by the Lord Himself, provides spiritual seekers with that map to the source of divinity itself, and, fortunately for us, this commentary by Paramahaṃsa Vishwananda helps us take each step along the way.

PARAMAHAMSA
SRI SWAMI VISHWANANDA

ABOUT PARAMAHAMSA VISHWANANDA

Paramahamsa Vishwananda carries the grace of two lineages which emphasise *bhakti*: loving devotion to God.

He is an *ācārya* in the Vaiṣṇava tradition, which promotes *bhakti* through ritual and service. He is also a *kriyā* Master and direct disciple of Mahāvatār Bābājī in the *kriyā-yoga* lineage. With the blessing of His *guru*, He introduced Atma Kriya Yoga which promotes *bhakti* through meditation.

Paramahamsa Vishwananda expertly weaves these two traditions together, one external and one internal, with the *bhakti* teachings of scriptures and the inspiration of *bhakti* saints to show everyone how to cultivate a uniquely personal, loving relationship with the Divine.

Since Paramahamsa Vishwananda is a *satguru* (one who can bring devotees to the level of God-realisation), the glory of God can be revealed through Him. Still, remaining humble and humorous, He makes the unfathomable, unknowable Lord not only real, but practical, tangible and personal. He brings the most profound and subtle truths down to earth, so that the same path that, traditionally, was pursued only by the few, is now accessible to all.

Dedicating His life to uplifting humanity, Paramahamsa Vishwananda's teachings can be found in His books, videos, spiritual practices, livestream *satsaṅgas* (spiritual Q&A), online *darśana* blessings, and His worldwide mission and organisation known as Bhakti Marga (the path of devotion).

paramahamsavishwananda.com

ABOUT THIS BOOK

It is rare when a book has the potential to become a lifelong spiritual companion. *Bhagavad Gītā Essentials* is designed to be just that: an essential part of your life. Small enough to carry with you wherever you go, yet profound enough to carry you all the way to God. It is succinct enough to read in a matter of hours, yet deep enough to contemplate for decades to come.

Bhagavad Gītā Essentials evolved out of two live discourses given by Paramahamsa Vishwananda: an 18-day course in 2014 and a 7-day course in 2016. The essence of these commentaries has been distilled to reveal the deeper meaning of this timeless scripture. All 701 *Saṅskṛt* verses of the *Bhagavad Gītā* are presented here along with translations that are infused with the beauty of *bhakti*: love and devotion for God.

In addition, this book has been specially designed to help you get the most out of its verses and commentary:

- Each chapter begins with highlights of the knowledge it contains and introduces key points to help you navigate your own journey.

- Within each chapter, the verses are grouped together under titles which help you stay connected to its themes.

- Each commentary selection is identified with numbers so you can look up its source in the References section found at the end of the book.

- Finally, definitions of key *Saṅskṛt* terms have also been included at the end of each chapter to help you better understand the philosophy behind the verses and commentaries.

How to Savour this Book

The *Bhagavad Gītā* offers a most precious treasure: the timeless discourse of Lord Kṛṣṇa which Paramahamsa Vishwananda's commentary unravels and delivers straight to the heart.

What you do with it depends on the value you give it. Receiving the *Gītā* with this in mind allows you to draw on its wisdom in the most powerful way.

There are many ways you can savour this book:

- Reading it cover to cover gives you an overview of the entire scripture.

- Reading only the verses from beginning to end allows you to stand next to Arjuna and take direct instruction from the Lord Himself.

- Concentrating on the introductory text and commentaries of each chapter helps you discover the secrets hidden within the verses.

• Simply letting the book fall open to any page allows the Divine to reveal something to you in the moment. Take it as a gift and contemplate on what you find.

Whether you read a verse a day, a chapter a week, the verses alone, only the commentary, or you just open the book to see what will be revealed to you in the moment, you'll surely want to keep this book close at hand and make it a part of your daily life.

Special Note from Paramahamsa Vishwananda

'The *Bhagavad Gītā* is not a novel. It's not just a book which you read whenever you have time. You have to soak your mind with it. Not only reading it one time.'

'You have to dive into it, because each line of the *Bhagavad Gītā*, each phrase which Kṛṣṇa has uttered, has a deeper meaning in your life. It's not outside of your life. He didn't say something alien to you. Actually, what He has spoken 5000 years ago is still relevant to now. If you see what Arjuna went through, everybody goes through the same thing. That's why you have to dive into it. Read it one time, two times, three times, hundreds of times. Become a living and walking *Bhagavad Gītā*.'

INTRODUCTION

The *Bhagavad Gītā* provides instruction and offers real, practical teachings on *yoga*, self-mastery and attaining perfection. We need such help because our incessant thoughts and desires inevitably lead to suffering. But by controlling and surrendering the mind to the Divine, we can become free from material conditioning. We return to our true Self and from there experience an eternal loving relationship with God. Through such teachings, the *Gītā* provides the ultimate solution to life's challenges, and offers a treasure map to the most priceless gem of all: the knowledge of how to attain real love and lasting happiness.

Although it is more than a philosophy, it can be helpful to have an overview of some of the philosophical principles this scripture embodies.

Philosophical Foundations of the *Bhagavad Gītā*

Sanātana-dharma (Hinduism) is founded on the idea that there is one Truth, one reality, one Supreme God, that is revealed in a number of ways. This explains the vast diversity and plurality that exists within this way of life. Various *gurus* and saints have come to humanity to reveal different traditions and pathways upon which the seeking individual can attain a first-hand experience of God. This has led to an immensely rich and profound spiritual culture which has lasted thousands of years.

But amongst all these elements, it is the *Bhagavad Gītā* which has emerged as the flagship scripture. In just 700 verses, it manages to explain all the key spiritual truths. The divine nature of the Self, reincarnation, *karma*, the nature of God, and so much more, are all neatly woven together in one discourse. Despite the wide range of thought within *Sanātana-dharma*, the *Gītā* has remained a unique source of authority in philosophical matters. This can be seen by the huge number of commentaries given by *gurus*, teachers and scholars.

Although given 5,000 years ago, the teachings of the *Bhagavad Gītā* describe eternal truths which are entirely relevant to this day and age. Each verse is saturated with meaning and should be seen not as mere philosophical statements, but as meditations designed to dispel ignorance. By regularly engaging with the teachings, one can develop the wisdom to move forward in life and progress on the spiritual path.

God in the *Gītā*

Each tradition within *Sanātana-dharma* views God in a different way, and amongst them, Vaiṣṇavism is one such tradition that holds Viṣṇu (Nārāyaṇa) as the Supreme Lord. He is the original Person, the source of creation, the ground of all that exists. Kṛṣṇa is an *avatāra*, a complete incarnation of the

Supreme Lord, who has entered this material world to uplift humanity. The *Gītā* therefore, is fundamentally a Vaiṣṇava scripture. Throughout it, we are repeatedly reminded of how everything depends on Kṛṣṇa, of how He is intrinsically present in the world, and at the same time, how He is beyond all of it.

In Kṛṣṇa, the *Gītā* shows that God is a deity who has a form, and who lovingly responds to His devotees. But at the same time, He does not simply reside in some distant Heaven. His presence pervades this material existence and He dwells within each living person. This entire world and the individual souls are an eternal part of His being. All of this becomes clear in the eleventh chapter where Arjuna is able to behold the cosmic form of Kṛṣṇa.

In the realm of material existence, only Kṛṣṇa and His Abode are exempt from the endless cycle of birth and death, creation and destruction. Kṛṣṇa is the highest reality since everything is supported, owned and controlled by Him, and everything that exists is only a part of His cosmic body.

(For further information on Hinduism, we recommend the book and course, *Understanding Hinduism*, by the Bhakti Marga Academy.)

The War to Restore Righteousness

The *Bhagavad Gītā* is part of a much larger scripture known as the *Mahābhārata* which details the history of the kings in the ancient Kuru dynasty.

It all takes place about 5000 years ago in India. Pāṇḍu ruled the kingdom of Hastināpura, but due to a curse, he retired to the forest with his wives, leaving his blind brother, Dhṛtarāṣṭra, to take the throne. Eventually children were born. The five sons of Pāṇḍu (Yudhiṣṭhira, Bhīma, Arjuna, Nakula and Sahadeva) were known as the Pāṇḍavas, while the hundred sons of Dhṛtarāṣṭra were called the Kauravas.

The righteous Pāṇḍavas were continuously persecuted by the jealous Duryodhana, the eldest of their Kaurava cousins. Eventually this ongoing feud led to the kingdom being divided between the two families. Unable to tolerate the growing success of the Pāṇḍavas, Duryodhana arranges a deceitful gambling match, the result of which forces the five brothers and their wife, Draupadī, into exile.

After thirteen long years, the Pāṇḍavas return to claim their kingdom, but despite repeated efforts for a peaceful resolution, Duryodhana refuses to compromise. In order to restore righteousness and vanquish the tyranny of the Kauravas, the Pāṇḍavas are left with no other choice but to wage war.

At this point, both sides gathered up their allies in preparation. Despite their affection for the Pāṇḍavas, many elders and relatives, such as their grandfather Bhīṣma and their teacher Droṇa, join the Kaurava army. All are profoundly aware of Duryodhana's arrogance and unrighteous behaviour, but filled with a sense of duty to the kingdom, they are ready to fight for him. Consequently, one family stands divided on the Kurukṣetra battlefield.

Arjuna and Duryodhana both approach Kṛṣṇa for help in the coming battle. Much to their surprise, Kṛṣṇa has taken an oath that He will not fight for any side. Instead, He presents two choices to both of them. In one hand, He offers his immensely powerful and illustrious army; in the other, He offers Himself, alone and unarmed. Arjuna is given first choice and, without doubt, chooses Kṛṣṇa. Duryodhana is both shocked and relieved. Without hesitation, he gleefully accepts the army that he thinks will assure him of victory.

Duryodhana assumes Kṛṣṇa to be an ordinary mortal, fallible and limited. He views Him as a means to fulfilling his desires. Arjuna, on the other hand, sees Kṛṣṇa as his dear friend and indeed as his world. He does not care for the army, the kingdom or for any victory, he simply wants Kṛṣṇa. It is this bond of Love that causes the Lord to serve Arjuna. As a result, the original Creator of the universe, the all-pervasive omnipotent personality that is Kṛṣṇa, takes on the role of a humble charioteer.

The Lord Takes the Lead

Arjuna's confusion and distress at the beginning of the battle provides the space for Kṛṣṇa to transcend His position as a charioteer, cousin and friend. He then assumes the role of the spiritual *guru* and takes responsibility for Arjuna's spiritual evolution. While we, as the reader of this timeless dialogue, take the place of Arjuna.

Kṛṣṇa is none other than the Supreme Lord Nārāyaṇa. Of His own Will, He enters into His creation to restore righteousness and awaken the hearts of His devotees. Within this one form of God, there is the potential for every kind of relationship with God. For example, as a child, Kṛṣṇa grew up in the forest of Vṛndāvana tending the cows. Wherever He went, His all-attractive persona captured the minds of the people. His mother Yaśodā attained the highest form of Love through maternal affection. His cowherd companions evolved through friendship with Him. The simple *gopīs* (cowherd girls) saw Him as their Lover and reached ecstatic states of devotion.

But the secret of His divine nature is not revealed to everyone. Through His divine *yoga-māyā*, the power of illusion, He conceals His true identity. Only those who have been graced to see Him can know Him as He truly is. Through Kṛṣṇa's grace, Arjuna is given these 'eyes to see' in Chapter 11.

The *Bhagavad Gītā* is built upon this profound relationship, demonstrating how devotion and a spirit of surrender allows one to see the Truth.

Your Part of the Story

The dialogue between Arjuna and Kṛṣṇa is an ancient hymn that has been sung for thousands of years. The poetic 700 *Saṅskṛt* verses detail a story of profound personal transformation. But it is not only the story of Arjuna the warrior. It is also the story of everyone on the path to God.

The Kurukṣetra War lasted 18 days; each of the 18 chapters of the *Gītā* reflects one of those days. Together, the story told in verse and the commentary given by the *guru*, shed a brilliant light of Love on the 18-step journey that every sincere spiritual seeker takes on the quest to attain the Lord.

A word to the wise: don't just read the story. Use this conversation between Kṛṣṇa and Arjuna as a guide on your own spiritual journey. Climb into the chariot and take a seat next to Arjuna at the feet of the *guru*. Become His disciple as well. Absorb your whole being in these wisdom teachings and you'll discover the mysteries of life, eternal truths of creation, and the true purpose of human existence.

By understanding and applying the wisdom given by Kṛṣṇa, and by meditating on the insightful commentary of Paramahamsa Vishwananda, you can stand beside Arjuna, and together, fight in the most important battle of all time.

The *Bhagavad Gītā* is a call to awaken the soul. It is a map for navigating the perilous journey from the head to the heart where we will find the most valuable treasure of all: the Lord Himself.

The scene is now set for one of the greatest encounters the world has ever seen.

Let the adventure begin...

CHAPTER ONE
ARJUNA-VIṢĀDA-YOGA
THE LAMENTATION OF ARJUNA

The *Gītā* begins with a vivid description of the scene on the Kurukṣetra battlefield. Key warriors on both sides are named. The blowing of conches and the beating of drums signal the start of this terrible war. It is at this point that the focus shifts to Arjuna and Kṛṣṇa. Eager to assess the enemy ranks, Arjuna asks Kṛṣṇa to take him to the middle of the battlefield so he can take a closer look at those he is about to fight.

Amongst the opposing army, he sees relatives, friends and revered elders. The sight of those who were once so dear to him causes Arjuna to lose his resolve. He can no longer see the point in engaging in this battle which will inevitably destroy his family. Confused about his duty and overwhelmed with compassion for his enemies, he begins to pour out his heart to Kṛṣṇa. Surely, he argues, this war cannot be based on righteousness. He repeatedly makes the point that killing one's own family for the sake of a kingdom will only produce dire consequences for the future. After making his case, the chapter ends with Arjuna casting aside his bow in grief.

VERSE 1: DHṚTARĀṢṬRA'S ENQUIRY

dhṛtarāṣṭra uvāca
dharma-kṣetre kuru-kṣetre samavetā yuyutsavaḥ |
māmakāḥ pāṇḍavāścaiva kim akurvata sañjaya || 1 ||

Dhṛtarāṣṭra says:
O Sañjaya, after they gathered on the holy field of Kurukṣetra, being eager for battle, what did my sons and the Pāṇḍavas do? (1)

'This verse starts with the word "*dharmakṣetra*." "*Dharma*" means righteous, "*kṣetra*" means the field – so this is the field of righteousness.'

'One of the meanings of this war is life, where the "good" side fights with the "not good" side. This war is not outside, it is also happening inside the human body. Your physical body is the *dharmakṣetra*. You have incarnated to do your *dharma* (duty) in this field.'

'Life is also a *dharmakṣetra*. You have come to fulfil your divine purpose. When you are in tune with your true Self, you realise your purpose in life...and that's what the word "*dharmakṣetra*" is reminding you of. Do your *dharma*! Awaken! This *dharma* can be done with the greatest gift which God has given: this field, this body. And when you start doing your *dharma*, you'll get good merit! But, if you run away from your *dharma*, then you turn towards the dark side.'

'This blind king, Dhṛtarāṣṭra, represents the mind – the mind which is blind and wants to always stay blind. The mind is hanging on to the outside so much that it has power only when it is focused on something exterior: on the material, on relationships, on gaining this or that. This is the nature of the mind. The mind is blind.'

'Both families were from the Kuru dynasty. But the king refused to recognise the Pāṇḍavas. The mind doesn't recognise the good qualities which are present in oneself. The mind can only look towards the senses, looking always towards the outside. The Self, and the positive qualities which are present inside, are not comprehended by it.'

VERSES 2-13: THE WARRIORS ARE INTRODUCED

sañjaya uvāca
dṛṣṭvā tu pāṇḍavānīkaṁ vyūḍhaṁ duryodhanas tadā |
ācāryam upasaṅgamya rājā vacanam abravīt || 2 ||

Sañjaya says:
O king! Duryodhana, seeing the Pāṇḍavas' army in military formation, approached his teacher, Droṇa, and said these words: (2)

paśyaitām pāṇḍu-putrāṇām ācārya mahatīṁ camūm |
vyūḍhāṁ drupada-putreṇa tava śiṣyeṇa dhīmatā || 3 ||

Duryodhana says:
O Master, behold this mighty army of the Pāṇḍavas, led by the son of Drupada, who is your intelligent disciple. (3)

atra śūrā maheṣvāsā bhīmārjuna samā yudhi |
yuyudhāno virāṭaśca drupadaśca mahārathaḥ || 4 ||

In that army are heroes and great archers like Bhīma and Arjuna; there are mighty warriors like Yuyudhāna, Virāṭa and Drupada. (4)

dhṛṣṭaketuś-cekitānaḥ kāśi-rājaśca vīryavān |
purujit-kunti-bhojaśca śaibyaśca nara-puṅgavaḥ || 5 ||

There is Dhṛṣṭaketu, Cekitāna, and the valiant king of Kāśī, Purujit, Kuntibhoja, and Śaibyā, all of whom are the best among men. (5)

yudhāmanyuśca vikrānta uttamaujāśca vīryavān |
saubhadro draupadeyāśca sarva eva mahārathāḥ || 6 ||

There is the valiant Yudhāmanyu and the strong Uttamaujas. There is also the son of Subhadrā, as well as the sons of Draupadī. All of them are mighty chariot-warriors. (6)

asmākaṁ tu viśiṣṭā ye tān-nibodha dvijottama |
nāyakāḥ mama sainyasya saṁjñārthaṁ tān bravīmi te || 7 ||

O best of *brāhmaṇas*, let me now familiarise you with our principle warriors who are the commanders of my army.
I shall name them to refresh your memory. (7)

bhavān bhīṣmaśca karṇaśca kṛpaśca samitiñjayaḥ |
aśvatthāmā vikarṇaśca saumadattis tathaiva ca || 8 ||

There is yourself, Bhīṣma and Karṇa, the victorious Kṛpā, Aśvatthāmā, Vikarṇa and Jayadratha, the son of Somadatta. (8)

anye ca bahavaḥ śūrā madārthe tyakta-jīvitāḥ |
nānā-śāstra praharaṇāḥ sarve yuddha-viśāradāḥ || 9 ||

And there are many other heroes who are determined to give up their lives for my sake. They are all experts in weaponry and experienced in the art of warfare. (9)

aparyāptaṁ tad asmakaṁ balaṁ bhīṣmābhirakṣitam |
paryāptaṁ tvidam eteṣāṁ balaṁ bhīmābhirakṣitam || 10 ||

This force of ours marshalled by Bhīṣma is immeasurable, while their strength controlled by Bhīma is limited. (10)

ayaneṣu ca sarveṣu yathā-bhāgam avasthitāḥ |
bhīṣmam evābhirakṣantu bhavantaḥ sarva eva hi || 11 ||

All of you therefore should make every effort to guard Bhīṣma, whilst stationed at your respective positions in the army. (11)

tasya sañjanayan harṣaṁ kuru-vṛddhaḥ pitāmahaḥ |
siṁhanādaṁ vinadyoccaiḥ śaṅkhaṁ dadhmau pratāpavān || 12 ||

Sañjaya says:
Then, the valiant grandsire Bhīṣma, the most senior of the Kuru clan, roaring like a lion, blew his conch to encourage Duryodhana. (12)

tataḥ śaṅkhāśca bheryaśca paṇavānaka-gomukhāḥ |
sahasaivābhyahanyanta sa śabdas-tumulo'bhavat || 13 ||

Suddenly, conches and kettle drums, trumpets, tabors and horns erupted forth and the sound was terrific. (13)

'Duryodhana represents this great pride that is born from the mind. When the mind is very active, one becomes proud of many things: proud of knowledge, proud of what one has.

'The army of the Pāṇḍavas was arrayed in a very special formation. Seeing this orderly formation, Duryodhana felt much nervousness and anxiety inside himself. Anxiety appears when one is proud. Even if pride appears very strong on the outside, in reality, it has a lot of weaknesses in it. Why does pride arise? Do you think it is out of strength? No! In reality, pride arises due to the weakness that one has inside. Even if somebody says, "Ah yes, I am very proud of this and I am very proud of that", you can feel that this pride is actually weakness. When pride arises, people think, "Yes, I am very confident!" No. It's the mind that perceives pride as confidence. In reality, one is running away from something, from the opposite of pride, which is humility. When one is running away from humility, one only appears to be very grand and confident.'

'When you start on the spiritual path, your pride sees all your good qualities, but then the mind becomes anxious. This pride tries to make you reason, tries to make you go sideways in a cunning way. That's why Duryodhana rushes to Droṇācārya, the great teacher of both the Kauravas and the Pāṇḍavas.

'Droṇācārya represents attachment to the material. He represents the greed in man. Droṇācārya also had good qualities. He was a great teacher of military science. Sometimes he would even advise Bhīṣma. He was the royal *guru*. But when the pride of Duryodhana saw the greed in Droṇācārya, he said to himself, "Let me go and feed his greed. Let me corrupt him."'

'Then he praises Bhīṣma. Bhīṣma represents the ego. He was very powerful. He was the great-uncle of the Kauravas and the Pāṇḍavas, and was considered the greatest of all in the Kuru dynasty. He was very virtuous. He was a renunciate... He was very devoted to his parents. He knew about the scriptures. He was devoted to his teachers. Above all, he was very dedicated to God. Due to this, there was a great ego.'

'The ego makes you think and feel that you are the best among men. You are the most knowledgeable of all. You have knowledge of everything. And that blinds you. Even if you have many good qualities, if you are egoistic, all these good qualities are nothing because it is all self-centred.'

'Duryodhana continues, "There are many more heroes who have sacrificed their lives for my sake." You see, pride has many friends, and most of these friends have qualities similar to him. Because of his arrogance, Duryodhana attracted similar people with similar qualities. Most of these qualities that were supporting him were in the form of his own ninety-nine brothers.'

'The Kauravas stand for this outside reality which is looking, fighting, always wanting something, but it's all material, it's all external, and that brings superficial joy: joy for a very short time and misery for a longer time.'

'When you start on your spiritual path, you have a battle: you perceive all the negative qualities within more strongly. Sometimes you'll awaken a quality which has never been there before. But this is the purification that one goes through; this is the Kurukṣetra that you go through, the *dharmakṣetra* that you go through. You uproot, one by one, all these qualities and transform them. You transform them until finally you have the Love of God that stays. That's realisation! To receive His grace. To manifest His Love and to beam His Love. And that's the duty of each human being.'

VERSES 14-20: KṚṢṆA IS INTRODUCED; THE CONCHES ARE BLOWING

tataḥ śvetair-hayair-yukte mahati syandane sthitau |
mādhavaḥ pāṇḍavaścaiva divyau śaṅkhau pradadhmatuḥ || 14 ||

Then Śrī Kṛṣṇa and Arjuna, stationed in their great chariot drawn by white horses, blew their divine conches. (14)

pāñcajanyaṁ hṛṣīkeśo devadattaṁ dhanañjayaḥ |
pauṇḍraṁ dadhmau mahā-śaṅkhaṁ bhīma-karmā vṛkodaraḥ || 15 ||

Śrī Kṛṣṇa blew His conch, Pāñcajanya, Arjuna blew his, named Devadatta, and Bhīma, the performer of terrible deeds, blew the great conch Pauṇḍra. (15)

ananta-vijayaṁ rājā kuntī-putro yudhiṣṭhiraḥ |
nakulaḥ sahadevaśca sughoṣa maṇi-puṣpakau || 16 ||

King Yudhiṣṭhira, the son of Kuntī, blew his conch Ananta-vijaya, and Nakula and Sahadeva blew their conches Sughoṣa and Mani-puṣpaka. (16)

kāśyaśca parameṣ-vasaḥ śikhaṇḍī ca mahārathaḥ |
dhṛṣṭadyumno virāṭaśca sātyakiś-cāparājitaḥ || 17 ||

Then the supreme archer, king of Kāśī, and the mighty warrior Śikhaṇḍī, Dhṛṣṭadyumna, Virāṭa; and the invincible Sātyaki, all blew their respective conches. (17)

drupado draupadeyāśca sarvaśaḥ pṛthivī-pate |
saubhadraśca mahā-bāhuḥ śaṅkhān dadhmuḥ pṛthak pṛthak || 18 ||

King Drupada, the sons of Draupadī, and the strong-armed son of Subhadrā, all blew their various conches again and again. (18)

sa ghoṣo dhārtarāṣṭrāṇāṁ hṛdayāni vyadārayat |
nabhaśca pṛthivīṁ caiva tumulo'bhyanunādayan || 19 ||

That tumultuous uproar, resounding through heaven and Earth, tore the hearts of Dhṛtarāṣṭra's sons. (19)

atha vyavasthitān dṛṣṭvā dhārtarāsṭrān kapi-dhvajaḥ |
pravṛtte śastra-sampāte dhanur udyamya pāṇḍavaḥ || 20 ||

After seeing the sons of Dhṛtarāṣṭra arranged in their formation, Arjuna, who had Hanumān as his banner crest, took up his bow in preparation for war. (20)

'Kṛṣṇa is seated in His chariot holding the reins, controlling the five horses. He is the Controller of all. Arjuna is seated with Him in the chariot and they blow their divine conches. This denotes that when one shows interest in changing, when the Lord perceives that one is making an effort to change, then the Lord Himself gives strength, power, energy and faith to that person who is willing to change. He gives one power to control the senses: the five horses pulling the chariot represent the five senses.'

'Imagine all these people blowing conches: so powerful and so strong must have been this sound at that time, that everything around started to tremble! And not only there on the battlefield, but also in the heavens. It didn't happen just in this physical world. It also happened in the spiritual world.'

'They used the conch to announce the beginning and the end of war. The sound is *oṁ*. This sound which vibrates, shows that at the end, no matter how big the battle is, how strong or difficult it is, one finds one's way. At the end, everything resounds in the cosmic sound. At the end, it is through this cosmic sound that one attains realisation. This cosmic sound is the word of God Himself. The conch and the bell are not just mere instruments. When one blows the conch, it awakens the divinity inside. It awakens clarity inside. It vibrates and the vibration also vibrates in your brain. The same is true of the bell.'

'When you go with full force on your spiritual path, nothing can move you! Nothing that people can say, nothing that people can do, can make you move from your path. That's what Christ says about having faith. About building your faith on a rock so that nothing can move you! If you build your house on sand, it will break. If you build your house on a rock, it will be very strong. This sound that we are talking about is the inner strength. When you have inner strength, it's not only in your heart. Your whole being will be full of energy! From head to toe, you'll be full of energy, because that energy is not from the outside, it is from deep within. This energy is from God Himself, from Kṛṣṇa Himself, and it beams out and gives you the support and the strength to move forward. But you should not look at your weakness, even if you see the weakness. It is part of you, yes! But hang onto your strength!'

VERSES 21-24: BETWEEN THE TWO ARMIES

hṛṣīkeśaṁ tadā vākyam idam āha mahī-pate |
arjuna uvāca
senayor-ubhayor madhye rathaṁ sthāpaya me'cyuta || 21 ||
yāvad etān nirīkṣe'haṁ yoddhu-kāmān avasthitān |
kair-mayā saha yoddhavyam asmin raṇa-samudyame || 22 ||

And he spoke, O king, these words to Śrī Kṛṣṇa...
Arjuna says:
O Kṛṣṇa, station my chariot between the two armies. I wish to look at those who are present here and know exactly who I have to fight in this great battle. (21-22)

yotsyamānān avekṣe'haṁ ya ete'tra samāgatāḥ |
dhārtarāṣṭrasya durbuddher yuddhe priya cikīrṣavaḥ || 23 ||

I am eager to see those who have gathered here to please the evil-minded son of Dhṛtarāṣṭra (Duryodhana). (23)

sañjaya uvāca
evam ukto hṛṣīkeśo guḍākeśena bhārata |
senayor-ubhayor madhye sthāpayitvā rathottamam || 24 ||

Sañjaya says:
O Dhṛtarāṣṭra, having been addressed by Arjuna, Śrī Kṛṣṇa stationed that best of chariots between the two armies. (24)

'Arjuna said to Kṛṣṇa, "move my chariot in between." So, this "in-between state" stands for neutral. You are neither on one side, nor the other. You are neither on the good side, nor on the bad side. For you to be able to observe, you have to be in that neutral state, that neutral point. Very often people take decisions in life being on one side. If you are on one side, there is always judgement, there is always confusion.'

'Testing times may arise in the form of troubles. Often one doesn't want to go through it, and so one tries to bypass it, and go sideways. But life is like this. Life is a great lesson. If you don't face your problem, if you don't face your negative quality and look at it in the eyes, you'll never become strong. If you always try to go sideways, you will not learn anything. Arjuna says, "Place me between them. Let me see – face to face, eye to eye – what are these qualities, what is this pain. Let me go above it, rise over, master it! I wish to see who I am to fight". Here it is not about fighting, it is about transcending. "What will I transcend? Which quality?" This is self-analysis. This is the point where Arjuna is analysing. Arjuna here represents self-observance. Observe all your qualities – your "good" qualities and your "not good" qualities – and then you can know how to overcome them, transcend them and transform them.'

VERSES 25-47: ARJUNA REFUSES TO FIGHT

bhiṣma droṇa pramukhataḥ sarveṣāṁ ca mahīkṣitām |
uvāca pārtha paśyaitān samavetān kurūn iti || 25 ||

In front of Bhīṣma, Droṇa, and all the other kings, Kṛṣṇa says: 'O Arjuna, behold all the Kurus who have assembled here.' (25)

tatrāpaśyat sthitān pārthaḥ pitṝn atha pitā-mahān |
ācāryān mātulān bhrātṝn putrān pautrān sakhīṁs tathā || 26 ||
śvaśurān suhṛdaścaiva senayor-ubhayor api |
tān samīkṣya sa kaunteyaḥ sarvān bandhūn avasthitān || 27 ||
kṛpayā parayā''viṣṭo viṣīdann idam abravīt |
arjuna uvāca
dṛṣṭvemaṁ svajanaṁ kṛṣṇa yuyutsaṁ samupasthitam || 28 ||
sīdanti mama gātrāṇi mukhaṁ ca pariśuṣyati |
vepathuśca śarīre me roma harṣaśca jāyate || 29 ||

Then Arjuna saw standing there, fathers and grand-fathers, teachers, uncles, brothers, sons, grandsons and friends. Having seen all his friends and different relatives there, Arjuna was filled with deep compassion and said these words in despair:
After seeing my own family and friends ready to do battle and kill one another, my limbs have become weak and my mouth is drying up. My body is trembling, and my hair is standing on end. (26-29)

gāṇḍīvaṁ sraṁsate hastāt tvak caiva pari-dahyate |
na ca śaknomy-avasthātuṁ bhramatīva ca me manaḥ || 30 ||

My bow, the Gāṇḍīva, is slipping from my hands and my skin is burning. I am unable to hold myself together, I am confused, and my mind is reeling. (30)

nimittāni ca paśyāmi viparītāni keśava |
na ca śreyo'nupaśyāmi hatvā svajanam āhave || 31 ||

O Kṛṣṇa, I see only calamity for the future. I cannot see any good in killing my own family in battle. (31)

na kāṅkṣe vijayaṁ kṛṣṇa na ca rājyaṁ sukhāni ca |
kiṁ no rajyena govinda kiṁ bhogair jīvitena vā || 32 ||

Nor do I desire victory, a kingdom or happiness. Of what use to us is a kingdom, enjoyment or even life itself? (32)

yeṣām arthe kāṅkṣitaṁ no rājyaṁ bhogāḥ sukhāni ca |
ta ime' vasthitā yuddhe prāṇāṁs tyaktvā dhanāni ca || 33 ||

The people for whose sake we desire those things stand ready to fight and give up their lives, and their wealth, for this war. (33)

ācāryāḥ pitaraḥ putrās tathaiva ca pitāmahāḥ |
mātulāḥ śvaśurāḥ pautrāḥ śyālāḥ sambandhinas tathā || 34 ||

Teachers, fathers, sons and also grandfathers, uncles, fathers-in-law and grandsons, brothers-in-law and other relatives stand before me. (34)

etān na hantum icchāmi ghnato'pi madhusūdana |
api trailokya rājyasya hetoḥ kiṁ nu mahīkṛte || 35 ||

O Kṛṣṇa, they may wish to slay me, but I have no desire to kill them, even if it were to rule the three worlds, much less for this Earth. (35)

nihatya dhārtarāṣṭrān naḥ kā prītiḥ syāj-janārdana |
pāpam evāśrayed asmān hatvaitān ātatāyinaḥ || 36 ||

If we kill the sons of Dhṛtarāṣṭra, what joy will be ours, O Kṛṣṇa? Sin alone will stain us if we kill these aggressors. (36)

tasmān nārhā vayaṁ hantuṁ dhārtarāṣṭrān svabandhavān |
svajanaṁ hi kathaṁ hatvā sukhinaḥ syāma mādhava || 37 ||

Therefore, it is not right that we slay the sons of Dhṛtarāṣṭra. How can we rejoice, O Kṛṣṇa, if we kill our own relatives? (37)

yady-apyete na paśyanti lobhopahata cetasaḥ |
kula-kṣaya-kṛtaṁ doṣaṁ mitra-drohe ca pātakam || 38 ||
kathaṁ na jñeyam asmābhiḥ pāpād asmān nivartitum |
kula-kṣaya-kṛtaṁ doṣaṁ prapaśyadbhir janārdana || 39 ||

Even though these people, whose minds are overpowered by greed, see no evil in destroying their family and betraying their friends, why should we, O Kṛṣṇa, who do recognise this evil, engage in such sinful deeds? (38-39)

kula-kṣaye praṇaśyanti kula-dharmāḥ sanātanāḥ |
dharme naṣṭe kulaṁ kṛtsnam adharmo'bhibhavaty-uta || 40 ||

If the family is destroyed, its ancient traditions perish, and when traditions perish, unrighteousness overtakes the whole clan. (40)

adharmābhi-bhavāt kṛṣṇa praduṣyanti kula-striyaḥ |
strīṣu duṣṭāsu vārṣṇeya jāyate varṇa-saṅkaraḥ || 41 ||

When unrighteousness prevails, O Kṛṣṇa, the women of the clan become corrupt; when women become corrupt, future generations will follow. (41)

saṅkaro narakāyaiva kula-ghnānāṁ kulasya ca |
patanti pitaro hyeṣāṁ lupta-piṇḍodaka-kriyāḥ || 42 ||

The mixing of social classes creates a living hell both for the family and for those who destroy it. Consequently, the ancestors of such a family will certainly fall because they will be deprived of their ritual offerings. (42)

doṣair etaiḥ kula-ghnānāṁ varṇa-saṅkara-kārakaiḥ |
utsādyante jāti-dharmāḥ kula-dharmāśca śāśvatāḥ || 43 ||

The sinful deeds of those who destroy their family and mix social classes ruin the ancient traditions of our clan. (43)

utsanna-kula-dharmāṇāṁ manuṣyāṇāṁ janārdana |
narake'niyataṁ vāso bhavatīty-anuśuśruma || 44 ||

We have heard, O Kṛṣṇa, that there is certainly a place in Hell for those who destroy such family practices. (44)

aho bata mahat pāpaṁ kartuṁ vyavasitā vayam |
yad rājya sukha lobhena hantuṁ sva-janam udyatāḥ || 45 ||

Alas! We have resolved to commit a great crime, in that we are ready to slay our own family, just to rule and enjoy the pleasures of a kingdom. (45)

yadi mām apratīkāram aśastraṁ śastra-pāṇayaḥ |
dhārtarāṣṭrā raṇe hanyus tan-me kṣemataraṁ bhavet || 46 ||

Even if the fully-armed sons of Dhṛtarāṣṭra were to slay me in battle, unresisting and unarmed, that would be better for me. (46)

sañjaya uvāca
evam uktvā'rjunaḥ saṅkhye rathopastha upāviśat |
visṛjya saśaraṁ cāpaṁ śoka saṁvigna mānasaḥ || 47 ||

Sañjaya says:
Having spoken these words on the battlefield, Arjuna threw aside his bow and arrows, and sat down on the seat of his chariot, his heart overwhelmed with grief. (47)

'You were born for a reason and that reason is to realise your Self, to awaken the divinity inside of you and to bring it to others; not merely to say, "Okay, I have a good life."'

'You are born with all your negative qualities. They are dormant inside you. Throughout many lifetimes you have carried them with you, but when the time comes for you to remove them, you just sit there and say, "No, I can't do it!" The same was true for Arjuna. He is just sitting there saying, "I can't do it!", because he is still holding onto his weaknesses.'

'Arjuna is overtaken by emotions which will stop him from fighting. So he becomes cowardly, very soft. If you are soft, you can't help anyone; you have to be strong. Here Kṛṣṇa reminds Arjuna that he will not move forward if he is weak. Yet Kṛṣṇa allows this feeling to awaken in Arjuna because He is purifying him. He is showing him, "Look at this clearly. It is not outside; it is inside of you. These people who you see outside of you, why do you feel this connection with them? Because they are inside your heart." These negative qualities that you see outside, in other people, they are not outside: they are inside of you. If you want to transcend them, you have to dig them out from the inside. You have to remove them from deep within. Not just superficially, by the mind saying, "Ah yes, I have changed, it is finished! Good! Now, God loves me! And I love God!" No, it doesn't work like that! Because loving God has to come from inside. For Him to manifest Himself, for Him to come to you, to run to you, a great amount of sincerity, strength and power has to be there!'

'In his confusion, Arjuna tries to find all kinds of excuses not to fight. He sees that Kṛṣṇa is just looking at him, not bothered about these things. Arjuna is using all kinds of words to please Kṛṣṇa, to make Kṛṣṇa agree with him. Like I explained earlier, when one is in a depressed state, one will look to everybody else to acknowledge one's depression. Arjuna is depressed and trying to make Kṛṣṇa say, "Poor you! We will not fight." He is trying to make Kṛṣṇa acknowledge that whatever he is saying is right. He is in a state of deep confusion and the Great Doctor is sitting there with him! Do you think that the Great Doctor would just sit there, start crying with him and say, "Oh, my God! Oh, Arjuna, you are right, let's go back!" Not a chance!'

'Kṛṣṇa is just listening and waiting for Arjuna to finish crying. It is like this in life. If you try to reason with a person who is in this state, it's of no use. The Lord is just watching and saying, "Okay, carry on. Do you have more? Send it! I am listening. I am patient."'

'In life, your *guru* is always with you, whether you are on the left side or on the right side, but you have to learn to listen. Here, Kṛṣṇa is standing with him in the battle. In the battle of life, the Master is with you, helping you to find your way out of this confusion.'

'This inner confusion which Arjuna is going through, is in all of us... You can't change the world outside. What you can change is yourself. But the willingness to change must be there. Because if you don't have the willingness to change, even reading or listening to the *Bhagavad Gītā* will not do anything inside of you. But if you have just a little percentage of that willingness, then the change will happen.'

'Arjuna is reduced to a very terrible state... In daily life, you see many people who go through that state. But it is a very important state, because in this state you are building your base in spirituality. If you are weak, you can't stand on the spiritual path. You have to become strong... Don't look only at the situation;

often certain situations happen in life that we don't want to see. Here Kṛṣṇa is saying, "Look at it! Face it and go beyond it!"'

'At the beginning of your spiritual path, it's not easy. You have to fight that mind.'

'In this battlefield of life, if you create an illusion to make yourself feel happy, then if anything appears in front of you, you try to find ways to run away from it. This is cowardice, going sideways, "putting it in a drawer". You will never be free, because sooner or later you will be facing the same thing again. But once you have faced it, it will never come back to you again.'

CHAPTER TWO
SĀṄKHYA-YOGA
THE ETERNAL NATURE OF THE SOUL

Despite Kṛṣṇa urging Arjuna to shake off his weakness, he continues to express his unwillingness to fight. Eventually, in a helpless state, Arjuna surrenders to Kṛṣṇa and begs for guidance. At this point, Kṛṣṇa assumes the role of the *satguru* [1] and teaches him about the nature of the Self – the *ātmā* [2] present in every individual. He describes how the *ātmā* is indestructible, eternal and beyond this material world. Just as we cast off old clothes and adorn ourselves with new ones, the soul sheds old bodies and takes on new ones. As a *kṣatriya* (warrior), therefore, Arjuna should have no reservation in carrying out his duty since ultimately nobody can be killed.

Having established Arjuna in this philosophical understanding, Kṛṣṇa proceeds to teach one of the fundamental concepts of the *Gītā*: *karma-yoga*. He explains that those of small intelligence perform various duties with the hope of gaining some limited reward; this attachment to results is what produces *karma* [3]. But Kṛṣṇa urges Arjuna to carry out his duty as a warrior without any attachment to the results. By engaging in righteous action without any selfish gain, one can be freed from all *karmic* consequences. With the senses restrained and the mind controlled, one is not distracted by the ways of the world. In this desire-less state, a *yogī* achieves perfect wisdom and peace.

This overview of *karma-yoga* [4] provides the centre piece for Kṛṣṇa's teachings over the next four chapters. We learn about the real meaning of action, what is true renunciation, as well as the ultimate state that is reached when practicing this *yoga*.

Chapter Two Intro: Key Terms

[1] **Satguru** – there are many types of *gurus* (teachers) who help one on the spiritual path, but the *satguru* is considered to be the highest. He is the Lord Himself, who has come to guide humanity to the ultimate goal.

[2] **Ātmā** – term interchanged with 'Self' and 'soul', which refers to an eternal, non-material, part of God.

[3] **Karma** – any action done with the body or mind that produces further consequences.

[4] **Karma-yoga** – the path by which one continues to act in the world with detachment. Such acts, therefore, do not create further consequences.

VERSES 1-9: ARJUNA SEEKS REFUGE IN KṚṢṆA AS THE GURU

sañjaya uvāca
taṁ tathā kṛpayāviṣṭaṁ aśrū pūrṇā-kulekṣaṇam |
viṣīdantam idaṁ vākyam uvāca madhusūdanaḥ || 1 ||

Sañjaya says:

Seeing Arjuna overcome with pity, depressed, bewildered, and his eyes filled with tears, Kṛṣṇa spoke these words: (1)

śrī bhagavān uvāca
kutas tvā kaśmalam idaṁ viṣame samupasthitam |
anāryājuṣṭam asvargyam akīrtikaram arjuna || 2 ||

Lord Kṛṣṇa says:

Where has this weakness come from, O Arjuna? It is not worthy of a noble person like you. Such faintheartedness will not lead to the attainment of Heaven but to dishonour. (2)

klaibyaṁ mā sma gamaḥ pārtha naitat-tvayyupapadyate |
kṣudraṁ hṛdaya daurbalyaṁ tyaktvottiṣṭha parantapa || 3 ||

Do not give in to this unmanliness, O Arjuna, it does not befit you. Throw away this weakness and arise, O vanquisher of enemies! (3)

arjuna uvāca
kathaṁ bhīṣmam ahaṁ saṅkhye droṇaṁ ca madhusūdana |
iṣubhiḥ pratiyotsyāmi pūjārhāv-arisūdana || 4 ||

Arjuna says:

O Kṛṣṇa, destroyer of enemies, how can I fire arrows against Bhīṣma and Droṇa in battle? These men are worthy of my worship. (4)

gurūn ahatvā hi mahānubhāvān
śreyo bhoktuṁ bhaikṣyam apīha loke |
hatvārtha kāmāṁs tu gurūn ihaiva
bhuñjīya bhogān rudhira-pradigdhān || 5 ||

It would be better to live a life as a beggar than to slay these great souls who are my teachers. Even if they are tainted with the desire for wealth, by slaying them I would only be enjoying blood-stained pleasures. (5)

na caitad vidmaḥ kataran no garīyo
yadvā jayema yadi vā no jayeyuḥ |
yān eva hatvā na jijīviṣāmas
te'vasthitāḥ pramukhe dhārtarāṣṭrāḥ || 6 ||

We do not know, which of the two is better for us — killing them or being killed by them. After slaying the sons of Dhṛtarāṣṭra standing here before us, there would be no point in living. (6)

kārpaṇya doṣopahata svabhāvaḥ
pṛcchāmi tvāṁ dharma samūḍha cetāḥ |
yacchreyaḥ syān niścitaṁ brūhi tan me
śiṣyas 'haṁ śādhi māṁ tvāṁ prapannam || 7 ||

With my heart overcome by weakness and my mind confused about my duty, I urge you to tell me clearly what is good for me. I am your disciple and I take refuge in you. Please teach me. (7)

na hi prapaśyāmi mamāpanudyād
yacchokam ucchoṣaṇam indriyāṇām |
avāpya bhūmāv-asapatnam-ṛddham
rājyaṁ suraṇām api cādhipatyam || 8 ||

Even if I win a prosperous kingdom unchallenged on this Earth or even if I have lordship over the gods, I cannot see how this grief drying up my senses can be dispelled. (8)

sañjaya uvāca
evam uktvā hṛṣīkeśaṁ guḍakeśaḥ parantapa |
na yotsya iti govindam uktvā tūṣṇīṁ babhūva ha || 9 ||

Sañjaya says:
Having spoken so to Śrī Kṛṣṇa, Arjuna, the conqueror of sleep and the vanquisher of enemies said, 'I will not fight' and became silent. (9)

'In the last chapter, we saw how Arjuna feels confused and how depressed he has become, because when the mind is focused and concentrated on the negative, everything becomes negative. We will see how Lord Kṛṣṇa gives Arjuna the knowledge of the *Gītā* and how He starts to talk to Arjuna about the knowledge of the Self.'

'Kṛṣṇa is a great psychologist; He doesn't directly go and give Arjuna everything. He goes slowly with him, step by step. He doesn't change him, but He gradually allows Arjuna to transform himself.'

'In this chapter, Kṛṣṇa becomes the *guru*. All this time, Arjuna has been looking at Kṛṣṇa as his cousin and his friend. But now, seeing this terrible, pitiful state of Arjuna, Kṛṣṇa starts to teach. At this moment, Kṛṣṇa becomes the *guru* and Arjuna, the disciple. But Arjuna's willingness to listen to Kṛṣṇa is very important!

'How can Kṛṣṇa tell something to Arjuna, if Arjuna doesn't want to listen? In the first chapter, you saw that Kṛṣṇa doesn't say much: He keeps quiet and listens to what Arjuna has to say. But when Arjuna is tired of talking, then Kṛṣṇa reveals to him the *Gītā*. Only when you can listen, can you change! If you can't listen, how will you change? You will never change. Life is like this: if you don't learn to listen and observe, you will not transform.'

'The instruction of the *guru* is like a seed which is planted in fertile land. If the disciple's heart is like a stone, nothing will grow from it.'

'When a disciple takes refuge in the *guru*, the disciple must completely accept the superiority of the Master. This is what Arjuna is accepting.'

'When you come to the Master, you have to come as an empty vessel so that you can be filled. That mind must be emptied to receive. You have to have this willingness to change to have the full benefit.

'If you start to think about what you are losing, you will never get anything, because on the spiritual path you may lose everything on the outside, but in reality, you are gaining everything.'

'Arjuna's eyes are brightened and his mind is completely transformed. His whole attitude has changed. With folded hands, he knows that by taking this role of the disciple, that the Lord, the God Almighty, the omniscient and the knower of all hearts, has taken the form of the supreme Master. And that He, who is full of Love, greatness, virtue, knowledge, He who is non-attached, who can't be touched by *karma* or by anything, is his dear friend. And from being his best friend, He has become the supreme guide and the supreme divinity.

'This is the greatness of the *guru*. The *guru* does not have just one role. He is not just a teacher. He takes different forms, a multitude of aspects. Because the life of the *guru* is not for Himself, but for others. The help and support, the knowledge, the power, and the affection that the *guru* has for the devotee, is amazing and exquisite.'

VERSES 10-30: THE ETERNAL NATURE OF THE SOUL

tam uvāca hṛṣikeśaḥ prahasann iva bhārata |
senayor ubhayor madhye viṣīdantaṁ idaṁ vacaḥ || 10 ||

O king, as Arjuna was grieving between the two armies, Kṛṣṇa, whilst smiling, spoke the following words. (10)

śrī bhagavān uvāca
aśocyān anvaśocas tvaṁ prajñāvādāṁśca bhāṣase |
gatāsūn agatāsūṁśca nānuśocanti paṇḍitāḥ || 11 ||

Lord Kṛṣṇa says:
Whilst grieving for those who should not be grieved for, your words appear wise. But the learned lament neither for the dead nor for the living. (11)

na tvevāhaṁ jātu nāsaṁ na tvaṁ neme janādhipāḥ |
na caiva na bhaviṣyāmaḥ sarve vayamataḥ param || 12 ||

There never was a time when I did not exist, nor you, nor any of these kings. Nor will there be any time in the future when all of us shall cease to be. (12)

dehino'smin yathā dehe kaumāraṁ yauvanaṁ jarā |
tathā dehāntara prāptir dhīras tatra na muhyati || 13 ||

Just as the embodied Self passes through childhood, youth and old age, so too at death It passes into another body. A wise man is not bewildered by these events. (13)

mātrā sparśās tu kaunteya śītoṣṇa sukha-duḥkhadāḥ |
āgamāpāyino'nityās tāṁs titikṣasva bhārata || 14 ||

The contact of senses with their objects, O Arjuna, give rise to feelings of cold and heat, pleasure and pain. They come and go; they are impermanent, so endure them without being disturbed. (14)

yaṁ hi na vyathayantyete puruṣaṁ puruṣarṣabha |
sama duḥkha sukhaṁ dhīraṁ so'mṛtatvāya kalpate || 15 ||

One who is unaffected by these, O best of men, and to whom pain and pleasure are the same, that steadfast person alone is worthy of immortality. (15)

nāsato vidyate bhāvo nābhāvo vidyate sataḥ |
ubhayor api dṛṣṭo'ntas tvanayos tattva darśibhiḥ || 16 ||

The unreal can never come into being, and the real never ceases to be. This is the conclusion of those who have seen the Truth. (16)

avināśi tu tad viddhi yena sarvam idaṁ tatam |
vināśam avyayasyāsya na kaścit kartum arhati || 17 ||

It is indestructible and pervades the whole material universe. None can cause the destruction of the imperishable Self. (17)

antavanta ime dehā nityasy-oktāḥ śarīriṇaḥ |
anāśino'prameyasya tasmād yuddhyasva bhārata || 18 ||

The material bodies of the Self are said to have an end, while the Self Itself is eternal, indestructible and incomprehensible. Therefore, fight O Arjuna. (18)

ya enaṁ vetti hantāraṁ yaścainaṁ manyate hatam |
ubhau tau na vijānīto nāyaṁ hanti na hanyate || 19 ||

One who believes that the Self can kill, and one who thinks It can be killed — both are in ignorance; for the Self neither slays nor is It slain. (19)

na jāyate mriyate vā kadācin nāyaṁ bhūtvā bhavitā vā na bhūyaḥ |
ajo nityaḥ śāśvato'yaṁ purāṇo na hanyate hanyamāne śarīre || 20 ||

The Self is never born and It never dies. It has always existed and will never cease to exist. It is unborn, eternal, everlasting and most ancient. It is not killed when the body is slain. (20)

vedāvināśinaṁ nityaṁ ya enam ajam avyayam |
kathaṁ sa puruṣaḥ pārtha kaṁ ghātayati hanti kam || 21 ||

Arjuna, if one knows this Self to be indestructible, unborn, unchanging and eternal, how and whom does one cause to be killed, and whom does one kill? (21)

vāsāṁsi jīrṇāni yathā vihāya navāni gṛhṇāti naro'parāṇi |
tathā śarīrāṇi vihāya jīrṇāny-anyāni saṁyāti navāni dehī || 22 ||

As a person casts off worn-out garments and puts on new ones, so does the embodied Self cast off Its worn-out bodies and enter into new ones. (22)

nainaṁ chindanti śastrāṇi nainaṁ dahati pāvakaḥ |
na cainaṁ kledayanty-āpo na śoṣayati mārutaḥ || 23 ||

Weapons do not cut the Self; fire does not burn It, water does not wet It, and wind does not dry It. (23)

acchedyo'yam adāhyo'yam akledyo'śoṣya eva ca |
nityaḥ sarva-gataḥ sthāṇur acalo'yaṁ sanātanaḥ || 24 ||

It cannot be cut; It cannot be burnt; It cannot be wetted, and It cannot be dried. It is eternal, all-pervading, fixed, immovable and everlasting. (24)

avyakto'yam acintyo'yam avikāryo'yam ucyate |
tasmād evaṁ viditvainaṁ nānuśocitum arhasi || 25 ||

This Self is said to be unseen, inconceivable and unchanging. When you understand this, you should no longer grieve. (25)

atha cainaṁ nitya jātam nityaṁ vā manyase mṛtam |
tathāpi tvaṁ mahābāho naivaṁ śocitum arhasi || 26 ||

Even if you consider this Self to repeatedly go through birth and death, O Arjuna, still you should not lament. (26)

jātasya hi dhruvo mṛtyur dhruvaṁ janma mṛtasya ca |
tasmād aparihārye 'rthe na tvaṁ śocitum arhasi || 27 ||

For death is indeed certain for everything that is born, and re-birth is certain for that which has died; therefore, you should not grieve for what is unavoidable. (27)

avyaktādīni bhūtāni vyakta-madhyāni bhārata |
avyakta nidhanānyeva tatra kā paridevanā || 28 ||

O Arjuna! All beings have a beginning that is unknown, a middle that is known and an end which is also unknown. So why lament over this? (28)

āścaryavat paśyati kaścid enam
āścaryavad vadati tathaiva cānyaḥ |
āścaryavac cainam anyaḥ śṛṇoti
śrutvāpyenaṁ veda na caiva kaścit || 29 ||

One person sees the Self as a wonder, likewise another speaks of It as a wonder; still another hears of It as a wonder. But even after hearing of It, no one truly understands It. (29)

dehī nityam avadhyo'yaṁ dehe sarvasya bhārata |
tasmāt sarvāṇi bhūtāni na tvaṁ śocitum arhasi || 30 ||

The Self is in all bodies, O Arjuna. It is eternal and indestructible, therefore it is not right for you to feel grief for any living being. (30)

'Now is the beginning of the *Gītā*. The real *Gītā* starts with the smile of the Lord. All that came before was just a preparation for this.'

'When the *guru* sees that the disciple is really ready, He has the same smile! The disciple can ask ten thousand times and the *guru* will give whatever He has to give. But when the disciple is truly ready, even without asking, all will be given.

This is the smile that Lord Kṛṣṇa gives to Arjuna. He says, "Ah! I see that now you are ready."'

'The *guru* will not tell you things which will elevate your ego or your pride. He will tell you things which you don't want to hear. This is how He crushes the pride out of you; He removes that ignorance out of you… He will show you the way. He will polish you, He will help you to control the mind, He will help you to conquer the senses and conquer the mind. He will help you to banish this unhappiness from you, so that automatically through discrimination, through reflection, through analysis, and the true knowledge of the Self, that true happiness, the permanent happiness, awakens inside of you.'

'If you want true wisdom, know that there is no birth and no death. You are the *ātmā*, you are eternal. For the *ātmā*, there is no beginning, there is no end. So why do you mourn? You have come here to attain a higher reality; you have come here to do a higher work than what you realise. Kṛṣṇa tells Arjuna that the wise never grieve in this way. The one who has the knowledge of the Self, the realised one, knows that the *ātmā* is eternal and that there is no point in mourning or grieving. The wise person knows that God is the embodiment of true knowledge... The wise person knows that it is only Him who is abiding in everything. He is the Self of all. He is the indestructible Absolute.'

[Kṛṣṇa says,] '"There was never a time when I did not exist, nor you! As I existed before everything, you were also with Me." This is the relationship that we have with God. We are always with Him and He is always with us, whether you want it or not. You can be the greatest atheist and you can say God doesn't exist; it doesn't bother Him.'

'You have an identity. You will always have it. You have ever existed with Him. You are never separate from Him. We all existed before our birth, before we manifested here in these bodies, and we will carry on existing long after these bodies have disappeared. That *ātmā* will always live even if everything gets destroyed.'

'The body goes through recycling, because it's made of the five elements, and the five elements go back into nature. But the Self remains untouched, unchanged, immutable, indestructible and it is eternal. It is not created. If something is not created, that means it can't die.'

'How you see the body is important. It doesn't mean that now that you have heard that the body is decaying and deteriorating, one shouldn't care about it. Then realisation will not come to you, because this body is the vehicle to attain that realisation.

'Even the Lord Himself manifests on Earth in a body. But you should not forget about the *ātmā* also. Nowadays people concentrate so much only on the external reality that they forget that they have a soul.'

'So awake, my dear soul. Realise your Self. You are the *ātmā*. Stop being in the sleeping state, because in a sleeping state you will not realise anything. You have to be awake to realise your Self.'

VERSES 31-38: THE DUTY OF A WARRIOR

sva-dharmam api cāvekṣya na vikampitum arhasi |
dharmyāddhi yuddhāc-chreyo 'nyat kṣatriyasya na vidyate || 31 ||

Furthermore, considering also your own personal duty, you should not hesitate. For a *kṣatriya* (warrior), there is nothing superior to fighting in a righteous war. (31)

yadṛcchayā copapannaṁ svarga dvāram apāvṛtam |
sukhinaḥ kṣatriyāḥ pārtha labhante yuddham īdṛśam || 32 ||

Happy are the *kṣatriyas*, O Arjuna, at such an opportunity. A war such as this, that comes of its own accord, opens the gates to Heaven. (32)

atha-cet tvam imaṁ dharmyaṁ saṅgrāmaṁ na kariṣyasi |
tataḥ sva-dharmaṁ kīrtiṁ ca hitvā pāpam avāpsyasi || 33 ||

But if you do not fight this righteous war, you will be turning away from your duty and will lose your honour. Therefore, you will accumulate sin. (33)

akīrtiṁ cāpi bhūtāni kathayiṣyanti te'vyayām |
saṁbhāvitasya cākīrtir maraṇād-atiricyate || 34 ||

Then people will forever speak of your disgrace, and for an honourable man, dishonour is worse than death. (34)

bhayād raṇād uparataṁ mansyante tvāṁ mahārathāḥ |
yeṣāṁ ca tvaṁ bahu-mato bhūtvā yāsyasi lāghavam || 35 ||

The great warriors will think that you have fled from the battlefield in fear. These men who held you in high regard will then speak in contempt of you. (35)

avācya vādāṁśca bahūn vadiṣyanti tavāhitāḥ |
nindantas tava sāmarthyaṁ tato duḥkhataraṁ nu kim || 36 ||

Your enemies will condemn your ability. They will use words which should never be uttered. What could be more painful than that? (36)

hato vā prāpsyasi svargaṁ jitvā vā bhokṣyase mahīn |
tasmād uttiṣṭha kaunteya yuddhāya kṛta-niścayaḥ || 37 ||

If slain, you shall gain Heaven; if victorious, you shall enjoy the Earth. Therefore, arise O Arjuna, and resolve to fight. (37)

sukha-duḥkhe same kṛtvā lābhālābhau jayājayau |
tato yuddhāya yujyasva nainaṁ pāpam avāpsyasi || 38 ||

Considering pleasure and pain, gain and loss, victory and defeat to be the same, prepare yourself for battle. If you act in this way, you will not incur sin. (38)

'Kṛṣṇa is saying everybody knows that they are not the body, everybody knows that they are not the mind, they are not the intellect, but yet, they still identify themselves with them. This is due to the lack of true knowledge, lack of true understanding. You have received this knowledge through books; reading wonderful books has given you this insight. You have heard many talks about it, but it has just remained as words which are pleasurable to you. It doesn't have any effect upon you. You are still running after the external pleasures; you are still running after things that are perishable.'

'If you are looking at the soul only from the point of view of the mind, do you think that the mind can understand the soul? A mind which is always moving around is, "*cañcala*", "restless," dancing and jumping like a monkey, from one thought to the other. How can the mind, which is in constant movement, be still and perceive the unmovable? The mind will always move from one thing to another until one has gone deeply into the *sādhana* (spiritual practice), deeply into meditation and calmed the mind. Only then, will the soul reveal itself. But before that, if the mind is still jumping around, the soul is unknowable.'

'"Considering pleasure and pain, gain and loss, victory and defeat to be the same": Remind yourself that this is all just a game. Take this pair of opposites as being equal. Even if they appear different, they are the same. A wise man should not be completely taken over by joy when something is happening, but just stay calm. And those who are wise don't complain when there is some trouble. They analyse the situation. They are in a balanced state in both situations: in a happy moment or in an unhappy moment.'

'When you do your duty in life, accepting what God is giving you to do, it draws you closer and closer to God-realisation. By accepting what God is giving you in your daily life, you are opening the gates to receive more. By showing that you are doing your duty by accepting what God gives you in life, you are showing God that you are ready for a greater purpose in this life, for greater work. Kṛṣṇa says, "If you run away from this, it will not bring you any good. It will hurt you. It will be unrighteous. Especially on such an occasion, where doing this duty will help you open all the doors to Heaven." He says, "Accept life. Accept whatever God gives you."'

VERSES 39-53: THE INTRODUCTION OF KARMA-YOGA

eṣā te'bhihitā sāṅkhye buddhir yoge tvimāṁ śṛṇu |
buddhyā-yukto yayā pārtha karma-bandhaṁ prahāsyasi || 39 ||

This knowledge which has been taught to you so far is based on Sāṅkhya [1]. Now listen to the teaching concerning karma-yoga. When you act with this knowledge, O Arjuna, you will be free from the bonds of action. (39)

nehābhikrama-nāśo'sti pratyavāyo na vidyate |
svalpam apyasya dharmasya trāyate mahato bhayāt || 40 ||

There is nothing to lose in this endeavour nor is there any failure. Even a little practise of this *yoga* saves one from great danger. (40)

vyavasāyātmikā buddhir ekeha kuru-nandana |
bahu-śākhā hyanantāśca buddhayo'vyavasāyinām || 41 ||

O Arjuna, on this path the resolute mind is one-pointed; but the thoughts of the irresolute are many-branched and endless. (41)

yām imāṁ puṣpitāṁ vācaṁ pravadanty-avipaścitaḥ |
veda-vāda-ratāḥ pārtha nānyad astīti vādinaḥ || 42 ||

Those who are unwise rejoice at the flowery words of the *Veda*, declaring 'there is nothing superior to this!' (42)

kāmātmānaḥ svarga-parā janma-karma-phala-pradām |
kriyā-viśeṣa bahulāṁ bhogaiśvarya gatiṁ prati || 43 ||

Such people are full of desires and have heaven for their goal. Seeking pleasure and power, they teach that the performance of various rituals leads to higher rebirth. (43)

bhogaiśvarya prasaktānāṁ tayāpahṛta cetasām |
vyavasāyātmikā buddhiḥ samādhau na vidhīyate || 44 ||

Those who cling to pleasure and power and are attracted to these teachings cannot develop the resolute will of a concentrated mind. (44)

trai-guṇya viṣayā vedā nistrai-guṇyo bhavārjuna |
nir-dvandvo nitya sattvastho nir-yoga kṣema ātmavān || 45 ||

The *Vedas* [2] deal with the three *guṇas* [3], O Arjuna. You must free yourself from these *guṇas* and from the pairs of opposites. Being ever established in the *sattva-guṇa* [4], do not care about acquiring things nor about protecting what has been acquired – instead, be established in the Self. (45)

yāvān artha udapāne sarvataḥ saṁplutodake |
tāvān sarveṣu vedeṣu brāhmaṇasya vijānataḥ || 46 ||

The purpose of a reservoir is easily met by an area flooded with water, in the same way the knowledge of the *Vedas* is easily met by a sage who is Self-realised. (46)

karmaṇy-evādhikāras te mā phaleṣu kadācana |
mā karma phala hetur bhūr mā te saṅgo'stva karmaṇi || 47 ||

You have a right to act, but not to the fruits of that action. Do not allow rewards to be your motive for action; at the same time do not be attached to avoiding action. (47)

yogasthaḥ kuru karmāṇi saṅgaṁ tyaktvā dhanañjaya |
siddhy-asiddhyoḥ samo bhūtvā samatvaṁ yoga ucyate || 48 ||

Established in *yoga* and abandoning attachment, perform your duty. See success and failure with an even mind. This equanimity is the meaning of *yoga*. (48)

dūreṇa hyavaraṁ karma buddhi-yogād dhanañjaya |
buddhau śaraṇam anviccha kṛpaṇāḥ phala-hetavaḥ || 49 ||

Arjuna, action done with attachment to the results is far inferior to this *yoga*. Seek refuge in that equanimous state. Those who are motivated by the fruits of action are petty-minded. (49)

buddhi-yukto jahātīha ubhe sukṛta duṣkṛte |
tasmād yogāya yujyasva yogaḥ karmasu kauśalam || 50 ||

Remaining equal-minded, one rises above righteous and unrighteous deeds. Therefore, devote yourself to this *yoga*, for *yoga* is the true way of performing action. (50)

karmajaṁ buddhi-yuktā hi phalaṁ tyaktvā manīṣiṇaḥ |
janma bandha vinirmuktāḥ padaṁ gacchanty-anāmayam || 51 ||

The wise who are established in this state, renounce the fruits of action, and are freed from the bondage of rebirth. They go to the Abode beyond all suffering. (51)

yadā te mohakalilaṁ buddhir vyati-tariṣyati |
tadā gantāsi nirvedaṁ śrotavyasya śrutasya ca || 52 ||

When your intellect has passed beyond the forest of delusion, you will be indifferent to what you shall hear in the future and what you have already heard. (52)

śruti vipratipannā te yadā sthāsyasi niścalā |
samādhāv-acalā buddhis tadā yogam avāpsyasi || 53 ||

When you are no longer perplexed by the words of the *Vedas* and remain unshaken with a concentrated mind, then you will have achieved success in *yoga*. (53)

'Here Kṛṣṇa is saying that you should do your work, but you should not attach to the fruit of the work. You have your duty. You have to work. But your work will bear fruits when you do it out of love, when you love what God has given you and happily do it knowing that you are serving Him. This is where work becomes worship. When you think of Him throughout the time you are working, then everything will be perfect, because it doesn't come from you. It comes from Him. It is Him who is working through you.'

'Realised souls are not attached to anything. Even if they do an action which is inappropriate in the minds of society, they are free from every *karma* related to it. Their ordinary speech, even their modes of sitting and walking, have a special characteristic: it is all through the vibration, and it is all for the sake of others, not for their own sake.'

'When you are attached, you become ineffective, because when you are only focused on trying to do things properly, you are not free! You don't have any freedom inside of you, because you are tense. Kṛṣṇa says, "If you do your action with the aim of serving the Lord, if you renounce this attachment to the result of the action, you will attain God-realisation. You can't renounce your actions, but do your actions with a selfless motive. Do them without egoism." If you try to renounce your actions by force, you will not succeed.'

'Take success and failure in the same way. Purify the mind. Only when the mind is purified, only when the mind is calm, only when the mind is focused and centred on the Supreme Lord, then you are free. If the mind is wandering in all directions, nothing good can come out of it. You are never sure, "Am I right or not?"... You have hundreds of questions that arise inside of your mind. This is an uncontrolled mind.'

'When you do your *sādhana*, first, try to calm your mind. What awakens is the first instinct, the first feeling, the first wave which awakens inside of you. That's what you have to learn to listen to, because it comes from your consciousness, it comes from your higher Self. If you can distinguish between the mind and your consciousness, you will always take the right decision. The mind always runs towards the pairs of opposites. It always wants to justify itself. So, control that mind. A controlled mind, which is not running left-right in all directions, will give you balance and equilibrium in life.'

VERSES 54-72: THE QUALITIES OF A REALISED PERSON

arjuna uvāca
sthita-prajñāsya kā bhāṣā samādhisthasya keśava |
sthita-dhīḥ kiṁ prabhāṣata kim āsīta vrajeta kim || 54 ||

Arjuna says:
O Kṛṣṇa, what are the defining qualities of one who has achieved this realisation? How does he speak? What is his language like? How does he sit and how does he move? (54)

śrī bhagavān uvāca
prajahāti yadā kāmān sarvān pārtha manogatān |
ātmany-evātmanā tuṣṭaḥ sthita-prajñās tadocyate || 55 ||

The Lord says:
When one gives up all desires arising in the mind, O Arjuna, when one satisfies himself by the Self alone, then one is said to be of steady wisdom. (55)

duḥkheṣv-anudvigna-manāḥ sukheṣu vigata spṛhaḥ |
vīta-rāga bhaya krodhaḥ sthita-dhīr munir ucyate || 56 ||

One whose mind is not perturbed by pain, who does not run after pleasures, who is free from desire, fear and anger – such a person is a sage of steady intellect. (56)

yaḥ sarvatrān-abhisnehas tat tat prāpya śubhāśubham |
nābhinandati na dveṣṭi tasya prajñā pratiṣṭhitā || 57 ||

He who has no attachment anywhere, who, when encountering the agreeable or the disagreeable feels neither attraction nor aversion – his wisdom is firmly established. (57)

yadā saṁharate cāyaṁ kūrmo'ṅgānīva sarvaśaḥ |
indriyāṇīndriyārthebhyas tasya prajñā pratiṣṭhitā || 58 ||

When one is able to withdraw the senses from the objects of senses on every side, as a tortoise withdraws its limbs, then one's wisdom is firmly established. (58)

viṣayā vinivartante nirāhārasya dehinaḥ |
rasa-varjaṁ raso'pyasya paraṁ dṛṣṭvā nivartate || 59 ||

Although the objects of the senses can be given up by one who practises abstinence, the attachment for them can still persist. But when one sees the Supreme Lord, such attraction is naturally renounced by the embodied soul. (59)

yatato hyapi kaunteya puruṣasya vipaścitaḥ |
indriyāṇi pramāthīni haranti prasabhaṁ manaḥ || 60 ||

The turbulent senses, O Arjuna, forcefully carry away the mind of even a wise person, despite him continually striving to control them. (60)

tāni sarvāṇi saṁyamya yukta āsīta matparaḥ |
vaśe hi yasyendriyāṇi tasya prajñā pratiṣṭhitā || 61 ||

Having controlled all the senses, one should abide in the state of meditation, having Me as the supreme goal; for one who has controlled his senses, wisdom is firmly established. (61)

dhyāyato viṣayān puṁsaḥ saṅgas teṣūpajāyate |
saṅgāt sañjāyate kāmaḥ kāmāt krodho'bhijāyate || 62 ||

When one deliberates upon sense-objects, attachment to them arises; from attachment comes desire, from desire arises anger. (62)

krodhād-bhavati saṁmohaḥ saṁmohāt smṛti-vibhramaḥ |
smṛti-bhraṁśād buddhi-nāśo buddhir-nāśāt praṇaśyati || 63 ||

From anger arises delusion; from delusion, there is loss of memory; from loss of memory the destruction of discrimination occurs; and with the destruction of discrimination, one is lost. (63)

rāga-dveṣa viyuktais tu viṣayān indriyaiś-caran |
ātma-vaśyair vidheyātmā prasādam adhigacchati || 64 ||

But one who is self-controlled, moving among the sense-objects with the senses under restraint, free from attraction and aversion, attains tranquillity. (64)

prasāde sarva-duḥkhānāṁ hānir asyopajāyate |
prasanna-cetaso hyāśu buddhiḥ paryavatiṣṭhate || 65 ||

In that state of serenity, all sorrow is overcome. For that person who has a serene mind, realisation soon becomes well established. (65)

nāsti buddhir-ayuktasya na cāyuktasya bhāvanā |
na cābhāvayataḥ śāntir aśāntasya kutaḥ sukham || 66 ||

There can be no realisation and no properly focused mind for one who does not engage in this practice. Without such a focused mind, there can be no peace, and without peace how can there be happiness? (66)

indriyāṇāṁ hi caratāṁ yan mano'nuvidhīyate |
tad asya harati prajñāṁ vāyur nāvam ivāmbhasi || 67 ||

The roaming senses experience their objects, and when the mind follows, one's understanding is carried away by them, just as a ship on water is carried away by the wind. (67)

tasmād yasya mahābāho nigṛhītāni sarvaśaḥ |
indriyāṇīndriyārthebhyas tasya prajñā pratiṣṭhitā || 68 ||

Therefore, O mighty-armed one, only when one has restrained their senses from their objects, does their wisdom become firmly established. (68)

yā niśā sarva bhūtānāṁ tasyāṁ jāgarti saṁyamī |
yasyāṁ jāgrati bhūtāni sā niśā paśyato muneḥ || 69 ||

What is night for all beings, is actually a time of awakening for the self-controlled, and when all beings are awake, it is night for the enlightened one. (69)

apūryamāṇam acala pratiṣṭhaṁ
samudram āpaḥ praviśanti yadvat |
tadvat kāmā yaṁ praviśanti sarve
sa śāntim āpnoti na kāmakāmī || 70 ||

Just as different rivers flow into the sea which remains full, steady and immovable, so too do desires flow into an enlightened person. It is he who attains peace and not the one who seeks to fulfil desires. (70)

vihāya kāmān yaḥ sarvān pumāṁś-carati niḥspṛhaḥ |
nirmamo nirahaṅkāraḥ sa śāntim adhigacchati || 71 ||

The one who has abandoned all desires and is free from any craving, and does not have any notion of 'I' and 'mine', that person alone attains real peace. (71)

eṣā brāhmī-sthitiḥ pārtha naināṁ prāpya vimuhyati |
sthitvā'syām antakāle'pi brahma-nirvāṇam ṛcchati || 72 ||

This is the realised state, O Arjuna. Once this is attained there is no delusion. By abiding in this state even at the hour of death, one attains the Abode of God. (72)

'Don't run behind the sense objects. Long for something permanent. Long for God's grace. Don't long for wealth, external comforts, the desire for name, fame, glory, pride, ego, vanity. All this will not make you free. It will make you more miserable, because it will keep you away from realising your Self. All this will awaken the egoistic self-importance, this big "I-ness" inside of you.'

'This big "I" will bring lots of expectations into your life. It will awaken lots of desires for many things.'

'If you are doing *yoga*, if you are doing spiritual things, humility has to be there, humbleness must be there. If there is no humility, you will never have peace.'

'The whole problem starts when you start thinking. When you start thinking, you start comparing. When you start comparing, you lose everything. There is no peace of mind. And when there is no peace of mind, everything is destroyed.'

'Whatever you have, be happy. God always gives you what you need. He also knows best when is the right time to give you what you need. If you learn to accept this, no matter what God will give you, it will be for your spiritual growth. Even all these desires will not have any effect on the person who is fully centred in the Divine, whose aim is clear. Nothing will affect one's mental state. If one is peaceful, there will be nothing to worry about. One knows that all is the will of God. One knows that all comes from God. It is He who gives, and it is He who takes.'

'When you are rebelling against somebody else, you are not rebelling against anybody except yourself. It's just because you can't see and accept your own fault that you are projecting it on people around you. That's what Kṛṣṇa is saying: from desire, anger comes forth and explodes! But when your mind is controlled, then you don't disturb anybody. You bring peace for the people around you also.'

'Those who have realised God, they reflect a different light. Whatever these great souls do is not for themselves… Whatever they do, they do in accordance with the will of God. They don't do it for their own pleasures, they don't do it for their own attachment or their own wants. Even if it appears that they are not doing anything, even if they are piling up a mountain of sand, they are always doing something for the benefit of the world… The same thing that they have inside of them, they give to others.'

'The *Bhagavad Gītā* is not just literature. These are not just nice words that Kṛṣṇa wanted to say to Arjuna to prove that he has to fight. In reality, the *Bhagavad Gītā* is life itself. It is your life from the moment you start to search.'

'When Bhagavān Kṛṣṇa is talking to Arjuna, He is not only talking to Arjuna, He is talking to everyone about how to transcend from just being a human being, and how to have this connection with Him, to build this relationship with Him. That's what *yoga* stands for. In the *Bhagavad Gītā* we talk about *yoga*, but *yoga* is this eternal relationship which we have with God. The world, everything that you see around, is trying to make you forget about this relationship, saying, "No, you are not this! This is all just a fantasy." Does the world teach you about your soul? No, it doesn't. Does the world teach you how to live your life? No, it doesn't. But the world wants to control you. Everywhere you see people wanting to control you. Society is like that.'

'So, long for the grace of the Lord, long for Him; don't let yourself be put under the spell of *māyā* [1]. Because *māyā* doesn't have any grip upon those who are centred in the Lord... they are free. They go everywhere. They radiate their peace, freedom, and true happiness freely to all, without expectation. They become a lantern to those seated in darkness. They become a guide to those who sit in darkness so that they can also start shining their light. This is the duty of a devotee, the duty of a *bhakta* [2]: once they have tasted that sweetness of the Love of God, and once they are strong enough, they should help others find that light.'

Chapter Two Verses: Key Terms

[1] **Sāṅkhya** – philosophy which states that there are two realities: the Puruṣa (Self) and *prakṛti* (matter). Through an analysis of *prakṛti*, one can realise oneself as the Puruṣa, which is utterly distinct from material nature.

[2] **Vedas** – the earliest body of Indian scripture, consisting of the *Ṛg Veda*, *Sāma Veda*, *Yajur Veda*, and *Atharva Veda*, which lay down the fundamental principles of Hinduism.

[3] **Guṇas** – the three qualities within *prakṛti* (matter): *sattva* (purity), *rajas* (activity) and *tamas* (darkness). The different *guṇas* work together to shape and influence the experience we have in the material world.

[4] **Sattva-guṇa** – quality of gentility, good conduct, enlightened understanding, purity and detachment.

Chapter Two Commentary: Key Terms

[1] **Māyā** – the influence of the material world that draws us away from our true relationship with God.

[2] **Bhakta** – one who is devoted to God.

CHAPTER THREE
KARMA-YOGA
UNDERSTANDING KARMA-YOGA

Despite the explanation of *karma-yoga*, Arjuna remains confused: If one has to renounce action, then why is he being urged to fight? Fundamentally Arjuna does not see the difference between *karma* and *karma-yoga*. *Karma* is any action done with the body or mind that produces further consequences. *Karma-yoga* is about performing action in a detached state, thereby being free of any such consequences.

Kṛṣṇa replies to Arjuna's question by saying that realisation of the Self can be achieved through two methods: by setting aside all duties and contemplating on the *ātmā* (*jñāna-yoga*), or by carrying out one's duties in a detached way (*karma-yoga*). But, out of the two, *karma-yoga* is the easiest. *Jñāna-yoga*, in the context of the *Gītā*, ultimately requires renunciation of external action, and action as a whole is incredibly difficult to renounce. The very nature of life causes us to act, we cannot escape it. Therefore, we should carry out our duty without any attachment to the results.

By following the example of Kṛṣṇa and other great personalities, action should be performed selflessly for the welfare of the world. Eventually the true *yogī* sees that, despite acting, oneself is not the doer. It is simply the various forms of the material world acting upon each other. Kṛṣṇa concludes chapter three by stating that the root cause of deviating from the path of *yoga* is desire. It clouds our vision and prevents us from realising true knowledge. As a result, we should strive to conquer this enemy through our spiritual practices.

VERSES 1-2: ARJUNA'S QUESTION

arjuna uvāca
jyāyasī cet karmaṇaste matā buddhir-janārdana |
tat kiṁ karmaṇi ghore māṁ niyojayasi keśava || 1 ||

Arjuna says:
If, O Kṛṣṇa, you consider intelligence to be superior to action, why do you urge me to engage in this terrible deed? (1)

vyāmiśreṇeva vākyena buddhiṁ mohayasīva me |
tad ekaṁ vada niścitya yena śreyoham-āpnuyām || 2 ||

You confuse me with statements that seem to contradict each other; tell me for certain the way I can reach the highest good. (2)

'In deep attention, Arjuna has been listening to Kṛṣṇa, but inside of himself, he is not fully cleansed. That doubt is still there, that mind is still active. He wants to understand in depth the knowledge that the Lord wants to give him... He is asking, "How can I do certain duties, have certain responsibilities, certain relationships, but not attach myself to them?"'

'Kṛṣṇa is talking to Arjuna, but in reality He is talking to everyone. Because He is not talking to a person, He is talking to the soul. People may differ in beliefs, they can differ in faith, but knowledge, true knowledge, is universal.'

'Even if Bhagavān Kṛṣṇa had talked about *jñāna-yoga* and had given Arjuna this great knowledge, they were not on the same wavelength. Their vibration is different. Bhagavān Kṛṣṇa is the Supreme Lord Himself. So, when He is talking, He is in His fullness. Whereas, Arjuna is listening, but he is still in a lower level. He has to rise to the same level so that he can understand.'

'Here, Kṛṣṇa is not just talking about the knowledge that you read in a book or that you hear from others. He is also talking about the inner knowledge: how to attain God consciousness.'

'Arjuna surrenders to the Lord. He is humbly submitting himself to the Lord and is willing to change himself... He is still hanging onto the mind, but with attentiveness and with the willingness to change. Arjuna is removing his own will, little by little. He is renouncing his own will so that his inner will, which is in accordance with the *guru*, which is in accordance with Śrī Kṛṣṇa Himself, will free him.'

'This chapter is about how one can work in daily life, accept what God has given, do one's *karma-yoga* outside, yet be separate from it; how to be focused and be free from that action. This chapter will allow you to realise that all the work that you have to do here can help you participate in your realisation.'

VERSES 3-16: THE INESCAPABLE NATURE OF ACTION

śrī bhagavān uvāca
loke'smin dvividhā niṣṭhā purā proktā mayā'nagha |
jñāna-yogena sāṅkhyānāṁ karma-yogena yoginām || 3 ||

Lord Kṛṣṇa says:
O sinless one, as I have mentioned in this world there are two paths: *jñāna-yoga* [1] for those who are ready to contemplate and analyse, and *karma-yoga* for those ready to act in detachment. (3)

na karmaṇām anārambhān naiṣkarmyaṁ puruṣo'śnute |
na ca saṁnyasanād-eva siddhiṁ samādhigacchati || 4 ||

Understand that no one achieves freedom from action simply by abstaining from it, and no one ever attains perfection by renunciation alone. (4)

na hi kaścit kṣaṇam-api jātu tiṣṭhaty-akarma-kṛt |
kāryate hy-avaśaḥ karma sarvaḥ prakṛti-jair-guṇaiḥ || 5 ||

No one can remain still even for a moment without performing action. Everyone is helplessly forced to act by the *guṇas* born from material nature. (5)

karmendriyāṇi saṁyamya ya āste manasā smaran |
indriyārthān vimūḍhātmā mithyācāraḥ sa ucyate || 6 ||

One who restrains the organs of action whilst still contemplating on the objects of the senses is deluded and a hypocrite. (6)

yastv-indriyāṇi manasā niyamyārabhate'rjuna |
karmendriyaiḥ karma-yogam asaktasya viśiṣyate || 7 ||

But, Arjuna, one who can subdue the senses with the mind and practise *karma-yoga* with the organs of action, free from attachment, is far superior. (7)

niyataṁ kuru karma tvaṁ karma jyāyo hy-akarmaṇaḥ |
śarīra-yātrā'pi ca te na prasiddhyed akarmaṇaḥ || 8 ||

You must perform your duty for action is superior to the avoidance of action. Understand that one cannot even maintain one's own body without action. (8)

yajñārthāt karmaṇo'nyatra loko'yaṁ karma bandhanaḥ |
tad-arthaṁ karma kaunteya mukta saṅgas-samācara || 9 ||

Apart from action done in a spirit of sacrifice, this world is bound by action. Therefore, Arjuna, being free from attachment, you must act with this purpose alone. (9)

saha yajñāiḥ prajāḥ sṛṣṭvā purovāca prajāpatiḥ |
anena prasaviṣyadhvam eṣa vo'stviṣṭa kāmadhuk || 10 ||

In the beginning, the Lord of all beings created humans, along with the sacrifice, saying: 'By this shall you prosper; this shall be the cow of plenty granting all your desires.' (10)

devān bhāvayetānena te devā bhāvayantu vaḥ |
parasparaṁ bhāvayantaḥ śreyaḥ paramavāpsyatha || 11 ||

By this, may you nurture the gods, and in return the gods will nurture you. In this way, nurturing one another, you will obtain the highest good. (11)

iṣṭān-bhogān-hi vo devā dāsyante yajñā-bhāvitāḥ |
tair-dattān apradāyaibhyo yo bhuṅkte stena eva saḥ || 12 ||

The gods, pleased by sacrifice, will bestow on you the enjoyments you desire. One who enjoys the gifts of the gods without offering them anything in return is verily a thief. (12)

yajñā-śiṣṭāśinaḥ santo mucyante sarva kilbiṣaiḥ |
bhuñjate te tvaghaṁ pāpā ye pacantyātma kāraṇāt || 13 ||

The righteous who eat the remnants of sacrifices are freed from all sins. But the sinful ones who cook only for their own gratification eat only sin. (13)

annād-bhavanti būtāni parjanyād-anna-saṁbhavaḥ |
yajñād-bhavati parjanyaḥ yajñāḥ karma samud-bhavaḥ || 14 ||

All beings are sustained by food; food is produced from rain; rain comes from sacrifice; and sacrifice is achieved through action. (14)

karma brahmod-bhavaṁ viddhi brahmākṣara samudbhavam |
tasmāt sarva-gataṁ brahma nityaṁ yajñe pratiṣṭhitam || 15 ||
This ritual action comes from the *Vedas* and the *Vedas* come from the Supreme Lord, therefore that all-pervading divinity is ever established in acts of sacrifice. (15)

evaṁ pravartitaṁ cakraṁ nānu vartayatīha yaḥ |
aghāyur-indriyā rāmo moghaṁ pārtha sa jīvati || 16 ||
O Arjuna, one who does not follow this cycle, which has been set in motion, lives in error. Revelling in the senses, he lives in vain. (16)

'The moment you are born in this world, you are born into the world of action, a world which is in constant movement. There is not a single moment when you are not working. Even when you think you are sitting and relaxing, you are still working. You are breathing, you are working. You are thinking, you are working.'

'One may say, "Oh, I will not do this work, because there will be no profit in it." But here the mind is still hanging onto the work. Kṛṣṇa says, that if *karma-yoga* is done with such an attitude, there is no freedom. He says, "No one ever attains perfection by mere renunciation of works". If one is fake with oneself, if one is not in truth towards oneself, freely and happily renouncing work, one will not be free. One will not do the work outside, but it will still play very much in the mind, saying, "I have renounced this, I am a great *yogī*. I do my meditation properly. My back is straight." But the mind always continues to play. This is not really doing meditation! And this is not really doing the job properly, focused on the Divine. It is not the outside that matters, it is God that matters. It is to find God in everything. Put Him first! If He is first, it is easy. But if He is not first, it is very difficult to let go, even if you pretend to let go! The ones who are only pretending are hypocrites!'

'You can't stop the senses. You can't stop the natural tendency of the senses, but you can control it. Even if you try to stop it, how would you do your *karma-yoga*? How would you do your action outwardly? It would never happen, because any form of action is through the senses. However, if the senses are under control, if the mind is under control, then one excels and rises above the senses.'

'If one reaches the state of a true *bhakta*, where all the activities of the body, mind and senses are completely surrendered, one sees that one is not the doer. One attains the Self; one becomes the Great Observer. One sees that one is the witness of all these activities. Instead of giving up the performance of their duties or stage of life, instead of running away, the devotees who practise the path of knowledge must renounce the sense of doership, the sense of possession, and the attachment to that desire. Lord Kṛṣṇa says, "One will not reach perfection by renouncing the act, but by transcending it, by transforming it into service to the Lord in whatever one does, and by being separate from self-gratification, self-glory." Be humble. Remove all this egoism inside of you. Remove all this pride inside of you and be free.'

'Do everything and offer everything upon the altar of the Lord. Surrender and dedicate all actions to the Lord, and then the action or the *karma* ceases to be a burden because it's being directed towards Him. So that's why Bhagavān has, first, given Arjuna the wisdom of the Self. First, He has told him what is the Self, what is the body, what is the mind. Now He is saying, "Utilise everything." How you will utilise it? Do your actions without complaining. Accept what God has given you, where God has put you; whatever job He has given you, accept it. Because where He has put you is where you have to be. Maybe you don't like it. Maybe you think that you could have done much better, but now you are here. What you could have had is in the past. You are not there. Learn to accept it right now without any complaints. Accept the result even if you don't agree with it, because in the mind, whenever you do something, you have a certain expectation. But you don't know about the result. Whatever result comes, learn to accept it. If you do that, this attitude will pave the way for *karma-yoga*, the *yoga* of action.'

VERSES 17-26: THE RESPONSIBILITY OF THE WISE

yastvātma-ratir-eva syād-ātma tṛptaśca mānavaḥ |
ātmanyeva ca santuṣṭas-tasya kāryaṁ na vidyate || 17 ||

But the person who delights in the Self, who is satisfied with the Self, who rejoices in the Self, for him there is nothing left to achieve. (17)

naiva tasya kṛtenārtho nākṛteneha kaścana |
na cāsya sarva-bhūteṣu kaścid artha vyapāśrayaḥ || 18 ||

For such a person there is nothing to gain from renouncing or performing action, nor is he dependent on any other being. (18)

tasmād asaktaḥ satataṁ kāryaṁ karma samācara |
asakto hyācaran karma param-āpnoti pūruṣaḥ || 19 ||

Therefore, always perform that work which ought to be done without attachment. For one who acts without attachment attains the Supreme. (19)

karmaṇaiva hi saṁsiddhim āsthitā janakādayaḥ |
loka saṅgraham-evāpi saṁpaśyan kartum arhasi || 20 ||

Verily, by *karma-yoga* alone did Janaka [2] and others reach perfection. Indeed, you should act bearing in mind the welfare of the world. (20)

yadyad-ācarati śreṣṭhas-tat-tad-evetaro janaḥ |
sa yat pramāṇaṁ kurute lokas-tad-anuvartate || 21 ||

Whatever an eminent person does, other people also do; whatever standard that one sets, the world follows. (21)

na me parthāsti kartavyaṁ triṣu lokeṣu kiñcana |
nānavāptam-avāptavyaṁ varta eva ca karmaṇi || 22 ||

For Me, O Arjuna, there is nothing in all the three worlds which needs to be done, nor is there anything for Me to gain. But despite this, I continually engage in action. (22)

yadi hyahaṁ na varteyaṁ jātu karmaṇyatandritaḥ |
mama vartmānuvartante manuṣyāḥ pārtha sarvaśaḥ || 23 ||

For if I did not continuously engage Myself in action, the world would follow My example. (23)

utsīdeyur-ime lokā na kuryaṁ karma ced aham |
saṅkarasya ca kartā syām upahanyām-imāḥ prajāḥ || 24 ||

If I did not perform action these worlds would perish; I would be the author of confusion and the cause of destruction for living beings. (24)

saktāḥ karmaṇy-avidvāṁso yathā kurvanti bhārata |
kuryād-vidvāṁs-tathāsaktāś-cikīrṣur loka-saṅgraham || 25 ||

Arjuna, just as the ignorant act with attachment to their work, so should the wise act without any attachment, thinking only for the welfare of the world. (25)

na buddhi-bhedaṁ janayed ajñānāṁ karma-saṅginām |
joṣayet sarva karmāṇi vidvān yuktaḥ samācaran || 26 ||

The wise should not disturb the minds of the ignorant who are attached to work. Instead by performing work with devotion, one should inspire others to do likewise. (26)

'The realised one doesn't look for any personal gratification. There is no obligation for him to do something or not do something! In the scriptures there are many rules about what one has to do, and what one has not to do. The *Vedas* are full of these rules. But here, Lord Kṛṣṇa says that the one who is completely surrendered and realise that it is only God, Lord Nārāyaṇa Himself, who is doing everything, is not bound by what he has to do or not do. He is not bound by his activities. He is not controlled by the senses. Nor is he controlled by the scriptures. The scriptures don't compel him to do or not to do anything. He doesn't have anything to abandon nor can he fail by not doing something. Why? Because he is guided. All his actions are guided by the Lord Himself. He is not bound by his own mind. Here Kṛṣṇa says to Arjuna, "This is another level now! This is a level where only God exists, where there is no 'I.'"

'This doesn't mean that God-realised souls don't act in the world. They do! But they are not bound by their actions. They help to maintain the balance in the world, but they have no attachment to what they do or to what they don't do. They go with their intuition. It's not them – they are guided. Everything happens, everything is taken care of, automatically. Such a state is the highest good for humanity. Not only for them, but also for the people around. They are centred in the Supreme. In this state, there is no creation of *karma*. Such a person renounces all!'

'Great heroes and great saints reached perfection during their lifetimes. You don't need ten lifetimes to do that. You only need one lifetime. You just need complete surrender. The willingness to surrender has to be there!'

'Here Bhagavān Himself is reminding: "Look at Me, dear Arjuna. I am free from these three worlds. *Māyā* doesn't have any power over Me. Illusion is far away. I am free from that and I don't need anything, because I have created everything. Everything comes from Me. I am in everything. But I'm doing My duty, not running away from My duty. I have taken this form for a purpose."'

'The Lord is the ideal person. He never neglects His duty, because He knows that if He does, others will take Him as an example… Thus, this will bring great imbalance to the world.'

'"Set an example, My dear Arjuna! People will follow that example and people will also be strong. Be strong in your faith! Be strong in your path so that you can also help others to find their way in life."'

'If God has given you a certain duty to do in life, if He has given you a family to look after, if your duty is the family, do your duty properly! If you are a mother, be a good mother! If you are a father, be a good father; if you are a husband or a wife, do your duty accordingly.'

'When you do your duty properly in the world, it can be a blessing to others. Your children watch you. Your children learn first from you. When they look at you, they imprint your example into their lives. And they will pass on this imprint to their children later on. If you are depressed, if you are weak, that's what you will give to your children, to humanity, to the world.'

'Kṛṣṇa says, "There is salvation for all!" Even if there is a very, egoistic person, there is salvation for him. There is also salvation for people who are into the mind. Nobody is completely lost. But He says, "Go slowly! Let them first see the changes inside of you. Be the example. They will change. Be patient! They will learn to be patient. Be loving! They will learn to love. Be strong!"'

VERSES 27-35: TRANSCENDING THE GUṆAS AND KARMA

prakṛteḥ kriyamāṇāni guṇaiḥ karmāṇi sarvaśaḥ |
ahaṅkāra vimūḍhātmā kartā'ham-iti manyate || 27 ||

All actions are being performed in every way by the *guṇas* within material nature. One whose mind is deluded by the sense of individuality, thinks, 'I am the doer.' (27)

tattva-vittu mahābāho guṇa-karma-vibhāgayoḥ |
guṇā guṇeṣu vartanta iti matvā na sajjate || 28 ||

But he who knows the truth, O mighty armed one, sees the difference between the *guṇas* and action. He recognises how they act on one another and, through this awareness, he remains unattached. (28)

prakṛter-guṇa saṁmūḍhāḥ sajjante guṇa-karmasu |
tān-akṛtsna vido mandān kṛtsnavinna vicālayet || 29 ||

Those who are deluded by the *guṇas* within material nature, are attached to the actions produced by them. However, one of perfect knowledge should not unsettle the ignorant who do not see the whole truth. (29)

mayi sarvāṇi karmāṇi saṁnyasyādhyātma-cetasā |
nirāśīr-nir-mamo bhūtvā yudhyasva vigata-jvaraḥ || 30 ||

Dedicating all your actions to Me, with a mind centred in the Self, free from desire and selfishness, with your emotions held in balance, you should engage in battle. (30)

ye me matam idaṁ nityam anu-tiṣṭhanti mānavāḥ |
śraddhāvanto'nasūyanto mucyante te'pi karmabhiḥ || 31 ||

Those people who have faith, who are free from envy and always practise this teaching of Mine, will be released from *karma*. (31)

ye tvetad abhyasūyanto nānutiṣṭhanti me matam |
sarva jñāna vimūḍhāṁstān viddhi naṣṭān acetasaḥ || 32 ||

But those who disregard My teaching and those who do not practise it — know them to be seriously deluded, devoid of reasoning, and therefore lost. (32)

sadṛśaṁ ceṣṭate svasyāḥ prakṛter-jñānavān api |
prakṛtiṁ yānti bhūtāni nigrahaḥ kiṁ kariṣyati || 33 ||

Everyone follows their nature, even an enlightened person, so what will repressing it do? (33)

indriyasyendriyasyārthe rāga-dveṣau vyavasthitau |
tayor-na vaśam āgacchet tau hyasya paripanthinau || 34 ||

Desire and aversion arise when the senses rest in the objects they perceive. One should not allow oneself to come under their sway, as they are obstacles on the spiritual path. (34)

śreyān sva-dharmo viguṇaḥ para-dharmāt svanuṣṭhitāt |
sva-dharme nidhanaṁ śreyaḥ para-dharmo bhayāvahaḥ || 35 ||

It is better to carry out one's own duty incorrectly, than it is to carry out the duty of another perfectly. Death is better in one's own duty, for the duty of another is filled with danger. (35)

'Lord Kṛṣṇa says that you just need to have faith and trust in Him and try to follow what He says. He is not imposing. He just says, "Try it!" He is talking to whoever believes in His word. Whoever trusts and tries to put into practise in their life what He is teaching, whoever tries to awaken His Love inside themselves and love as He loves the world, they will be released from the bondage, from the effect of the three *guṇas*. They will be free from the cycle of birth and death. He is giving His assurance to everybody, to the people of all nationalities, creeds, colours, and castes. He is giving His assurance saying, "If you try to follow what I say, you will be free! You'll attain supreme bliss! If you surrender all your actions to Me, it doesn't matter what you do, you'll be transformed. And I assure you that if this is done, if you are practising your *sādhana* or if you are not practising your *sādhana*, you'll attain salvation!"'

'Kṛṣṇa emphasises that the evil which is described in the scriptures comes from attraction and aversion. On the other hand, normal deeds, inspired by faith and devotion, make one strong, make one renounce all evil deeds, and make one free. Letting go of the vices which are cherished in the heart, one should devote oneself to God, devote oneself to devotional practices, by keeping the mind focused on the Divine. If one does such an action, it will only bear good deeds. Even if someone is in the world outside and can't let go of the world, but the mind, from time to time, runs to the Divine – for even five minutes a day – just by doing that, one will be free!'

'Very often people come and say, "Swamiji, what is my *dharma*?" I say, "Well, look, what do you do?" "I work in an office." I say, "Okay, that's your *dharma*. Accept it!" But they don't want to hear that. Do you know what they want to hear? "Your *dharma* is to be spiritual." But they don't know that spirituality is also in their duty of daily life, in what God has given them to do!'

'If you don't accept the outside, what God has given, you will never be able to handle a greater duty when it is given to you. God will not even give you a greater duty to do! That's why He has placed each one in the world differently. Each one has his own right place and if one sees this perfection of the Lord, one will do one's *dharma* at that place, at that time.

'For some, it is meant to live completely for God! But for some, no. They are still on the way. They are still in preparation; they are still in kindergarten. Very often, you will see this in children: when they look at grown-ups, they also want to be a grown-up. They don't know what it is to be an adult because they see it only from the outside and say, "Oh, it's a party! When will we grow up?" They are so eager to grow up. But then one doesn't let time carry oneself. One doesn't learn to trust in the will of the Divine, that God has put everyone where they have to be.'

'Each one is right where one has to be. Learn to accept this! If you start to fight it, of course, your mind will say, "Oh, how wonderful it would be if I moved there." But if you do not go to the right place, this will create a complete imbalance inside of you. And when this confusion starts happening inside of you, you go backwards. Stay wherever you are and accept the will of God, accept that He has put you there, and let yourself flow with it, until He clearly calls you to go elsewhere. If it is meant to be, He will call you, and when you develop this trust, then you are free!

'Kṛṣṇa says to Arjuna, "Be centred in your duty! Even if it is without any merit, don't try to run away. This would be the reaction of a cowardly person. Better is death in your own duty!" When God calls you to your true *dharma* to do what you have come to this world to do, if you die in that, it is your salvation!'

VERSES 36-43: DESIRE IS THE GREAT ENEMY OF THE WISE

arjuna uvāca
atha kena prayukto'yaṁ pāpaṁ carati pūruṣaḥ |
anicchann-api vārṣṇeya balādiva niyojitaḥ || 36 ||

Arjuna says:
But what is it, Kṛṣṇa, that causes one to stray even against one's own will, as if compelled by some force? (36)

śrī bhagavān uvāca
kāma eṣa krodha eṣa rajoguṇa samudbhavaḥ |
mahāśano mahā-pāpmā viddhyenam-iha vairiṇam || 37 ||

Lord Kṛṣṇa says:
It is the desire born of the *guṇa* of *rajas* [3] and the resulting anger. That is the all-devouring, sinful enemy of the world. (37)

dhūmenāvriyate vahnir-yathādarśo malena ca |
yatholbenāvṛto garbhas-tathā tenedam-āvṛtam || 38 ||

Just as a fire is enveloped by smoke, a mirror is covered by dust, and an embryo by the amnion, so is this world enveloped by desire. (38)

āvṛtaṁ jñānam etena jñānino nitya vairiṇā |
kāma-rūpeṇa kaunteya duṣpūreṇānalena ca || 39 ||

O Arjuna, knowledge is veiled by desire, and desire is therefore the great enemy of the wise. Desire burns like an insatiable fire. (39)

indriyāṇi mano buddhir-asyādhiṣṭhānam-ucyate |
etair-vimohayaty-eṣa jñānam-āvṛtya dehinam || 40 ||

The senses, the mind, and the intellect are said to be desire's abode. Through these, desire deludes the embodied Self by concealing Its wisdom. (40)

tasmāt-tvam-indriyāṇyādau niyamya bharatarṣabha |
pāpmānaṁ prajahi hyenaṁ jñāna vijñāna nāśanam || 41 ||

Therefore, O Arjuna, you should control the senses first, and slay this source of sin that destroys both knowledge and discrimination. (41)

indriyāṇi parāṅyāhur-indriyebhyaḥ paraṁ manaḥ |
manas-astu parā buddhir-yo buddheḥ paratas-tu saḥ || 42 ||

The senses are superior to matter, the mind is superior to the senses, the intellect is higher than the mind, and the Self is even greater than the intellect. (42)

evaṁ buddheḥ paraṁ buddhvā saṁstabhyātmānam ātmanā |
jahi śatruṁ mahā-bāho kāma-rūpaṁ durāsadam || 43 ||

O Arjuna, knowing that which is greater than the intellect and steadying yourself by your spiritual strength, slay this enemy in the form of desire, which is difficult to overcome. (43)

'Desire is everywhere, in many kinds and in many forms. All the actions of people are due to these desires. Desires are like dust which accumulates on the surface of a mirror, and then the mirror can no longer reflect any object. Even so, the mind gets soiled by impurities in the form of sin. It is no longer able to reveal the true nature of things or its own true duty. That's why someone with an impure and sinful mind cannot correctly judge things. They don't know what is "good" and what is "bad". In this deep ignorance, the light of Truth is covered. Knowledge gets covered by ignorance... It is desire alone which makes the mind restless. It is through desire that one becomes evil and does sinful acts.'

'There are two forms of desire. The desire of the mind drags one completely to the outside. The other desire, the longing of the heart, is the gateway to Heaven. When you train yourself to transform the desires of the mind through meditation, and perform your duty, and accept the will of God, then these desires, which can't be killed, are transformed from *rajasic* to *sattvic* in nature. Don't go into the game of desires. Let's say you feel anger: in place of acting on that anger, in place of putting fuel into that fire, try to control yourself. The anger will leave you and transform itself.'

'When anger arises in the heart of man, it deprives him of his power of discrimination. He is unable to think, so he will not heed the consequences of whatever he does in a fit of anger. He doesn't realise what he is doing. When the anger grows, one's memory starts to get confused, and when the brain starts to get confused, one loses all control. One forgets about relationships; one forgets about everyone around. One also forgets what one has to do, or not to do. In this state, one is unable to plan; one doesn't have any determination. One loses all reasoning. When one doesn't control the senses, one is reduced to this state. And when a man is reduced to this state, it becomes easy for him to abandon the path of duty, the path of *dharma*. It becomes easy for that person to lose himself.'

'If someone doesn't take advantage of this human life to realise and attain God-realisation, attain the grace of God, or receive His Vision, this life is wasted… In this lifetime itself, you can attain God. This is mercy. God loves you! God cares for you! God incarnates! God traces your life and makes everything possible for you to realise Him! But He can't force you to do it. He shows you the way to come to Him, through His Love. He says, "I am waiting for you! Please come, realise, awaken! First do your effort, control yourself! I will help you."'

'Lord Kṛṣṇa says, "First control the senses: they are easier to control, because they are outside. Control too much sleep. Control what you are eating. Control what you are doing in your actions. Control the mind. Don't let the mind dwell on the attraction of worldly perishable things, which will bring you sorrow." Use all the senses, transforming them by serving God, by hearing His glory, by chanting and by concentrating on the Divine Names, on the different Names of God. Use the hands, the touch, to serve God through the action. Like that, you don't go into the game of worldly enjoyments. Keep yourself busy with the right things. If you start running after these desires, if you entertain them in the mind, it will destroy knowledge and discrimination.'

'Desire destroys the greater knowledge inside, the knowledge of the Divine. It is through this knowledge that the Divine acts inside people. If this knowledge is veiled, then life will be very difficult, because one will not be guided by knowledge and discrimination. One will always feel self-pity and sadness.

'Kṛṣṇa says to Arjuna, "Be knowledgeable about the Self! Have the power to discriminate! Because, if you have knowledge and the power to discriminate, desire has no power." You can uproot desire itself and transform it.'

'In *karma-yoga*, if you do everything in this world with an attitude of surrender, you will attain Him. Kṛṣṇa says to Arjuna, "Without controlling the senses, it will not be possible. If you give in, you will bring about your own damnation. But with control, you will free yourself. It is in your hands!" God will help you when you start helping yourself. Once you take your first step, He will give you courage; He will give you support; He will bring you to where you have to be.'

Chapter Three Verses: Key Terms

[1] **Jñāna-yoga** – the path of external renunciation, where outside activity is given up in pursuit of inner enquiry.

[2] **Janaka** – a great king who achieved realisation through the practice of *karma-yoga*. An ideal example of one who acts in the world but is detached from his actions.

[3] **Rajas** – the *guṇa* relating to the quality of passion, activity, endeavour, anxiety and frustration. People predominated by this *guṇa* are impelled by their desires and live a life of intense, restless action.

CHAPTER FOUR
JÑĀNA-VIBHĀGA-YOGA
THE PATH OF KNOWLEDGE

Chapter four begins with Kṛṣṇa telling Arjuna how He originally taught this ancient knowledge of *karma-yoga* to Vivasvān, the Sun-god. Due to the passage of time it was lost and now it is being revived once again. It is at this point that Kṛṣṇa declares emphatically His identity as the *avatāra*, the Lord who has descended to protect *dharma* [1] and vanquish evil.

The discourse then shifts back to a discussion on *karma-yoga* and how we can understand the true nature of action. The overall point is that action which produces results (*karma*) is not connected with one's external activity but rather the state of consciousness we are in. Our thoughts, feelings and desires also produce *karmic* results. If we are free of desire and detached no matter how much activity we are engaged in, there are no *karmic* consequences to our actions. However, even if we do our best to abstain from any external activity, so long as we have desires and attachment, we will always be creating further results. In other words, the level of renunciation and the amount of *karma* produced cannot be simply gauged from one's outside behaviour.

Following on from this, Kṛṣṇa discusses the ritual fire sacrifice or *yajña* [2]. Traditionally this *yajña* is seen as a way of satisfying the gods and fulfilling material desires. But Kṛṣṇa explains that this *yajña* should not be understood as just an external act, but an internal process of restraint and dedication. Controlling the senses, breath and taking up vows are all different forms of *yajña*. Rather than focusing on the external ritual for material gain, *karma-yoga* is all about the inner *yajña* which eventually leads to knowledge of the Self (*Brahma-jñāna*). Once this goal is achieved, the realisation of who we truly are destroys the possibility of incurring any additional *karma*.

Chapter Four Intro: Key Terms

[1] **Dharma** – everything in this world is part of a natural cosmological order. As a result, each individual has a set purpose in line with this order. *Dharma* is the fulfilment of this purpose.

[2] **Yajña** – this is the *Vedic* fire sacrifice. Various ritual offerings are made in an effort to appease the different gods and gain results. Throughout the *Gītā*, however, Kṛṣṇa introduces *yajña* as being more about the internal sacrifice of spiritual practice rather than just a fire ritual.

VERSES 1-6: THE REVIVAL OF ANCIENT WISDOM

śrī bhagavān uvāca
imaṁ vivasvate yogaṁ proktavān aham avyayam |
vivasvān manave prāha manur-ikṣvākave'bravīt || 1 ||

Lord Kṛṣṇa says:
I taught this imperishable *yoga* to Vivasvān [1]; Vivasvān taught it to Manu; Manu declared it to Ikṣvāku. (1)

evaṁ paramparā prāptam imaṁ rāja-ṛṣayo viduḥ |
sa kāleneha mahatā yogo naṣṭaḥ paraṅtapa || 2 ||

Handed down through disciplic succession, the royal sages received this knowledge. But due to the passage of time, Arjuna, this *yoga* was lost to the world. (2)

sa evāyaṁ mayā te'dya yogaḥ proktaḥ purātanaḥ |
bhakto'si me sakhā ceti rahasyaṁ hyetad-uttamam || 3 ||

It is this same ancient *yoga* which I now teach to you, as you are My devotee and My friend; it is indeed the highest mystery. (3)

arjuna uvāca
aparaṁ bhavato janma paraṁ janma vivasvataḥ |
katham etad vijānīyāṁ tvam ādau proktavān iti || 4 ||

Arjuna says:
Your birth was recent, and the birth of Vivasvān was long ago. How is it possible that You taught this in the beginning? (4)

śrī bhagavān uvāca
bahūni me vyatītāni janmāni tava cārjuna |
tānyahaṁ veda sarvāṇi na tvaṁ vettha parantapa || 5 ||

Lord Kṛṣṇa says:
Many births of Mine have passed, O Arjuna, and so it is with you also. I know them all, but you do not know them. (5)

ajo'pi sann-avyayātmā bhūtānām īśvaro'pi san |
prakṛtiṁ svām-adhiṣṭhāya saṁbhavāmy-ātma māyayā || 6 ||

Though I am unborn and unchanging, and although I am the Lord of all beings, by using My own nature (*prakṛti*), I enter into this world by My own free will. (6)

'Here Kṛṣṇa is revealing His eternal relationship. He says, "This ancient *yoga* that I am revealing to you, I am giving to you out of the Love which I have for you. This is the same *yoga* which I have given to the Sun-god billions of years ago, and I am now giving it to you. Nothing has changed. Even if you have forgotten it, due to passing from generation to generation and it has disappeared in time, here it is on this battlefield, for you are My devotee and you are My friend."'

'When you are in tune with the Divine, the Divine reveals to you your true *dharma* of life: the reason you have incarnated on Earth. Then all the illusion, all the other *dharma* which you have thought about, disappears! Only then, you have true knowledge of how to serve the Lord. Only then, can the Lord reveal Himself to you. Therefore, Arjuna should not entertain any doubt about the Truth of the Lord when He says, "I gave this knowledge to the Sun-god. I existed before everything was created or manifested."'

'This secret was only given to people by their *gurus* when they were ready. If you give this *Brahma-jñāna* (knowledge of the Self) to people who are not ready to grasp it with their hearts, they will not know what to do with it. If their minds are too focused on the outside world, it will not make any sense to them; it will just be meaningless.

'Kṛṣṇa sees this quality of a *bhakta* inside of Arjuna, this longing! That's what the *guru*, the Teacher, the Master looks for in the devotees, in the disciples. He checks to see if the "soil" is ready, if all the wild grass has been removed and if the disciples are ready to do their *dharma* or not. If people are in a state of confusion, if they are given such knowledge and such blessing, they will fall into deeper confusion. But if one is wholeheartedly surrendered to the *guru*, one doesn't need to worry about anything. Everything will be taken care of.'

VERSES 7-8: KṚṢṆA DECLARES HIMSELF AS THE AVATĀRA OF THE AGE

yadā yadā hi dharmasya glānir-bhavati bhārata |
abhyutthānam-adharmasya tadā'tmānaṁ sṛjāmy-aham || 7 ||

Arjuna, whenever there is a decline in *dharma* (righteousness), and an increase of *adharma* (unrighteousness), it is then that I manifest Myself. (7)

paritrāṇāya sādhūnāṁ vināśāya ca duṣkṛtām |
dharma saṁsthāpan-ārthāya saṁbhavāmi yuge yuge || 8 ||

For the protection of the good, for the destruction of the wicked, and to establish *dharma*, I incarnate Myself from age to age. (8)

'Here Bhagavān Kṛṣṇa is saying He comes forth from age to age whenever righteousness is covered by unrighteousness, whenever evil starts to predominate in the world and when it is threatening and destroying cultures and the world. For the good and benefit of this world, Bhagavān manifests Himself and He manifests by His own willpower.'

'People can't understand the Ultimate, God Himself, the Lord of all creation, the One who is ever-pure, who is awakened and ever-free, who is playing every role in His creation. It is too difficult for the mind to understand. Even if one tries to understand it, it's far beyond the mind. He (Kṛṣṇa) says, "Even if you become a great *yogī*, even if you are centred in the Self, you will realise only one step of realisation. My true nature, the Self of the Self, can't even be realised by *yogīs*." That's why He says, "I am veiled. I came into birth by My *māyā*: when I will it, I manifest. I'm ever-free to take any form, at any time. I am not bound by time or by space. I am not bound by anything, not even by the scriptures."

'God is ever-free, He can do whatever He wants. Some people would ask, "How can this be possible? This is just a human being, how can He be God?" Arjuna is asking the same question: "How can He be God?" Here you see the doubting human mind. But God is beyond that. Even if He appears to be very human, He is not human. The saints and sages can only have a glimpse of that reality. What He shows to the sages is only a little aspect of Himself. This raises them to a very high degree of spirituality, but not to the Ultimate Himself.'

'Kṛṣṇa says, "I manifest Myself from time to time, taking various forms, appearing in different places. Sometimes I remain unknown to the world, incognito. Yet whatever I do, I do it for the sake of uplifting mankind."'

'Humans are blinded by one *māyā* which we call "illusion". You are blinded by this *māyā* until you are ready. When you make yourself ready through *sādhana* (spiritual practice), the veil of *māyā* is removed. Through your *sādhana*, when you're surrendered to your *sādhana*, you are moving away from external desires and the objects of senses which hold you back, drag you down, and root you here to this world.

'By doing your *dharma* and by doing your *sādhana* with the aim of attaining the Lord, the Lord allows this first veil of *māyā* to be removed from your eyes. Then you see differently, and you perceive the glory of the Lord everywhere. However, you are not perceiving Himself everywhere because by His own will, He veils Himself by another *māyā*, *yoga-māyā* [1], so people won't recognise Him and realise who He is. This is due to God's humility. He says, "I veil Myself with another *māyā*, *yoga-māyā*, so that even if you do your *sādhana*, even if you try your best to see who I am, until I will it, you will never see Me. You can try as much as you want, you can be the greatest *yogī*, but you will not know Me until I will it." Here He reveals that this *yoga-māyā* is different from the *māyā* that covers mankind.'

'Even being the Lord of the whole universe, He humbles Himself for the sake of humanity, so that He can uplift humanity. This is wonderful. He willingly chooses to veil Himself. He chooses to put a limitation on Himself in order to incarnate, but He is not bound by any limitation. He appears to be limited, but He is not.'

VERSES 9-15: HOW SURRENDER LEADS TO FREEDOM

janma karma ca me divyam evaṁ yo vetti tattvataḥ |
tyaktvā dehaṁ punar-janma naiti māmeti so'rjuna || 9 ||

Whosoever knows the truth of My divine birth and deeds, O Arjuna, is not reborn again. After leaving the body they come to Me. (9)

vīta rāga-bhaya-krodhā man mayā mām upāśritāḥ |
bahavo jñāna tapasā pūtā mad-bhāvam āgatāḥ || 10 ||

Freed from desire, fear and anger, absorbed in Me, taking refuge in Me, and having been purified by the austerity of knowledge, many have attained their eternal relationship with Me. (10)

ye yathā māṁ prapadyante tāṁs-tathaiva bhajāmy-aham |
mama vartmānuvartante manuṣyāḥ pārtha sarvaśaḥ || 11 ||

In whatever way one surrenders to Me, in the same way I approach them. Everybody follows My path in all respects, O Arjuna. (11)

kāṅkṣantaḥ karmaṇāṁ siddhiṁ yajanta iha devatāḥ |
kṣipraṁ hi mānuṣe loke siddhir-bhavati karmajā || 12 ||

Those who desire the fruits of their action perform sacrifices to the gods; for in this human world, results are quickly attained by such religious rituals. (12)

cātur-varṇyaṁ mayā sṛṣṭaṁ guṇa karma vibhāgaśaḥ |
tasya kartāram api māṁ viddhy-akartāram avyayam || 13 ||

I created the four *varṇas* [2] based on their work and *guṇas*. Despite creating this system, I am still unchanging and free from action. (13)

na māṁ karmāṇi limpanti na me karma phale spṛhā |
iti māṁ yo'bhijānāti karmabhir-na sa badhyate || 14 ||

Actions do not taint Me, nor do I have a desire for the fruits of actions. One who understands this about Me, is not bound by *karma*. (14)

evaṁ jñātvā kṛtaṁ karma pūrvair-api mumukṣubhiḥ |
kuru karmaiva tasmāt tvaṁ pūrvaiḥ pūrvataraṁ kṛtam || 15 ||

Having known this, the ancient seekers of liberation also performed action, similarly you should also engage in your duty just as people in the past have done. (15)

'Those who do their work with an attitude of surrender, knowing that only God is the doer, will attain Him. Whoever surrenders sees that whatever Lord Kṛṣṇa does is for the good of this world. Every activity of His is for the upliftment of humanity. He has also given the *Gītā* for this. Whoever surrenders to the Word of the *Gītā* and practises its teaching wholeheartedly, with love in their hearts, is free, and attains Him.'

'But it's not just about saying, "I love God!" You also have to serve Him. You have to have this deep knowledge through meditation that He is the core of the Self in each person. You have to train the mind to see Him in everybody and in everything. Therefore, one is not waiting to die to attain Him, to realise Him. No. Now, in this moment, do everything to see Him, do everything to feel His Love. Whether you attain Him now or not, don't be concerned about it. Let Him give you whatever is needed. Learn to accept it. It's not only after you leave the body that you will attain God. No. First you attain Him now in every moment of your life.'

'True happiness can be given only by the Lord Himself. Only when you long for Him, He reciprocates the feeling that you have inside of you, not just one time, but one hundred times more... You think that you are thinking of Him. No. He is thinking of you. You think that you are going to Him; He is running towards you. You think of Him, you long for Him, but in His heart, He is pining for you.'

VERSES 16-23: DEFINING ACTION AND INACTION

kiṁ karma kim akarmeti kavayo'py-atra mohitāḥ |
tatte karma pravakṣyāmi yaj-jñātvā mokṣyase'śubhāt || 16 ||

What is action? What is inaction? Even the wise are confused about this. I shall now explain to you what action is. Knowing this, you will be freed from suffering. (16)

karmaṇo hyapi boddhavyaṁ boddhavyaṁ ca vikarmaṇaḥ |
akarmaṇaśca boddhavyaṁ gahanā karmaṇo-gatiḥ || 17 ||

For verily one must understand what is action (*karma*), what is forbidden action (*vikarma*), as well as what is inaction (*akarma*). Action is indeed hard to understand. (17)

karmaṇya karma yaḥ paśyed akarmaṇi ca karma yaḥ |
sa buddhimān manuṣyeṣu sa yuktaḥ kṛtsna karma-kṛt || 18 ||

He who sees inaction in action and also action in inaction is wise among people. He is fit for liberation and performs all his designated duties. (18)

yasya sarve samārambhāḥ kāma saṅkalpa varjitāḥ |
jñānāgni dagdha karmāṇāṁ tam āhuḥ paṇḍitaṁ budhāḥ || 19 ||

He whose every action is free from personal gain has his sins burnt up by the fire of knowledge. He is described by the wise as a sage. (19)

tyaktvā karma phalā-saṅgaṁ nitya tṛpto nirāśrayaḥ |
karmaṇy-abhi-pravṛtto'pi naiva kiñcit karoti saḥ || 20 ||

A person who has renounced attachment to the fruits of action is dependent on no one and is ever-content in the Self. He does not act despite being engaged in activity. (20)

nirāśīr yatacitt-ātmā tyakta sarva parigrahaḥ |
śarīraṁ kevalaṁ karma kurvan-nāpnoti kilbiṣam || 21 ||

Free from expectation, with a controlled mind, having no sense of ownership and acting only to maintain the body, one does not incur sin. (21)

yadṛcchālābha santuṣṭo dvandvātito vimatsaraḥ |
samaḥ siddhāvasiddhau ca kṛtvāpi na nibadhyate || 22 ||

When one is content with what comes without effort, one has transcended the pairs of opposites, is free from envy, and is balanced in success and failure; despite acting, one is not bound. (22)

gata-saṅgasya muktasya jñānāvasthita cetasaḥ |
yajñāyā-carataḥ karma samagraṁ pravilīyate || 23 ||

For the liberated person, who is free from attachments, whose mind is established in wisdom, and acts only for sacrifice, *karma* is entirely dissolved. (23)

'Thinking involves performance of action; the mind wandering around is still action. You can't stop that. But you can transcend these worldly activities. You can see that everything is predominated by the Lord.'

'If you perform "inaction" without the direction and supervision of a Master, you will not achieve anything. You can sit for meditation, you can control your speech, you can control the body, but this is not true calmness, because there is a motive behind it. Even if the mind, speech and body are controlled, if the motive is egoistic, if there is an expectation, it will not lead you anywhere.

'The realised ones, the enlightened souls have the true knowledge: they know which action to perform, and which motive to use, so it will lead them to complete renunciation, and not only superficially. So that's why those who are seeking to liberate themselves should surrender to a *guru*, who will lead them out of this game of action, inaction, and prohibited action. Prohibited action means action done with deceit, hypocrisy, violence, greed, pride. On the other hand, when people do work with devotion, they are humble. When one is surrendered to the *guru*, automatically one is humble; one is ready to accept what the *guru* says, which means one has to remove one's own will and ways of seeing and embrace what the *guru* is giving.

'Of course, the *guru* has to have certain qualities, otherwise he can't help you progress. In the world nowadays, there are so many *gurus*, so many teachers. There are many *gurus* who teach *yoga*. But if these *gurus* don't teach you to attain the perfection of the soul, and if they just focus on the perfection of the body or the mind, it's not enough. That's why I said that it's very important to know the *guru* who can help you advance and attain the ultimate reality. There are many learned people in the world who know all the scriptures. Their head is full of book knowledge, but this doesn't give them liberation, it doesn't free them. These people fail to determine what their true nature is. That's why it is necessary to approach a true *guru* and surrender to Him.

'Nowadays, there are many schools of *yoga*; each one claims that their *yoga* is better than the others. But when one is realised, one sees that all ways are right, because God puts people where they have to be. So if there is true realisation, there is no judgement. If one has divine knowledge, one should not have any judgement towards anyone; one should not have any enmity or aggressiveness towards anyone.

'If people are doing their *sādhana*, either for their own benefit or to gain something from the world, this can be considered prohibited action and they won't gain anything from it. Whereas a true *guru* teaches one to love God beyond everything and to surrender to God. Then one is free.'

'The wise people perform all their duties in a renounced way. They renounce the fruit of the action and the thinking, "I am doing this." If you think that you are doing it, you will expect the result. But if your mind is not on "I, I, I", if the mind is upon Him, thinking, "He is doing it through me", no matter what result will come, it will be the fruit of that action which the Lord has performed through you.

'When the Lord performs a certain action through you, there is always perfection in it, and you will always have peace of mind. You will be free from *karma*, because you are not creating the *karma*. As the Lord is free from *karma*, so shall you be.'

VERSES 24-33: THE DIFFERENT TYPES OF YAJÑA

brahmārpaṇaṁ brahma-havir brahm-āgnau brahmaṇā hutam |
brahmaiva tena gantavyaṁ brahma karma samādhinā || 24 ||

For those absorbed in God, Brahman [3] is the instrument, Brahman is the oblation; Brahman is the one who offers into the fire which is also Brahman. Brahman alone is to be reached by one who meditates upon Him in one's actions. (24)

daivam-evāpare yajñāṁ yoginaḥ paryupāsate |
brahmāgnāv-apare yajñāṁ yajñenaivopa-juhvati || 25 ||

Some *yogīs* resort only to sacrificing to the demigods [4], but others sacrifice into the fire of Brahman and perform sacrifice for its own sake. (25)

śrotrādīn-indriyāṇy-anye saṁyamāgniṣu juhvati |
śabdādīn-viṣayān-anya indriyāgniṣu juhvati || 26 ||

Some offer hearing and the other senses into the fires of restraint. Others offer sound and the other objects of the senses into the fires of the senses themselves. (26)

sarvāṇ-īndriyāṇi-karmāṇi prāṇa karmāṇi cāpare |
ātma-saṁyama yogāgnau juhvati jñāna-dīpite || 27 ||

Others offer the actions of the senses and life breath (*prāṇa*) into the fire of *yoga* which is based on self-control and illumined by true knowledge. (27)

dravya yajñās-tapo yajñā yoga yajñās-tathā'pare |
svādhyāya-jñāna yajñāśca yatayaḥ saṁśita vratāḥ || 28 ||

Observing strict vows, some sages offer material objects as sacrifice, some make offerings through austerity and *yoga*, while others offer their scriptural study and knowledge as sacrifice. (28)

apāne juhvati prāṇaṁ prāṇe'pānaṁ tathā'pare |
prāṇāpāna-gatī ruddhvā prāṇāyāma parāyaṇāḥ || 29 ||

Still there are others who offer their exhalation into the inhalation, and the inhalation into the exhalation. In this way they achieve the state where all breathing stops. (29)

apare niyatāhārāḥ prāṇān prāṇeṣu juhvati |
sarve'pyete yajñā-vido yajñā kṣapita kalmaṣāḥ || 30 ||

Others who restrict their eating offer the practice of breath-control (*prāṇāyāma*). All these *yogīs* know the meaning of sacrifice and through their sacrifices become free of sinful reactions. (30)

yajñā-śiṣṭāmṛta bhujo yānti brahmā sanātanam |
nāyaṁ loko'sty-ayajñāsya kuto'nyaḥ kurusattama || 31 ||

The remnants of sacrifice is the nectar of immortality. By taking it, one attains that eternal Abode of the Lord.
Understand, Arjuna, that one cannot live happily in this world without sacrifice, and what can be said of the next? (31)

evaṁ bahu vidhā yajña vitatā brahmaṇo mukhe |
karmajān viddhi tān sarvān evaṁ jñātvā vimokṣyase || 32 ||

In this way, many forms of sacrifice have been laid down in the *Vedas*. All of them are based on action; once you understand this, you shall be liberated. (32)

śreyān dravyamayād yajñāj-jñāna yājñāḥ parantapa |
sarvaṁ karmākhilaṁ pārtha jñāne parisamāpyate || 33 ||

The sacrifice of wisdom is superior to the ritual material sacrifice. O Arjuna, all action has its end in wisdom. (33)

'There is a saying that goes, "God is always with people, whether people want it or not. But people are not always with God." However, someone who is realised has already attained the state of realising that everything, wherever one goes, whatever one does, is only Him. Whatever one is doing, it is Him doing it: every step, every thought, everything. If one doesn't self-judge oneself, one will see that it is only the Lord Himself taking every step, doing every action.'

'If the aim is to attain God, it doesn't matter where you are or what you are doing, however, it's very important how you are doing your duty, how you are doing the offering, with what aim, and with what attitude you are doing it. If it is with pride, it doesn't reach Him.'

'There is not only one way, but the aim is one! The aim is only God! And if everybody understands this aim, one will be free; it doesn't matter where one is. That's why at the beginning, Lord Kṛṣṇa Himself says to Arjuna that each one has been placed in the right place to do their duty. And if one does one's duty properly, with the attitude of surrendering to the Divine, the Divine will free that person. That's why He says, "Arjuna accept your duty! And be free."'

'*Yajña* doesn't only mean when you sit and pour *ghī* in the fire. Whatever you do is a sacrifice upon the altar of the Lord. It's a continuous offering.

'That's what Bhagavān is asking for right now: to sacrifice these material things and to sacrifice the way you see things. Transform. Know that everything is the Divine only. Find the Divine inside of you. Find the Divine in every action you are doing. Release yourself. Let the Self take over. Let God take over your life. Let yourself be consumed by the Love of God. That's what realisation is. When your heart is consumed with the Love of God, you will have that awareness. And that's what Atma Kriya Yoga [2] does inside: it elevates you to that realisation.'

VERSE 34: THE IMPORTANCE OF THE GURU

tad viddhi praṇipātena paripraśnena sevayā |
upadekṣyanti te jñānaṁ jñāninas-tattva-darśinaḥ || 34 ||

One should approach a spiritual Master with submission, extensive enquiry and service. Such realised souls can instruct you, for they have seen the Truth. (34)

'Here Bhagavān Kṛṣṇa Himself is saying that if you just take a book and read it, it will not lead you anywhere. Here He is giving the importance of the Master.'

'Surrender to the Feet of the Master. Serve the Master with your heart filled with love and humility. Earn that grace from the Master. Make yourself ready, make yourself willing, make yourself worthy. Let the Master guide you. The Master has already reached one with the Divine.'

'Often people say, "No, you don't need a Master in life, you don't need a *guru*, you can do it by yourself." They are all stupid. Walk in a jungle without a guide, and you will be lost.'

'Even if something is very near, just like realisation IS there, one needs a guide. This is the importance of a Master.'

'The *guru* wants the disciples to reach a certain level. They know that they have a certain mission, a certain goal, and a certain *dharma* to fulfil and to achieve; if they are not doing it, the Master has to be strict. This strictness doesn't mean that the Master doesn't love the disciple. He does. It's like when an abscess grows on the leg of a child. First the parents use the medicine to cure the child, but if it's not getting cured, the parents will not hesitate to cut the limb of the child to save the child's life. If it's even necessary to cut off the leg of the child, they will do it. How difficult this would be! But the parents care for their children. In the same way, the *guru* is sometimes strict so that all the "evil-doers" will be destroyed, so that you can grow and rise spiritually.'

'When the mind is upset, one doesn't…see that the *guru* is doing everything for the benefit of the disciple's progress – even if He has to sacrifice Himself, as did Christ. The *guru* is always sacrificing Himself for the sake of His disciples and devotees.'

VERSES 35-42: THE FRUIT OF KARMA-YOGA IS REALISED KNOWLEDGE

yaj-jñātvā na punar-moham eva yāsyasi pāṇḍava |
yena bhūtāny-aśeṣeṇa drakṣyasy-ātman-yatho mayi || 35 ||

Once you receive this knowledge, Arjuna, you will never again be deluded. Through that knowledge you will see all beings, without exception, as the Self and then as part of Me. (35)

api ced-asi pāpebhyaḥ sarvebhyaḥ pāpa-krttamaḥ |
sarvaṁ jñāna plavenaiva vṛjinaṁ santariṣyasi || 36 ||

Even if you are the most sinful of all sinners, you can cross over this miserable condition by the boat of knowledge. (36)

yathaidhāṁsi samiddho'gnir-bhasmasāt kurute'rjuna |
jñānāgniḥ sarva karmāṇi bhasmasāt kurute tathā || 37 ||

Arjuna, just as a blazing fire turns wood to ashes, so does the fire of knowledge turn all *karma* to ashes. (37)

na hi jñānena sadṛśaṁ pavitram iha vidyate |
tat-svayaṁ yoga saṁsiddhiḥ kālenātmani vindati || 38 ||

In this world nothing purifies one more than knowledge. Those who have perfected the practice of *karma-yoga* will have this knowledge revealed to them. (38)

śraddhāvāllabhate jñānaṁ tatparaḥ saṁyatendriyaḥ |
jñānaṁ labdhvā parāṁ śāntim acireṇādhigacchati || 39 ||

One who has faith will gain this knowledge, if they are dedicated and have controlled the senses. Having attained it, one quickly realises supreme peace. (39)

ajñāś-cāśraddadhānaśca saṁśayātmā vinaśyati |
nāyaṁ loko'sti na paro na sukhaṁ saṁśayātmanaḥ || 40 ||

But for the ignorant, the faithless and the sceptical there is only destruction. The doubting person does not belong to this world or the next, and will never find happiness. (40)

yoga-saṁnyasta karmāṇaṁ jñāna saṁcchinna saṁśayam |
ātmavantaṁ na karmāṇi nibadhnanti dhanañjaya || 41 ||

O Arjuna, when one is established in *karma-yoga*, with doubts dispelled by knowledge, having a steady mind, such a person is not bound by action. (41)

tasmād-ajñāna saṁbhūtaṁ hṛtsthaṁ jñānāsinātmanaḥ |
chittvainaṁ saṁśayaṁ yogam-ātiṣṭhottiṣṭha bhārata || 42 ||

Therefore, with the sword of knowledge, cut this doubt present in your heart, which has arisen from ignorance. Protected by this *yoga*, arise and fight, O Arjuna. (42)

'The Truth about the soul is deeply mysterious because it cannot be known by the mind. It is only a few who have a controlled mind, who are centred in the Lord, who are fully dedicated to the spiritual path, who receive the grace of realisation.'

'Many people practise meditation, but only a few really attain realisation. And who are these few? The ones who are completely surrendered.'

'You have a human body, and in this human body, God has given you the power to find Him! This means that He has great hope for you! He has great hope that you can do it! He is waiting for you. If you let yourself be weak, He can't help you. But if you make yourself strong, He will carry you.'

'If you are not ready, the true knowledge doesn't come to you. If you are not ready, the *guru* doesn't reveal Himself to you. But when you are ready, you are guided to where you have to be. The soul sends an invisible "email" to Mother Nature and as the *guru* receives that "email", He says, "Ah, this one is ready!"'

'When one has faith, one is ready to evolve, ready to change and ready to transform. Faith makes you conquer and control the mind and senses.'

'It is through faith that He brings you on your spiritual path, to get better and to grow… It is through faith that you can have respect for your Teacher. It is through faith that you can accept what the Teacher is giving you, and in that faith, humility and peace of mind awaken.'

'Many claim they know better. They come and then they leave, due to that pride. They don't want to let go of their pride. They don't want to let go of their ego. They don't want to change.'

'By surrendering to the Feet of the Master, all the errors of lives are removed. Once you have this right knowledge about the *ātmā*, the Truth will be revealed. That supremacy of the Lord will be revealed, not outside, but first inside of yourself.'

Chapter Four Verses: Key Terms

[1] **Vivasvān** – also referred to as the Sun-god, who was given divine knowledge by Kṛṣṇa at the beginning of the age.

[2] **Varṇas** – the different social classes within *Vedic* culture, namely the *brāhmaṇas* (sages and priests), *kṣatriyas* (warriors and royal leaders), *vaiśyas* (merchants responsible for commerce), and *śūdras* (responsible for general labour). In order to ensure a prosperous society, these different groups were allocated different responsibilities for the welfare of everyone at large.

[3] **Brahman** – in this context, this term is used to describe the supreme reality, God or Nārāyaṇa.

[4] **Demigods** – term interchangeable with '*devas*', which refers to the limited celestial beings who occupy different heavenly realms within the material universe. Although not perfected beings, they are generally associated with positivity.

Chapter Four Commentary: Key Terms

[1] **Yoga-māyā** – the specific potency of God that conceals His true identity.

[2] **Atma Kriya Yoga** – given by Paramahamsa Sri Swami Vishwananda for humanity to realise the teachings of the *Bhagavad Gītā*. It brings constant awareness of the Divine in every action and consists of a series of techniques which include meditation, *prāṇāyāma*, *āsanas*, *mudrās*, *japa*, and OM Chanting.

CHAPTER FIVE
KARMA-SANNYĀSA-YOGA
TRUE RENUNCIATION

Kṛṣṇa acknowledges that renunciation of external action (*jñāna-yoga*), and acting without attachment (*karma-yoga*), are two spiritual paths, but nonetheless they both deliver the same goal: they both lead to knowledge of the Self. For this reason, they are ultimately non-different. However, due to the ease of practise, *karma-yoga* is judged to be the better of the two.

This knowledge of the Self makes us realise that despite performing all kinds of activity, in truth we do nothing. All action is simply the senses engaging with the world and does not contaminate our true nature. Established in this state, we become untouched by the movements of life. We develop equanimity, beyond pain and pleasure. Eventually we rise beyond every form of judgment and see the same divinity in all living beings. Such *yogīs*, who are detached and have conquered desire, master the mind, which is the ultimate cause of pain and suffering in the material world.

VERSES 1- 7: JÑANA-YOGA AND KARMA-YOGA ARE ULTIMATELY THE SAME

arjuna uvāca
sannyāsaṁ karmaṇāṁ kṛṣṇa punar-yogaṁ ca śaṁsasi |
yac-chreya etayor-ekaṁ tan-me brūhi suniścitam || 1 ||

Arjuna says:

Kṛṣṇa, You recommend the renunciation of action and at the same time instruct me on *karma-yoga*. Tell me conclusively which is the better of the two. (1)

śrī bhagavān uvāca
sannyāsaḥ karma yogaśca niḥśreyasakarāv-ubhau |
tayos-tu karma saṁnyāsāt karma-yogo viśiṣyate || 2 ||

Lord Kṛṣṇa says:

Renunciation of action and *karma-yoga*, both lead to the highest state. But of the two, *karma-yoga* is superior to the renunciation of action. (2)

jñeyaḥ sa nitya saṁnyāsī yo na dveṣṭi na kāṅkṣati |
nir-dvandvo hi mahābāho sukhaṁ bandhāt-pramucyate || 3 ||

One who neither resents nor desires anything is a true renunciate. Whoever is free from the pairs of opposites is easily liberated from bondage, O Arjuna. (3)

sāṅkhya-yogau pṛthag-bālāḥ pravadanti na paṇḍitāḥ |
ekam-apy-āsthitaḥ samyag-ubhayor-vindate phalam || 4 ||

Only the inexperienced speak of *jñana-yoga* and *karma-yoga* as separate. One who is firmly established in either path, attains the fruit of both. (4)

yat-sāṅkhyaiḥ prāpyate sthānaṁ tad-yogair-api gamyate |
ekaṁ sāṅkhyaṁ ca yogaṁ ca yaḥ paśyati sa paśyati || 5 ||

That state which is attained by the *jñana-yogī* is also attained by the *karma-yogī*. The one who sees that both are really one is truly wise. (5)

sannyāsas-tu mahābāho duḥkham-āptum-ayogataḥ |
yoga-yukto munir -brahma na cireṇādhigacchati || 6 ||

But renunciation is hard to achieve without *karma-yoga*. The sage who follows this *yoga* quickly attains realisation. (6)

yoga-yukto viśuddhātmā vijitātmā jitendriyaḥ |
sarva-bhūtātmā bhūtātmā kurvann-api na lipyate || 7 ||

One who is devoted to the path of action, who is pure of mind, who is self-controlled, who has conquered the senses, sees the Supreme Self in all beings. Even while acting, one remains untainted. (7)

"Arjuna is still examining what Kṛṣṇa said in the previous chapters about *jñāna-yoga*, the path of knowledge, and *karma-yoga*, the path of action. The Lord says, "Both paths are okay." But the mind of Arjuna is still troubled, because if Kṛṣṇa considers knowledge superior to action, why does He also urge him to fight? If knowledge is superior to action, then Kṛṣṇa should just say, "Okay, renounce everything, go and sit in a cave!" This doubt is still playing in Arjuna's mind, so he is unable to really understand what Kṛṣṇa is trying to tell him. He continues to look at this from the point of view of the mind, asking Lord Kṛṣṇa, "Which one will be better for me? Which path should I adopt to attain this true wisdom, to attain the wisdom of the Self?" And in which way should he be disciplined – by meditating on this knowledge or by doing his duty without any personal expectation, without any attachment, dedicating all his action to God? Arjuna is sitting there in his chariot, on the battlefield, sincerely asking, "Which path, Lord?"'

'Here the Lord says that both *yogas* will bring you to supreme bliss. When you are disciplined in your *sādhana* and doing it for the sake of attaining God, you will attain salvation. But Kṛṣṇa gives priority to *karma-yoga* saying to Arjuna, "You are a *karma-yogī*, you are married, you have a family, you have children, you are a warrior! It's not meant for you to go sit and meditate in a cave." It is interesting to note here that Kṛṣṇa is talking to everybody in this world saying, "Find Me in whatever you do! I am in your house! The moment you sit to do your *sādhana*, I am there. I am also in the work that you are doing."'

'Most people usually work in order to get something, so there is always an expectation. But when work is only done to serve God, to please Him, one beholds the Absolute Lord in whatever one does. Then, there is a mixture of both *yogas*, *karma-yoga* and *jñāna-yoga*, because the *karma-yogī* is acting as a true renunciate. On the other hand, there are many people who pretend to renounce, who appear to renounce, yet they haven't renounced anything. The renunciation that Lord Kṛṣṇa is referring to is not a superficial renunciation. It means to renounce very deeply and sincerely. It's of no use to say, "I have renounced everything! I have renounced the outside world," and then sit there and think, "Oh, I wish I had this" or "I wish I had that". When you renounce something, you have to let go of it in the mind itself.

'There are many people who are still living in the world outside, yet they are true renunciates; they are free! They are not attached to the fruits of their actions. Kṛṣṇa says, "That's the best path!" It's not because one wears a robe that one becomes a renunciate. One becomes a renunciate when one renounces the expectations, this aggressiveness of the mind; when one has control over the senses; when one perceives that the aim of life is only to serve God in everything. This is true renunciation! The true renunciate can be a *karma-yogī*, someone who is doing one's duty in the outside world, yet who is completely surrendered to the Divine.'

'Renouncing everything for something will not bring you peace, because there will be always an expectation. And when this expectation is not fulfilled, what will arise? Frustration. And frustration will lead you to anger. Anger will lead you to mental stress.'

'You have incarnated in this world to do certain things, and once you are here, you can't run away. Even a saint who has renounced everything, sitting in the cave, in a hut, is performing action too. Saints are constantly praying for the world, for everyone. This is their duty.'

VERSES 8-17: THE SELF IS UNTOUCHED BY ACTION

naiva kiñcit karomīti yukto manyeta tattva-vit |
paśyañ-śṛṇvan spṛśañ jighrann-aśnan gacchan svapañ-śvasan || 8 ||

Despite seeing, hearing, touching, smelling, eating, moving, sleeping, and breathing, the one who is engaged in *yoga* practise and sees the truth, declares within himself: 'I do nothing'. (8)

pralapan visṛjan gṛhṇann-unmiṣan nimiṣann-api |
indriyāṇīndriyārtheṣu vartanta iti dhārayan || 9 ||

Even while speaking, releasing, grasping, opening, and closing the eyes, he is always aware it is just the senses operating among sense-objects. (9)

brahmaṇyādāya karmāṇi saṅgaṁ tyaktvā karoti yaḥ |
lipyate na sa pāpena padma-patram ivāmbhasā || 10 ||

One who acts without attachment, surrendering one's actions to the Lord, is not tainted by sinful actions, just as a lotus leaf is unaffected by water. (10)

kāyena manasā buddhyā kevalair-indriyair-api |
yoginaḥ karma kurvanti saṅgaṁ tyaktvā'tma śuddhaye || 11 ||
Renouncing all attachment to action, and using the body, the mind, the intellect and the senses, the *yogīs* act only to purify themselves. (11)

yuktaḥ karma phalaṁ tyaktvā śāntim-āpnoti naiṣṭhikīm |
ayuktaḥ kāma-kāreṇa phale sakto nibadhyate || 12 ||
Giving up the fruits of action, the *yogī* attains everlasting peace. But the one who is attached to the results of action, impelled by desire, is subject to bondage. (12)

sarva karmāṇi manasā saṁnyasyāste sukhaṁ vaśī |
nava-dvāre pure dehī naiva kurvan-na kārayan || 13 ||
Mentally renouncing all actions and being in full control, the embodied Self lives happily in the city of nine gates (i.e., the body), neither acting nor causing the body to act. (13)

na kartṛtvaṁ na karmāṇi lokasya sṛjati prabhuḥ |
na karma phala saṁyogaṁ svabhāvastu pravartate || 14 ||
The master of the body — the Self, does not initiate activities, nor does It induce people to act, nor does It create the fruits of action. It is a person's inherent nature that does all this. (14)

nādatte kasyacit-pāpaṁ na caiva sukṛtaṁ vibhuḥ |
ajñānenāvṛtaṁ jñānaṁ tena muhyanti jantavaḥ || 15 ||
The all-pervading Lord does not take on the sin or merit of any person. Knowledge is covered by ignorance and so, beings are deluded. (15)

jñānena tu tad-ajñānaṁ yeṣāṁ nāśitam ātmanaḥ |
teṣām ādityavad-jñānaṁ prakāśayati tat param || 16 ||
But for some, the ignorance covering the Self is destroyed by knowledge; this knowledge acts like the sun and reveals a higher reality. (16)

tad-buddhayas tad-ātmānas-tan-niṣṭhās tat-parāyaṇāḥ |
gacchanty-apunarāvṛttiṁ jñāna nirdhūta kalmaṣāḥ || 17 ||
When one strives for the supreme goal, with their mind, faith and intelligence fully absorbed in it, the knowledge gained frees them from contamination. They go to the place from which there is no return. (17)

'Those who are always aware of the ultimate reality remain constantly absorbed in the true Identity of God. As their minds are always focused on the Divine, they are not attached to pride and say, "I am doing this," or "I am doing that." No! They are always aware that it is the Divine who is doing everything through them. And if one is fully focused on the Self, focused on God and serving Him, there will be no duality. When duality disappears from the mind, there will be no trace of evil qualities like lust, greed, anger, infatuation or egoism. All these negative qualities, these "one hundred Kauravas", will be killed, will disappear and vanish! The heart will be purified and the mind will be constantly under control. Even when they walk in the outside world, whatever they do doesn't touch them at all. There is no anger in their hearts and no judgement in their minds. They are free! That's a true *yogī*! That's a true devotee of the Lord.'

'Here Lord Kṛṣṇa uses the example of the lotus leaf. The lotus is born from muddy water, which is very dirty, but when it rises to the surface of the water, the water doesn't touch it. Have you ever seen lotus leaves? Even if you put water on them, it quickly falls off. He meant here that you have to be like the lotus leaf, so that nothing can cling to you. When you do your *sādhana*, only God should be there. If God is your aim, if God becomes everything for you, no negativity will be able to cling to you. Like water can't stay on a lotus leaf and runs off it, if one is completely surrendered to the Divine, all the negative qualities, all the kinds of attachments which one has in this world, will disappear. Even the attachment to gaining Heaven will disappear.'

'On the other hand, every action which is done with expectation, with the aim of self-gratification or with ego, will bring pain to oneself. And due to the *karma* created from this one binds oneself to the cycle of birth and death and this will destroy life itself. And the more one is attached to this *karma*, the more difficult it is to remove it. It's like creating and building up layers of *karma*.'

'A true *karma-yogī* considers everything as coming from God, belonging to God and only for God's service. Everything: the body, the senses, the mind and the intellect, belong to God. So the *karma-yogī* performs all his duties absolutely unselfishly, with a disinterested spirit. In this way, one is completely purified. In such a state, the Divine takes full control of oneself and one is totally under the inspiration and guidance of God, living and working as His instrument. Even the small "I" which is aware of God, is only Him.'

'Kṛṣṇa says, "By mere renunciation of the mind, one gets attached to the 'nine-gated city', the body." But when the mind is fully absorbed in the Divine through service, when the mind is tamed and controlled through discrimination and reasoning, it turns automatically within. Then, when the mind turns within, the intellect awakens and through this intellect, through this wisdom, the heart opens up to Love. Through that Love, one is fully absorbed in the Supersoul, in God consciousness within one's soul. In this state, it is the soul itself that is perceiving: at first the mind was looking at the soul, and now the soul is looking at the Supersoul.'

'Those who are under the control of the *indriyas*, the sense organs, and the sense enjoyment claim doership. They are not aware of the divine Self within themselves due to this ignorance. Here the Lord says, "I am beyond this." All this game of the outside reality is done by *prakṛti*. Everything which is manifested, which is tangible, is *prakṛti*. But this doesn't affect Him or touch Him. He is the Great Observer. He is the soul of souls who is not touched by anything.'

'Lord Kṛṣṇa emphasises that as you are the *ātmā*, you also are out of this game: you are not the doer. It is just the human mind that gives you the limited perception that you are the doer.'

'The natural function of the heart is to beat and to pump the blood throughout the body. The natural function of the eyes is to see. The natural role of fire is to burn. The natural role of water is to wet. All these have been created through *prakṛti*, only through His will! So Mother Nature carries on Her own work. But when one gets realised, one rises above material nature. However, if the *jīva* has not risen above material nature, if one doesn't realise that one is hanging onto the *guṇas*, how can one be free? If people don't realise their true essence as being part of the Supreme, if they don't see the divinity within themselves, if they get stuck in the duality of like and dislike, good and evil, then they unite themselves with material nature and limit themselves to only that outward reality.'

'Very often people think that God is only "good" and doesn't have any imperfections inside of Him. But how can He be God, if He doesn't have any imperfections? He is the source of everything! He has all the "good" inside Him and He has all the imperfections inside Him. And He is also above all these qualities! That's what makes Him God, because He is beyond this duality, beyond His own will, beyond His own creation.'

'Once the eyes are open, one will perceive that light, not only in oneself, but everywhere, because that light which the divinity carries is not limited; it is not only here in yourself, but it is in everything… When you are fully absorbed into the Divine, you don't need anybody's confirmation. That automatically will shine through you. You will glow. Here the glow is not an external glow, but a glow from the inside out, and that glow reflects upon you. That glow will consume every trace of ignorance in the body, in the mind, everywhere. And that's what will set you free.

'The first thing that one has to do is perceive Kṛṣṇa within oneself. When you sit down in your meditation you are absorbed and seeing the *guru* and God within you. So, this is where the inner *guru* reveals Himself. So, this wisdom, this awakening, will make you luminous and will transform your gloomy self into a luminous Self. You will start to shine. You will transform everything around. The misdeeds, misapprehension, the impure thoughts; everything will be purified. So, when everything is glowing with this luminous light, this uncreated light of Kṛṣṇa within you, then how can there be sin? Once you have attained that level, nothing can bring you back. You can't fall back. You will stay immersed in that divine bliss even being in the world itself.'

VERSES 18-26: THE STATE OF EQUANIMITY

vidyā vinaya saṁpanne brāhmaṇe gavi hastini |
śuni caiva śvapāke ca paṇḍitāḥ sama-darśinaḥ || 18 ||

The sages perceive with equal vision, a good and learned *brāhmaṇa*, a cow, an elephant, a dog and a dog-eater. (18)

ihaiva tair-jitaḥ sargo yeṣāṁ sāmye sthitaṁ manaḥ |
nir-doṣaṁ hi samaṁ brahma tasmād-brahmaṇi te sthitāḥ || 19 ||

Those who have reached this equanimity have risen beyond the conditions of the material world. The Self is pure and unchanging, and because such persons are situated in the Self, they are the same. (19)

na prahṛṣyet priyaṁ prāpya nodvijet prāpya cāpriyam |
sthira-buddhir-asaṁmūḍho brahma-vid brahmaṇi sthitaḥ || 20 ||

One who neither rejoices at gaining what is pleasant, nor grieves at receiving what is unpleasant, whose mind is fixed and undeluded, he has knowledge of the Self and he dwells in the Self. (20)

bāhya-sparśeṣv-asaktātmā vindaty-ātmani yat sukham |
sa brahma-yoga-yuktātmā sukham akṣayam aśnute || 21 ||

When the mind is detached from external sensations, one finds happiness in the Self, and when through *yoga* the mind is on the Lord, one enjoys endless bliss. (21)

ye hi saṁsparśajā bhogā duḥkha-yonaya eva te |
ādy-antavantaḥ kaunteya na teṣu ramate budhaḥ || 22 ||

The pleasures that arise from contact with the external world are a source of suffering. They have a beginning and an end, O Arjuna, and so the wise do not rejoice in them. (22)

śaknotīhaiva yaḥ soḍhuṁ prāk-śarīra vimokṣaṇāt |
kāma krodhodbhavaṁ vegaṁ sa yuktaḥ sa sukhī naraḥ || 23 ||

A person who can resist the impulses arising from desire and anger whilst still in the body, is a true *yogī* and a joyful person. (23)

yo'ntaḥ sukho'ntarā rāmas-tathāntar jyotir-eva yaḥ |
sa yogī brahma-nirvāṇaṁ brahma-bhūto'dhigacchati || 24 ||

One who is joyful within, whose pleasure is within, and is illumined within, is a true *yogī*. He is liberated within the Supreme and he attains the Supreme. (24)

labhante brahma-nirvāṇam ṛṣayaḥ kṣīṇa kalmaṣāḥ |
chinna-dvaidhā yatātmanaḥ sarva bhūta hite ratāḥ || 25 ||

The sages who are free from the pairs of opposites, who are self-controlled and are devoted to the welfare of all beings, become cleansed of all impurities and attain the bliss of the Supreme. (25)

kāma krodha viyuktānāṁ yatīnāṁ yata-cetasām |
abhito brahma-nirvāṇaṁ vartate viditātmanām || 26 ||

To those who are free from desire and anger, whose minds are controlled, and who have attained self-mastery, liberation is close at hand. (26)

'Here "*brāhmaṇa*" doesn't mean a priest or somebody who is born into a certain caste. No, Kṛṣṇa says here, "You are *brāhmaṇa* when you have realised God, when you have realised your relationship with Him, when you have attained Him."'

'Those who have this true knowledge...are fully aware that every duty is only service to the Lord.'

'The sages, the *sādhus*, the saints, perceive only the oneness: they see God equally in each person. They see beyond outward appearances and respect each person's role as being in accordance with the will of God. They have this deep knowledge which allows them to see that there is perfection everywhere! There is nothing that is imperfect! Imperfection is due to the ignorance in the minds of men. But if one has transcended one's human nature and realised the divine Self, and the divine qualities manifest through one, then one sees that the whole creation which has come out of Him, is a projection of His own will.'

'The one who is ignorant finds fault everywhere and proclaims, "I am better than you. What I believe is best! My God is better than your God. Why do you have so many gods?" Then due to ignorance people fight over all these things. But the truly wise ones, who have realised themselves, whose knowledge is not based on mere study of scriptures or on books, who have perceived the Truth within themselves, who have perceived the Divine, God within their true Self, don't find fault anywhere.'

'People can give them either honour or dishonour. People can criticise them because of lack of understanding. But to the saint, it doesn't make any difference. For the one who is seated in God consciousness, it doesn't matter if life brings joy or sorrow. His faith is never shaken!'

'One who takes delight in the sense enjoyment of the outside world, whose mind is always running towards judgement and criticising everything, will never experience this supreme, blissful state. The joy born of dispassion, the bliss which the realised soul attains, is far greater than any so-called joy and happiness of the outside reality. People's happiness level always varies, doesn't it? Today they "wake up with the right foot", and they are happy; tomorrow they "wake up with the left foot" and they are not happy. The ones who are constantly awake in the divine Self, who are constantly in the blissful state, always "wake up with the right foot", even if the left foot touches the ground first. They are constantly meditating on God, so they perceive only this One reality, Nārāyaṇa. They eat – Nārāyaṇa. They sleep – Nārāyaṇa. They talk – Nārāyaṇa. They dance – Nārāyaṇa. They laugh – Nārāyaṇa. There is not a single moment when Nārāyaṇa is not present, for each breath is Nārāyaṇa.'

'No one is responsible for your happiness or your unhappiness except yourself. You are the cause of your own happiness. When you are surrendered wholeheartedly to God, when your mind, body and spirit are fully in accordance with the will of God, serving God, meditating on Him, this becomes the source of your true happiness and bliss! But when the mind runs towards the external reality thinking, "Yes, this is it!", when one is finding great joy in the outside world, this will bring deep sorrow to oneself. The one who enjoys the sense objects, automatically becomes evil-minded, greedy, lustful and angry. One will have to go through enormous suffering in this life and even later on, in future lifetimes. And then one will ask, "What have I done to God to suffer so much? Why me, and not my neighbour?"'

'God is the Supreme Light of all lights. The whole universe is illumined by His effulgence. He is the Supreme soul in all beings. A true *yogī* is ever conscious of such a God. He sees the Ultimate as His own Self. He remains constantly absorbed in His Love, His Peace and His Light. Even though the world appears real, the true *yogī* sees beyond the external reality. He sees beyond what normal people see. He sees the source. He sees within his own Self the Supreme Light, the Light of God, '*antarātmā*', '*antara-jyoti*'. '*Antara-jyoti*' is the inner Light; '*antarātmā*' is the Supreme Light within the core of his soul itself. Then, one starts to emanate the inner Light and becomes a source of salvation, not only for oneself, but for others.'

'Wherever one goes, one brings this Light to the people. These ones don't think only for themselves. They say, "I have reached that realisation. I want every soul to realise themselves. I want everybody to understand how the mind is and I want everybody to be free." That's what the *guru* does. The *guru*s have already realised and attained the Supreme Lord, but yet, they come down of their own accord to help, and to uplift humanity... You have to change. You have to transform. You have a life. You are a living identity. You have to move out of this ignorance and be aware of the knowledge of the Self.'

'When you take shelter at the Feet of the Master, you have the reflection of the Master upon you. As you come into the Light of the Master, the Light of the Master shines upon you... Reflect your Master. Let the Light you have received from your spiritual path enlighten others also.'

VERSES 27-29: INTRODUCING YOGA PRACTICE

sparśān kṛtvā bahir-bāhyāṁś-cakṣuś-caivāntare bhruvoḥ |
prāṇāpānau samau kṛtvā nāsābhyantara cāriṇau || 27 ||
yatendriya mano-buddhir-munir mokṣa parāyaṇaḥ |
vigat-ecchābhaya krodho yaḥ sadā mukta eva saḥ || 28 ||

Shutting out all external contacts, focusing the gaze between the eyebrows, suspending the inward and outward breaths within the nostrils, and having controlled the senses, mind, and intellect, the sage who desires liberation gives up desire, fear and anger, and attains it. (27-28)

bhoktāraṁ yajñā tapasāṁ sarva loka maheśvaram |
suhṛdaṁ sarva-bhūtānāṁ jñātvā māṁ śāntim-ṛcchati || 29 ||

And knowing Me as the supreme enjoyer of all sacrifices and austerities, as the Lord of all the worlds, and the Friend of every being, one attains peace. (29)

'Usually the human mind hangs onto the outside reality, but when the mind is tamed, it starts to look within. Then, the focus of the mind is towards the true knowledge of the soul. When you sit in meditation, the mind starts to perceive everything in a different way; the mind looks up to the soul, to the Great Observer. And when the soul is turned into itself, it rests in the greater Supersoul, who is Nārāyaṇa. When the soul rests in the Supersoul, it still continues its activities in the world, but it is the Supersoul who is doing this activity. At this point, one is fully absorbed into the Supersoul. One is fully absorbed into this awareness, that God alone is the reality, nothing else.'

'He says, "I am your best Friend, I am the Friend of every being. Those who attain that peace, those who attain that level of consciousness, they realise that whatever I am doing is not for My sake. Whatever I am doing is for your sake and for the sake of uplifting humanity." That's the humbleness of God. He lowers Himself so that you can be dear to Him.'

CHAPTER SIX
DHYĀNA-YOGA
KṚṢṆA DESCRIBES MEDITATION

Now that renunciation and the nature of action have been thoroughly explained, chapter six begins to describe *dhyāna-yoga* or meditation.

Kṛṣṇa up till now has provided a step by step path beginning with *karma-yoga*. Once this is successfully practised, one achieves inner tranquillity. This creates the desired state for *dhyāna-yoga*, where the mind is made to focus within and have the direct perception of the *ātmā*.

Kṛṣṇa gives Arjuna the practical techniques upon which one can best attempt to master the mind through the practice of meditation. Gradually, through intense self-control and repeated practise, one is able to perceive the *ātmā* and experience limitless joy, free from suffering. Responding to Arjuna's fears of failure, Kṛṣṇa explains that the fruits of this *yoga* are never lost. If one does not achieve the goal in this life, one will inevitably be given the right circumstances to carry on one's spiritual development.

The chapter concludes by stating that the one who is absorbed in the path of *yoga*, given by Kṛṣṇa thus far, is superior to all other spiritual seekers, but amongst all such *yogis*, the one who dwells on Kṛṣṇa is the highest of all. It is this last verse which marks the beginning of a new line of discourse in the *Gītā*: one where Kṛṣṇa places Himself explicitly as the Supreme Lord and teaches Arjuna the way of *bhakti* (devotion).

VERSES 1-4: THE TRUE RENUNCIATE

śrī bhagavān uvāca
anāśritaḥ karma-phalaṁ kāryaṁ karma karoti yaḥ |
sa saṁnyāsī ca yogī ca na nir-agnir-na cākriyaḥ || 1 ||

Lord Kṛṣṇa says:
One who performs their prescribed work without expecting the fruits of their action is a true renunciate and a *yogī*; not one who does not light the sacrificial fire and avoids their duty. (1)

yaṁ sannyāsam-iti prāhur-yogaṁ taṁ viddhi pāṇḍava |
na hy-asaṁnyasta saṅkalpo yogī bhavati kaścana || 2 ||

O Arjuna, understand that renunciation is the same as *yoga*. For no one becomes a true *karma-yogī* without giving up the desire for pleasure. (2)

ārurukṣor-muner-yogaṁ karma kāraṇam ucyate |
yogārūḍhasya tasyaiva śamaḥ kāraṇam ucyate || 3 ||

For the sage who is still seeking to make progress in *yoga*, action is said to be the way; when one has become advanced in *yoga*, renunciation is the way. (3)

yadā hi nendriyārtheṣu na karmasv-anuṣajjate |
sarva saṅkalpa saṁnyāsī yogārūḍhas-tad-ocyate || 4 ||

When one loses all attachment for sense-objects and to performing action, and when he has abandoned all desires, then he is considered to have reached the heights of *yoga*. (4)

'Very often you will see people calling themselves renunciates, but still they enjoy everything, they are bothered about everything. They are renunciates only on the outside, but inside they have a certain motive or a certain aim behind their actions.'

'On the other hand, people who live in the world, but are not attached to it, who dedicate their life to serving others, to helping people, helping the animals, protecting the animals, they are the true *sannyāsīs*.'

'Those who are doing every action without expecting something in return, selflessly; those who love unconditionally; those who are devoid of pride and ego and expectation; those who have renounced the mind (because it is the mind that desires and always longs for recognition); they are the true *sannyāsīs*. It's not the colour or the clothes that they are wearing; that's not *sannyāsa*. It's not the external *sannyāsa*. It is the internal.'

VERSES 5-9: THE MIND IS OUR BEST FRIEND OR OUR WORST ENEMY

uddhared-ātman-ātmānaṁ nātmānam avasādayet |
ātmaiva hy-ātmano bandhur-ātmaiva ripur-ātmanaḥ || 5 ||

One should raise oneself by one's own mind and not allow oneself to fall, for a controlled mind is one's friend, but an uncontrolled mind is one's enemy. (5)

bandhur-ātmā'tmanas tasya yenātmaivātmanā jitaḥ |
anātmanastu śatrutve vartetātmaiva śatruvat || 6 ||

The mind is a friend to one who has mastered it. But for one whose mind is uncontrolled, it becomes the worst of enemies. (6)

jitātmanaḥ praśāntasya paramātmā samāhitaḥ |
śītoṣṇa sukha-duḥkheṣu tathā mānāpamānayoḥ || 7 ||

If one gains self-control and tranquillity, then the Supreme Self is realised. He is perfectly balanced in heat and cold, pleasure and pain, honour and dishonour. (7)

jñāna vijñāna tṛptātmā kūṭastho vijitendriyaḥ |
yukta ity-ucyate yogī sama-loṣṭāśma kāñcanaḥ || 8 ||

The *yogī* who is fully content with knowledge and realisation of the Self, who dwells in a transcendent state, whose senses are controlled, will see earth, stone and gold the same. (8)

suhṛn mitrāry-udāsīna madhyastha dveṣya bandhuṣu |
sādhuṣv-api ca pāpeṣu sama-buddhir viśiṣyate || 9 ||

One who regards well-wishers, friends, an enemy, one who is indifferent, a mediator, the hateful, relatives, and even the righteous and the unrighteous, as the same, is truly advanced. (9)

'The mind is the best friend of one who has conquered the mind. Who has conquered what? It is the Self that conquers the mind.'

'So, what happens? The thoughts and subsequent actions, which are always under the command of the mind, change. Now, the mind is being controlled by the soul. When the mind is running somewhere else, the soul says, "Come back here!", and puts you on the right track.'

'If you don't control the mind, if you don't succeed in your endeavour, the mind will become your worst enemy. This is when, very often, people go into deep depression. They collapse. They can't handle anything. Even if they have all knowledge, but yet they…have let the mind poison them.'

'When the mind and the senses are controlled, they don't run after the sense objects, so one can direct the senses to where one wants; this is "self-mastery". If the mind and senses are under control, they can be focused on God, on the image of the Divine, which will lead one towards God-realisation.

'The ones who are completely surrendered to God,…through the control of the mind, they don't get disturbed by anything. They are not touched by pleasure or pain, honour and dishonour, or anything. These opposites don't affect them at all, because they see the Divine in everything. This is the quality of someone who has merged into his own Self. He reflects calmness, peace, tranquillity and joy. These qualities emanate from the ones who are not agitated by anything; they are free.'

'True *yogīs* are here on Earth to love: they always stay in that loving state and in that loving state, there is no judgement. It's not like human love, where you put someone high up on a pedestal, and then the moment you hear or see something that you don't like about the person you think you love, then you become aggressive, and depressive – you become all the "sives" – expansive, expressive, oppressive, and possessive... Whereas the ones who excel are above all this, as they look at everything equally and rejoice in God consciousness. They see that it is God who is doing this multitude of activities through His creation. It is God who has manifested Himself and is enjoying Himself while He is doing everything.'

'There is no need to judge when you are absorbed in Divine Love. The only thing to do is to love. That's why I chose "Just Love" Otherwise I would tell you, "Think about Love, think Love." No, I said, "Just Love", don't bother about anything. Don't worry. Your aim is to love. This is your *dharma*.'

VERSES 10-17: THE PRACTICE OF MEDITATION

yogī yuñjīta satatam ātmānaṁ rahasi sthitaḥ |
ekākī yatacittātmā nirāśīr aparigrahaḥ || 10 ||

Remaining alone in a solitary place, controlling his mind and body, free from any desire and sense of ownership, the *yogī* should constantly engage the mind in meditational absorption. (10)

śucau deśe pratiṣṭhāpya sthiram-āsanam ātmanaḥ |
nāty-ucchritaṁ nāti-nīcaṁ cailājina kuśottaram || 11 ||

In a clean place, he should make a firm seat which is neither too high nor too low, covering it with cloth, deer-skin and *kuśa* grass [1]. (11)

tatraikāgraṁ manaḥ kṛtvā yata-cittendriya kriyaḥ |
upaviśyāsane yuñjyād-yogam-ātma viśuddhaye || 12 ||

Sitting on that seat, focusing the mind in concentration, with thoughts and senses restrained, one should practise *yoga* for self-purification. (12)

samaṁ kāya-śiro-grīvaṁ dhārayann-acalaṁ sthiraḥ |
saṁprekṣya nāsikāgraṁ svaṁ diśaś-cānavalokayan || 13 ||

He should hold the body, head and neck erect, in a motionless and steady posture, focusing one's gaze on the tip of the nose without looking around. (13)

praśāntātmā vigata-bhīr-brahmacāri vrate sthitaḥ |
manaḥ saṁyamya mac-citto yukta āsīta mat-paraḥ || 14 ||

Being serene and fearless, firm in the vow of celibacy, and holding the mind in check, he should fix his thoughts on Me. Sitting in meditation, he should hold Me to be the goal of life. (14)

yuñjann-evaṁ sadā'tmānaṁ yogī niyata-mānasaḥ |
śāntiṁ nirvāṇa paramāṁ mat-saṁsthām adhigacchati || 15 ||

Applying themselves constantly in this way, the *yogī* with a controlled mind attains a peace which culminates in liberation, thereby abiding with Me forever. (15)

nāty-aśnatas-tu yogo'sti na caikāntam-anaśnataḥ |
na cāti svapnaśīlasya jāgrato naiva cārjuna || 16 ||

Arjuna, *yoga* is not for one who overeats, nor for one who fasts excessively; nor is it for one who sleeps too much, nor for one who stays awake for lengthy periods. (16)

yuktāhāra vihārasya yukta ceṣṭasya karmasu |
yukta svapnāvabodhasya yogo bhavati duḥkhahā || 17 ||

***Yoga* becomes the destroyer of sorrow for one who is moderate in eating, recreation, the performance of action, sleep and wakefulness. (17)**

'Kṛṣṇa is saying you should practise your *sādhana* for self-purification. Without self-purification, you can't advance. This purification is very important. He is emphasising purification through meditation. Purify yourself by chanting the Name of God, meditate on the Lord, meditate on His glory, meditate on His form, meditate on His Name.'

'For a *yogī* to sit in Times Square is easy, because that one has transcended everything. But people who have not yet transcended, still have to find this quiet place in the outside where they will not be disturbed, where the mind will not run left and right.'

'The time and the place of meditation are very important, because when you set a certain time to meditate, you are inviting God to be there with you. It's like if you invite a friend to come to your place and then you are not there to welcome your friend. How would it be? Or you are invited somewhere, you are ringing the bell and you see all the lights off. Then someone turns the light on and you see the person in pyjamas saying, "Ai! I thought it was tomorrow!" How would it be? You would be shocked, no? So, here it is the same thing. When you set a certain time to sit for meditation, you are inviting God to manifest Himself at that moment. And you can have this expectation that, as you sent the invitation, God will come and be eagerly waiting for you inside yourself at that time.'

VERSES 18-32: THE GOAL OF MEDITATION

yadā viniyataṁ cittam-ātmany-evāvatiṣṭhate |
niḥspṛhaḥ sarva-kāmebhyo yukta ity-ucyate sadā || 18 ||

When the subdued mind rests in the Self alone, free from all material desire, one is said to be well established in *yoga*. (18)

yathā dīpo nivātasthe neṅgate sopamā smṛtā |
yogino yata-cittasya yuñjato yogam-ātmanaḥ || 19 ||

The controlled mind of a *yogī* who meditates on the Self is compared to a lamp which does not flicker in a windless place. (19)

yatroparamate cittaṁ niruddhaṁ yoga-sevayā |
yatra caivātmanā'tmānaṁ paśyann-ātmani tuṣyati || 20 ||
sukham-ātyantikaṁ yat-tad-buddhi-grāhyam-atīndriyam |
vetti yatra na caivāyaṁ sthitaś-calati tattvataḥ || 21 ||

When the mind, restrained by the practice of *yoga*, perceives the Self, one discovers Its bliss. When one experiences that intense joy which is known to the intellect, but unknowable to the senses, one remains fixed in this state, never wavering from it. (20-21)

yaṁ labdhvā cāparaṁ lābhaṁ manyate nādhikaṁ tataḥ |
yasmin sthito na duḥkhena guruṇā'pi vicālyate || 22 ||

When one has attained this state, one realises there is nothing higher. As a result, one cannot be moved from this position even by terrible suffering. (22)

taṁ vidyād duḥkha saṁyoga viyogaṁ yoga saṁjñitam |
sa niścayena yoktavyo yogo 'nirviṇṇa cetasā || 23 ||

You should understand that this deliverance from suffering is the very purpose of *yoga*. Therefore, *yoga* must be practised with determination and with a mind free from despondency. (23)

saṅkalpa prabhavān kāmāṁs-tyaktvā sarvān-aśeṣataḥ |
manasaivendriya-grāmaṁ viniyamya samantataḥ || 24 ||

It should be done while renouncing all desire for material things and restraining the senses through the mind alone. (24)

śanaiḥ śanairu-paramed buddhyā dhṛti-gṛhītayā |
ātma-saṁsthaṁ manaḥ kṛtvā na kiñcid-api cintayet || 25 ||

With the firm resolution of the intellect, step by step one should become centred within; having focused the mind upon the Self, one should think of nothing else. (25)

yato yato niścarati manaś-cañcalam asthiraṁ |
tatas-tato niyamyaitad-ātmanyeva vaśaṁ nayet || 26 ||

Wherever the fickle and unsteady mind wanders, one should bring it back under control, keeping it fixed on the Self alone. (26)

praśānta manasaṁ hyenaṁ yoginaṁ sukham-uttamam |
upaiti śānta rajasaṁ brahma-bhūtam akalmaṣam || 27 ||

When the *yogī* has his passions subdued and is focused on the Lord without worldly contamination, when his mind is still, he experiences the highest happiness. (27)

yuñjann-evaṁ sadā'tmānaṁ yogī vigata kalmaṣaḥ |
sukhena brahma saṁsparśam atyantaṁ sukham-aśnute || 28 ||

Thus, freed from mental impurities, and constantly engaged in the practice of *yoga*, the *yogī* easily attains the supreme bliss of knowing the Lord. (28)

sarva-bhūtastham ātmānaṁ sarva-bhūtāni cātmani |
īkṣate yoga-yuktātmā sarvatra sama-darśanaḥ || 29 ||

Through this *yoga*, one gains that equal vision. One sees the Lord in all beings and all beings within the Lord. (29)

yo māṁ paśyati sarvatra sarvaṁ ca mayi paśyati |
tasyāhaṁ na praṇaśyāmi sa ca me na praṇaśyati || 30 ||

For one who sees Me everywhere and everything in Me, I am not separated from him and he is never separated from Me. (30)

sarva-bhūta-sthitaṁ yo māṁ bhajaty-ekatvam-āsthitaḥ |
sarvathā vartamāno'pi sa yogī mayi vartate || 31 ||

However a person lives, if he realises this unity and worships Me as the One dwelling in all beings, he rests in Me as a true *yogī*. (31)

ātmaupamyena sarvatra samaṁ paśyati yo'rjuna |
sukhaṁ vā yadi vā duḥkhaṁ sa yogī paramo mataḥ || 32 ||

O Arjuna, one who sees the pleasure and pain of all others as one's own is the highest *yogī*. (32)

'Here Kṛṣṇa makes an analogy between a still mind and an unmoving flame: the mind is "motionless like the light of a lamp in a windless place." A flame is always moving, but when it is sheltered, blocked from all sides, it doesn't move, it doesn't flicker; it is stable, it shines, it radiates light! Like that, when one is fully absorbed in the divine Self, God within oneself, nothing can deviate one from the path and automatically one starts to shine all the divine qualities.'

'When through deep meditation, one has perceived the true reality, "which is perceived by the intelligence and is beyond the senses"; when one has perceived and attained this bliss through meditation on God; when God has revealed this supreme aspect of Himself within oneself, "established therein, the soul can no longer fall away from the spiritual truth of its being." In this state, one perceives this oneness and the everlasting, imperishable joy and bliss emanating from God within oneself. One is God-realised, one is a true *yogī* and one is never disunited from God. Whatever one does in life, whether it is having children, eating, drinking, or sleeping, if one is centred in that state, nothing can touch that person. One stays ever free. That's why you see that in ancient times, the sages were all *karma-yogīs*, they were all married, even the *gurus*, and their wives were supporting their work. All those greater mothers also attained the same state of God-realisation as their husbands, due to their surrender, their service, their *bhakti* and the dedication that they had to their husbands.

'Lord Kṛṣṇa says that the ones who have attained this supreme state, whatever they do in the outside world, they are completely free, even if it may appear that they are limited. One might ask, "If you are a *yogī*, why do you need to sleep? If you are a *yogī*, why do you need to eat?" But as they are established in the Self, they are beyond duality, they are beyond the judgement of right and wrong, they are beyond the judgement of being husband and wife, they are beyond the duality of man and woman, they are beyond heat and cold, they are beyond "good" and "bad" and other opposites.'

'Everything that you do, once you have attained bliss, is infused with that bliss... When bliss awakens inside of you, it starts to consume you and it is forever. It will keep growing. There is not an end to that bliss... All the saints of the Lord are absorbed in that bliss.'

VERSES 33-36: ARJUNA'S DOUBT

arjuna uvāca
yo'yaṁ yogas-tvayā proktaḥ sāmyena madhusūdhana |
etasyāhaṁ na paśyāmi cañcalatvāt sthitiṁ sthirām || 33 ||

Arjuna says:
O Kṛṣṇa, due to the mind being so unsteady, this *yoga* which has been taught by You appears impractical and unstable. (33)

cañcalaṁ hi manaḥ kṛṣṇa pramāthi balavad-dṛḍham |
tasyāhaṁ nigrahaṁ manye vāyoriva suduṣkaram || 34 ||

The mind is fickle, turbulent, powerful and stubborn. It is more difficult to control than the wind. (34)

śrī bhagavān uvāca
asaṁśayaṁ mahābāho mano dur-nigrahaṁ calam |
abhyāsena tu kaunteya vairāgyeṇa ca gṛhyate || 35 ||

Lord Kṛṣṇa says:
The mind is undoubtedly chaotic and hard to subdue, O Arjuna. But by repeated practise and renunciation it can be brought under control. (35)

asaṁyatātmanā yogo duṣprāpa iti me matiḥ |
vaśyātmanā tu yatatā śakyo'vāptum upāyataḥ || 36 ||

In my opinion, it is hard for a person with an unrestrained mind to take up this path. However, it can be done through proper means by one who strives for it with a subdued mind. (36)

'Arjuna's question was how to gain control of this unsteady mind. Bhagavān has replied to him saying that it is possible to do so through constant practise of mental discipline and observance, to observe the mind, to observe how the mind is thinking, to keep the mind on the path of reflection...that will free oneself from attachment. But He is saying that one must practise. Wherever you focus your mind, that mind takes a shape. It's like liquid. It doesn't have a form itself, but it takes the form of a receptacle. You pour water in a bottle, it takes the form of a bottle.'

'Such is this mind also. If you feed that mind with negativity, it will become negative. "If you are sitting here, O Arjuna, and telling Me, 'No, no, I can't do it, I can't do it, I can't do it', you will not be able to." If you sit and say, "I can't, I can't, I can't", you are building a brick wall where you are closing yourself inside. You are blinding yourself, you are finding thousands of excuses for not doing your *sādhana*, for not practicing your *kriyā*. Here Bhagavān says, "Practice is very important. Don't find excuses." Stop saying, "I can't, I can't, I can't"; sing, "I can, I can, I can" and, "I will, I will, I will." And when you sit down in your meditation, have this pure conviction that the Almighty Lord Himself is with you.'

'Kṛṣṇa says that when your mind is jumping from one thing to the other, don't run into your weakness, don't run into your fear! Don't think that your desire for God is too much or too far away. One should always be alert and not allow the mind to think about anything but God. He has given so many divine forms, He has given so many Divine Names to enable mankind to completely focus on Him. When you sit for meditation, if you perceive your mind going somewhere else, let it go, but then bring it back. Show your power over it through the intellect. Show that the Great Observer is more powerful than the mind. That's why you can bring back your thought and control it. Remind yourself continuously, even if you don't notice when the mind ran away and slipped out. When it slips out, don't dwell on the object that has attracted the mind: instead bring the mind back and fix it "in the Self." Fix it on God! God dwells in the identity of the soul as the Supersoul.'

VERSES 37-46: THE FATE OF THE FAILED YOGĪ

arjuna uvāca
ayatiḥ śraddhayopeto yogāc-calita-mānasaḥ |
aprāpya yoga-saṁsiddhiṁ kāṁ gatiṁ kṛṣṇa gacchati || 37 ||

Arjuna says:
O Kṛṣṇa, what becomes of that person who has conviction, but due to the wanderings of the mind and lack of diligent effort, fails to attain perfection on this path? (37)

kaccin-nobhaya-vibhraṣṭaś-chinnābhram iva naśyati |
apratiṣṭho mahābāho vimūḍho brahmaṇaḥ pathi || 38 ||

Having no success in both the material world and the path to God, is he not like a broken cloud, lost and without any position? (38)

etan-me saṁśayaṁ kṛṣṇa chettum arhasy-aśeṣataḥ |
tvad-anyaḥ saṁśayasyāsya chettā na hy-upapadyate || 39 ||

O Kṛṣṇa, please remove this doubt of mine completely for there is no one else who can dispel it. (39)

śrī bhagavān uvāca
pārtha naiveha nāmutra vināśas tasya vidyate |
na hi kalyāṇa-kṛt kaścid durgatiṁ tāta gacchati || 40 ||

Lord Kṛṣṇa says:
Neither in this world nor in the next, O Arjuna, is he ever lost. For verily, no one who does good ever comes to grief. (40)

prāpya puṇya-kṛtāṁ lokān uṣitvā śāśvatīḥ samāḥ |
śucināṁ śrīmatāṁ gehe yoga-bhraṣṭo 'bhijāyate || 41 ||

Having attained to the realms of the righteous and dwelt there for many long years, one who has fallen from *yoga* is born again in the house of the pure and prosperous. (41)

athavā yoginām eva kule bhavati dhīmatām |
etaddhi durlabhataraṁ loke janma yadīdṛśam || 42 ||

Or one is born into a family of wise *yogīs*; but such a birth in this world is very difficult to obtain. (42)

tatra taṁ buddhi saṁyogaṁ labhate paurva-dehikam |
yatate ca tato bhūyaḥ saṁsiddhau kurunandana || 43 ||

Then, O Arjuna, one regains the same disposition of mind which was acquired in their previous body, and from there one strives again for success in *yoga*. (43)

pūrvābhyāsane tenaiva hriyate hyavaśo'pi saḥ |
jijñāsur-api yogasya śabda-brahmātivartate || 44 ||

Due to the practise done previously he is pulled to that position, even against his will. Understand that one who merely enquires about *yoga*, transcends the ritualistic principles of the scriptures. (44)

prayatnād yatamānastu yogī saṁśuddha-kilbiṣaḥ |
aneka-janma saṁsiddhas tato yāti parāṁ gatim || 45 ||

By striving earnestly, the practicing *yogīs* who are purified of their faults, attain perfection after many births and reach that supreme goal. (45)

tapasvibhyo'dhiko yogī jñānibhyo'pi mato'dhikaḥ |
karmibhyaścādhiko yogī tasmād yogī bhavārjuna || 46 ||

The *yogī* is considered to be superior to those who perform austerity, superior to the intellectuals, and even superior to the ritualists; therefore, O Arjuna, become a *yogī*. (46)

'If you don't reach it in one life, it doesn't get wasted, because spirituality is not tangible. Spirituality is not something which is made up of matter, but it is made up of faith inside of you. What is happening right now is a continuation from what you have started before. And if in this life you don't attain it, it will still carry on in the next life.'

'Those who have faith in God, they are not lost. This is His assurance.'

'The surroundings create an effect on people. Even if one has grace, it can stay dormant inside one's heart. Deep inside one has the feeling, "I am incomplete." However, due to the environment, due to the surroundings, due to the mind's activities, they only get drawn to the outside reality. They get tempted and controlled by the outside reality, and then they don't have the grace to find their path in this lifetime. However, through the grace that they received, through the *puṇya* that they accumulated, they are born again on this Earth in spiritual families which will contribute to their spiritual growth… This means that the ones who try their best, never lose. They enjoy celestial regions for long years and are born again on Earth to continue on their spiritual advancement.'

'In this life, through *sādhana*, through following the words of the Master, the one who has faith in one's practice, who has faith in God, transcends the enjoyment of this world, as well as the next one. And due to the fruits of past good *puṇya*, one continues practising and advancing on the path to Enlightenment.'

'Sometimes people take a spiritual path, they get initiated, they follow the Master, and then they feel that that path is not their path. Then, they go away not knowing that God had placed them on that path for a reason... Due to their difficulty in following what the Master had asked from them, that grace that they received even just to be in the presence of the Master will become dormant inside of them until they are truly ready. Then, they will be called back again. And if they die, they will be called again in their next life.'

'The soul sees the path that will lead one to the spiritual family – *vasudhaiva-kuṭumbakaṁ* – this unification of one family... A real family is one that shares with you, who stands with you, however you are, who supports you on your way. That's real family.'

VERSE 47: THE HIGHEST OF ALL YOGĪS

yoginām api sarveṣāṁ mad-gatenāntarātmanā |
śraddhāvān bhajate yo māṁ sa me yuktatamo mataḥ || 47 ||

But more than all the *yogīs*, he who has faith and worships Me, is deemed by Me to be the highest of all. (47)

'The *bhaktas*, the devotees of the Lord, are the true *yogīs*. Devotees who love Him and serve Him are united with Him in *yoga*. And so, they are the true *yogīs*. The true *yogīs* have a zeal inside of them, a longing; they have an urge inside of them to seek the grace of the Lord, which normal people don't have.

'Here Bhagavān Kṛṣṇa is praising the *bhakta*. He is praising the devotee who is surrendered to Him. He is praising the greatness of a devotee... They don't just believe, but they have conviction of the existence of the Supreme Lord. The *bhaktas* have full conviction that their existence here is to serve the Lord and the saints. Their faith is unshakeable. Those who have unshakable faith are dear to the Lord.'

Chapter Six Verses: Key Terms

[1] **Kuśa grass** – a type of grass considered sacred in India. It is generally used for purification or as a conduit for energy during *pūjā* and ritual ceremonies. It can also be used to construct a seat for meditation.

CHAPTER SEVEN
JÑĀNA-VIJÑĀNA-YOGA
KNOWLEDGE OF KṚṢṆA

The first six chapters have focused on how one can attain realisation of the Self through desireless action. The practice of *karma-yoga* allows one to internally withdraw from the world and gain mastery over the senses. Eventually, through *dhyāna-yoga* one gains knowledge of the *ātmā* (*Brahma-jñāna*) and becomes firmly established in this state. But throughout Kṛṣṇa's discourse, Arjuna has been both confused and doubtful about just how successful one can be on this path.

Chapter seven marks the beginning of a new phase in the *Gītā*'s teaching, where the next six chapters shift the emphasis to devotion (*bhakti*) on Kṛṣṇa as a means of freeing oneself from the bondage of *karma*. It is where Arjuna gradually becomes aware of the divine personality who creates, sustains and destroys all that exists. So far there have been incidental references to Kṛṣṇa as the Supreme Lord, but now this truth is revealed explicitly to Arjuna.

In this chapter, Arjuna learns how this world and the individual souls rest upon Kṛṣṇa, forming a part of His cosmic form. Not only does Kṛṣṇa support creation, but He is actually immanent within each and every aspect of it. He is the fragrance of the earth, the brilliance of fire and the life of life itself.

Kṛṣṇa states that this material world is very difficult to cross over, but by surrendering to Him one can easily break free of it. Various people approach Kṛṣṇa, but out of these it is the pure devotee who is most dear. Such a person enjoys a mutual loving relationship and sees the Truth that Kṛṣṇa is all things. But those without this knowledge, worship other gods, failing to see that they are empowered by Kṛṣṇa alone. Kṛṣṇa points out that the ignorant cannot recognise His divinity and are fooled by His external form. Only those who are pure and engage in virtuous acts can sincerely worship Him as the Lord.

VERSES 1-3: THE RARITY OF KNOWING KṚṢṆA

śrī bhagavān uvāca
mayyāsakta manāḥ pārtha yogaṁ yuñjan madāśrayaḥ |
asaṁśayaṁ samagraṁ māṁ yathā jñāsyasi tacchṛṇu || 1 ||

Lord Kṛṣṇa says:

Now listen Arjuna, how one can have full knowledge of Me without any doubts, by dedicating his *yoga* practise to Me, and absorbing his mind on Me. (1)

jñānaṁ te'haṁ savijñānam idaṁ vakṣyāmy-aśeṣataḥ |
yajjñātvā neha bhūyo'nyajjñātavyam avaśiṣyate || 2 ||

I will explain this knowledge to you fully, along with the process of its immediate realisation. Once you understand this, there is nothing else that needs to be known. (2)

manuṣyāṇāṁ sahasreṣu kaścid yatati siddhaye |
yatatām-api siddhānāṁ kaścin māṁ vetti tattvataḥ || 3 ||

Among thousands of men, perhaps one strives for perfection; even among those who strive for perfection, only one may know Me; and among those who know Me, maybe one alone knows Me in truth. (3)

'How great it is to be born as a human. Because no other creature has the faculty of longing for the Lord, of attaining the Lord, of achieving God-realisation. No other creature has this choice. You will not see a bird saying, "Oh, today I will not do anything. I will just sit and meditate on God." Rarely is one given the gift to realise God.'

'Sadly, human beings don't realise the greatness of the blessing, the grace of being born on Earth – even if they are reminded thousands of times, "Rise above this illusion, don't attach yourself to this illusion." The attachment to worldly enjoyment lasts only during this life and then you are bound by imperfection. Kṛṣṇa says, "Love God." Yet, out of the thousands who love God, only a handful, only a few, can really reach perfection. As it is said in the *Bible*, "Many are called; few are chosen."'

'When one sees Him within the core of one's own heart, within one's own Self, through this supreme knowledge, one will perceive the Supreme Lord everywhere. The *bhaktas*, the devotees, who have achieved such perfection, see that there is no difference anywhere. Wherever they go, whichever form of the Divine they worship, they perceive only one reality… Kṛṣṇa says that this is very rare. This is why there are so many groups, so many denominations, that bring abomination into the world, because of this lack of perception that it is the same Supreme Lord who has different Names and different forms, who is present everywhere. That's why there is complete judgement, "My path is better than yours."

'Some devotees have the grace of becoming true Vaiṣṇavas. However, one doesn't become a true Vaiṣṇava just by wearing a *tilaka* and a *dhotī*. The true Vaiṣṇavas who are striving to attain the Lord, change inside and let the divine qualities awaken inside them. They are completely detached from the outside world and are not attached to anything. Whatever they have, they offer it in devotion to the Lord. They don't desire anything but Him. They have super faith, and when they sit in their *sādhana*, they don't think, "Oh my goodness, when will I finish?" The Lord will reveal Himself within these great ones.

'When you look at the life of saints, you see that they are so fully absorbed into Kṛṣṇa that nothing else matters to them, nothing in the outside reality disturbs them. Bhagavān Kṛṣṇa says that there were many great kings who achieved such a state. They still continued doing their everyday duties, but their minds were fully focused on the Lord. However, Lord Kṛṣṇa says that even among those, only a few perceive and know Him "in reality." One can know Him in the scriptures, yet only the one who is fully surrendered, can know Him as the supreme reality. And these blessed ones are truly very few.'

VERSES 4-6: THE HIGHER AND LOWER NATURES OF GOD

bhūmir-āpo'nalo vāyuḥ khaṁ mano buddhir-eva ca |
ahaṅkāra itīyaṁ me bhinnā prakṛtir-aṣṭadhā || 4 ||

Earth, water, fire, air, ether, mind, intellect and the ego; make up the eight parts of My material nature. (4)

apareyamitastvanyāṁ prakṛtiṁ viddhi me parām |
jīvabhūtāṁ mahābāho yayedaṁ dhāryate jagat || 5 ||

This is My lower nature. But, Arjuna, know that My higher nature is different. It is made up of the embodied souls, which sustain this universe. (5)

etad-yonīni bhūtāni sarvāṇītyupadhāraya |
ahaṁ kṛtsnasya jagataḥ prabhavaḥ pralayastathā || 6 ||

Know that all beings originate from these two natures of mine. Understand therefore that I am the origin and the dissolution of this whole universe. (6)

'The whole universe comes out of Kṛṣṇa and disappears back into Kṛṣṇa. This is a law of creation, which manifests through His two *Śaktis* – *aparā-prakṛti* and *parā-prakṛti*. Everything is taking place in His cosmic body.'

'*Prakṛti*, His *māyā*, makes everybody jump and dance to Her tune and think that this tune is the higher reality. However, this eightfold *prakṛti* is just one aspect of His *māyā*: it is called *aparā-prakṛti*, where the mind is veiled and can't perceive the eternal reality. These "eightfold" principles are the Lord's "material nature (*prakṛti*)". It is through this *prakṛti*, this *māyā*, that the Lord manifests Himself and manifests His whole creation. It is because of this *māyā*, which created the whole outside world, that human beings get trapped, carried away and rooted in ignorance, forgetting that there is a higher, supreme reality.'

'Who are you? This mind? This ego? This intellect? People who dwell in the lower nature of *māyā*, perceive the difference between themselves and God. They don't realise themselves. Then they stay in ignorance. And due to ignorance they have this pain, this sadness, this suffering of separation.'

'Everything is His *māyā*, His own creation. Through these two *prakṛtis* – *aparā-prakṛti* and *parā-prakṛti* – He manifests and sustains His own creation, where He plays all the different roles. The one who has realised such a state, doesn't sing the "Glory Song": "I am beautiful. I am the most important. I am the greatest. There's nothing but me." Rather he sings, "Kṛṣṇa, You are beautiful.

Kṛṣṇa is everything. Kṛṣṇa is here, Kṛṣṇa is there and Kṛṣṇa is everywhere." Such are the wise ones, who are always seated in this deep realisation and perceive this reality, this true knowledge.'

VERSES 7-12: KṚṢṆA'S TRANSCENDENCE AND IMMANENCE

mattaḥ parataraṁ nānyat kiñcid-asti dhanañjayaḥ |
mayi sarvam idaṁ protaṁ sūtre maṇi-gaṇā iva || 7 ||

There is nothing higher than Me, O Arjuna. All of this rests upon Me, like pearls on a thread. (7)

raso'ham-apsu kaunteya prabhāsmi śaśi-sūryayo |
praṇavaḥ sarva vedeṣu śabdaḥ khe pauruṣaṁ nṛṣu || 8 ||

I am the taste of water; I am the radiance of the Sun and Moon. I am the sacred syllable *oṁ* in the *Vedas*; I am the sound in ether, and the valour in men. (8)

puṇyo gandhaḥ pṛthivyāṁ ca tejaścāsmi vibhāvasau |
jīvanaṁ sarva bhūteṣu tapaścāsmi tapasviṣu || 9 ||

I am the fragrance of the earth; I am the heat of fire; I am the life of all living beings, and the austerity of ascetics. (9)

bījaṁ māṁ sarva bhūtānāṁ viddhi pārtha sanātanaṁ |
buddhir-buddhimatām asmi tejas-tejasvinām aham || 10 ||

Know Me, Arjuna, to be the original seed of all beings.
I am the intelligence of the intelligent, and the energy of the energetic. (10)

balaṁ balavatāṁ cāhaṁ kāma-rāga vivarjitam |
dharmāviruddho bhūteṣu kāmo'smi bharatarṣabha || 11 ||

O Arjuna, I am the strength of the strong which is without passion and desire. I am that desire in all living beings which does not go against righteous principles. (11)

ye caiva sāttvikā bhāvā rājasāstāmasāśca ye |
matta eveti tān-viddhi na tvahaṁ teṣu te mayi || 12 ||

Know that all the states of *sattva*, *rajas* and *tamas* have their origin in Me alone. But I am not in them; they are in Me. (12)

'All the universes are strung together like pearls on a necklace that He Himself wears. Nothing exists beyond Him. He is the sole reality. Like the thread holding the pearls, God is holding and sustaining His entire creation. And He is in each part of His creation.'

'He is the strength and the essence of men, because He is the Supersoul. He is the soul of souls. He is the one who pervades the soul itself and there is none beyond Him. If one reaches such a state, one fully realises Kṛṣṇa, one attains Him fully.'

'"It is Me who inspires one to rise above desire. I am the one who gives the strength to rise above duality and see the oneness. I am also the one who is striving for awakening. It is Me who gives one the awareness to see the limitation and to divert from the limitation, so that one can perceive beyond *prakṛti*. I am this eternal perfection seated beyond any duality."'

'"But I am not in them, they are in Me." Do you understand that? This means that even though God pervades everything, He is not touched by anything. Even in His cosmic body, He is ever-free from His own lower nature, from the qualities of *rajasic*, *tamasic*, and *sattvic*. These qualities are said to be "secondary, subjective becomings of nature." They evolve not from *yoga-māyā*, *parā-prakṛti*, but from… *aparā-prakṛti*, the *prakṛti* that blind men, the *prakṛti* that makes one become attached to the outside reality. The supreme quality is beyond that. That's why He says, "I am not in them."'

'Even the *ātmā* Itself is a lower manifestation of the Lord. That's why the *ātmā* is always permanent and It is always there serving the Supreme. Have you ever seen great souls who have realised themselves? What do they do? They always pray and they always tell everybody else to pray. All the great sages are always constantly praying to the Supreme Lord. They realise that they are always next to Him and that they are here to serve Him. They don't say, "Yes, I am the Ultimate. There is nothing to pray to." They say, "There is this Supreme Lord that we all are turning towards."… Once one awakens, one will perceive that the Lord remains always the Lord. The servant remains always the servant.'

VERSES 13-15: SURRENDER ALLOWS US TO CROSS OVER MĀYĀ

tribhir-guṇa-mayair-bhāvair-ebhiḥ sarvam idaṁ jagat |
mohitaṁ nābhijānāti māmebhyaḥ param-avyayam || 13 ||

The entire universe is deluded by these three conditions originating from the *guṇas*, and fails to recognise Me, who is unchanging and beyond. (13)

daivī hyeṣā guṇamayī mama māyā duratyayā |
māmeva ye prapadyante māyāmetāṁ taranti te || 14 ||

For this divine *māyā* of Mine consisting of the three *guṇas* is hard to overcome. But those who take refuge in Me alone, cross over it easily. (14)

na māṁ duṣkṛtino mūḍhāḥ prapadyante narādhamāḥ |
māyayāpahṛta jñānā āsuraṁ bhāvam āśritāḥ || 15 ||

But the unrighteous, the foolish, the lowest of people, those whose wisdom has been stolen away by *māyā* and those who have taken the nature of demons, do not seek refuge in Me. (15)

'The one who is full of sorrow, who is deluded by the glamour of outside world, who rejoices in the objects of the senses, who is constantly focused on the outside reality, who is always longing for outward perfection, can't perceive true perfection, true knowledge, the glory of God, the mystery of God, because the mind is so full of doubts and misconceptions. There are even people who are constantly hanging onto the qualities of the three *guṇas*. Until they rise above the three *guṇas*, they will never realise themselves and reach the goal of life. Bhagavān is emphasising, "I am above that. When you realise that I am the cosmic soul, when you realise within the core of your Self that I am the essence of all, then you will rise above this kind of judgement; you will rise above the *sattvic*, *rajasic* and *tamasic* qualities." Then you can completely identify yourself with the Lord.'

'There is no judgement of others, because one knows that God is doing His work through each person. In one person, He is a banker; in another, He is a sweeper; in another, He is tapping on the iPad; and in another, He is playing the drums. But the one who is a fool doesn't realise this.'

[The Lord is saying:] '"As I am not touched by *māyā*, so My devotees who are surrendered to Me are free. *Māyā* stops controlling them. Those who chant My Name; those who by any means try to control their mind; those who are fully absorbed in My service, forgetting themselves completely; those who think only on Me; they are My devotees, and they cross beyond the *guṇas*. The *guṇas* don't have any effect on them, because they become as Me. I start to shine upon them and they start to reflect My divine qualities, My cosmic qualities, and wherever My cosmic qualities are shining, *māyā* doesn't have any power." Here Bhagavān is saying, 'Even if it appears as if Māyā controls everything, I am the Lord of Māyā and I control Her.'"'

❁ VERSES 16-22: FOUR CATEGORIES OF DEVOTEES

catur-vidhā bhajante māṁ janāḥ sukṛtino'rjuna |
ārto jijñāsur arthārthī jñānī ca bharatarṣabha || 16 ||

Four types of devotees worship Me, O Arjuna: The distressed, the seekers of knowledge, those who desire wealth, and the *jñānī* [1] who truly has knowledge. (16)

teṣāṁ jñānī nitya-yukta eka bhaktir-viśiṣyate |
priyo hi jñānino'tyartham ahaṁ sa ca mama priyaḥ || 17 ||

Of these, the *jñānī* who is steadfast and ever-devoted is the best. I am very dear to him and he is dear to Me. (17)

udārāḥ sarva evaitaṁ jñānī tvātmaiva me matam |
āsthitaḥ sa hi yuktātmā māmevānuttamāṁ gatim || 18 ||

Those who approach Me are all noble people, but I see the *jñānī* as My very Self, for such a person is steady and exclusively devoted to Me as the highest goal. (18)

bahūnāṁ janmanām ante jñānavān māṁ prapadyate |
vāsudevaḥ sarvam iti sa mahātmā sudurlabhaḥ || 19 ||

At the end of many births, the one who has true knowledge surrenders to Me, realising that 'Kṛṣṇa is everything'. Such a person is very rare. (19)

kāmais tais tair hṛta-jñānāḥ prapadyante'nya-devatāḥ |
taṁ taṁ niyamam āsthāya prakṛtyā niyatāḥ svayā || 20 ||

Enslaved by their inherent nature, and deprived of insight by various desires, the worldly-minded turn to other demigods, observing various disciplines. (20)

yo yo yāṁ yāṁ tanuṁ bhaktaḥ śraddhayārcitum icchati |
tasya tasyācalāṁ śraddhāṁ tām-eva vidadhāmy-ahaṁ || 21 ||

Understand that whichever manifestation of a demigod any devotee desires to worship with faith, it is I that makes that faith unshakeable and firm. (21)

sa tayā śraddhayā yuktas tasyārādhanam īhate |
labhate ca tataḥ kāmān mayaiva vihitān hi tān || 22 ||

Endowed with that faith, one engages in the worship of a particular *demigod*, obtaining their desired objects, but these objects are in fact given by Me alone. (22)

'Lord Kṛṣṇa says that there are four kinds of *bhaktas*, four kinds of devotees who come to Him. The first kind of devotees, "*ārto*", are the suffering ones.

'"*Jijñāsur*" is the second kind of devotee, whose sole motive is to know God and to attain God-realisation in this life. Unlike the first kind of devotees, they care not for the outside world. They are completely the opposite. They don't care about the objects of the senses. Everything they do in their work, in their daily routine, is only for one thing: to attain the Lord, nothing else.'

'Here Lord Kṛṣṇa says that this kind of devotee is also very dear to Him. They worship the Lord, but they still perceive God as being outside themselves, separate from themselves. They don't perceive the Divine, they don't perceive Kṛṣṇa within themselves. They serve Him when He is present as a deity, but they can't see beyond that. They don't know that the Supreme Lord is beyond everything, is seated everywhere, in all His creation. Of course, they know it, but only in the mind; they have not perceived it.

'The third kind of devotees, "*arthārthi*", are those who know that everything comes from God, yet they are still very attached to wealth, honour, name, fame and glory. They seek God only to fulfil their desires. They pray, they do their *sādhana*, they do everything with that one aim. These devotees have great faith and devotion and know deep within that only God can fulfil their desires. But they long only for God's gifts and their faith is based on that. They do everything for personal gain, not selflessly. They know that God is the embodiment of Truth. They pray to Him for security, for they know that He is the only one who can protect and save them.

'The fourth type of devotee, the "*jñānī*", the realised souls, are the ones who abide completely in the reality of God consciousness. For them, there is nothing other than Him, Kṛṣṇa. All their desires have ceased, including the desire to meet Kṛṣṇa or to realise Kṛṣṇa, because they perceive Kṛṣṇa within themselves, in the core of their heart. Wherever they are, whatever they do, is an act of worship to the Lord. In such a state of devotion and surrender, they realise that there's only the Lord Himself in them who is doing everything.'

'Here Bhagavān Kṛṣṇa Himself says that it is okay for ignorant people to worship other deities, not knowing His true nature. If they have faith, it is actually Him that makes that faith strong. For the sake of people's faith, He manifests Himself in different aspects, He takes different forms. If the devotee worships Him through *yajña*, due to the love and faith that they have, even if it is for the demigods, He limits Himself and manifests Himself into that aspect. Such is the mercy of God that by His own will, He happily limits Himself and takes any aspect, any form... Through faith, you can transform a block of marble and make Bhagavān Himself install Himself fully in it. Then that marble statue is no longer just a statue. Your faith has transformed the statue and made it come alive: the Lord Himself has become alive in the statue. Many people may say, "In Hinduism, they pray to statues." But people don't know that they are not just statues. They are deities. They are alive. Through faith, they become alive.'

VERSE 23: WHAT YOU WORSHIP DETERMINES YOUR DESTINATION

antavattu phalaṁ teṣāṁ tad bhavaty-alpa medhasām |
devān devayajo yānti mad-bhaktā yānti mām api || 23 ||

But the reward gained by these people of limited understanding is temporary. The worshippers of the demigods will go to the demigods, but My devotees will come to Me. (23)

'Here Kṛṣṇa says people who pray or do big sacrifices just for the sake of selfish gain, whatever business they have done with the demigods, when they leave this plane, when they die, their soul migrates to the celestial world for a small holiday.'

'The demigods will give you what you ask for, but it's a business. You go to those celestial realms for some time, and then you come back, you are born on Earth again because you missed the opportunity to realise God when you were here before. You missed the opportunity to attain Him through devotion to Him alone. Like that, many souls get trapped in this delusion. That's why there is birth and death, death and birth; one continues in this cycle, one life after another. One stays in this dormant state of illusion. Even the Lord stays dormant within the hearts of these people, waiting for them to become conscious of Him. He is waiting, life after life, until they come face to face with God's reality, until they have the chance to surrender to the *guru* wholeheartedly, in body, mind and spirit.'

VERSES 24-30: PERCEIVING THE TRUTH OF KṚṢṆA

avyaktaṁ vyaktim āpannaṁ manyante mām abuddhayaḥ |
paraṁ bhāvam ajānanto mamāvyayam anuttamam || 24 ||

Not knowing My higher nature as imperishable and supreme, the ignorant think of Me as an impersonal being who has now become manifest. (24)

nāhaṁ prakāśaḥ sarvasya yoga māyā samāvṛtaḥ |
mūḍho'yaṁ nābhijānanti loko mām ajam avyayam || 25 ||

I do not reveal Myself to everybody, but I cover Myself with My *yoga-māyā*. This deluded world does not recognise Me as unborn and infallible. (25)

vedāhaṁ samatītāni vartamānāni cārjuna |
bhaviṣyāṇi ca bhūtāni māṁ tu veda na kaścana || 26 ||

O Arjuna, I know all the beings that have come before, that are here now, and those that have yet to come; but no one knows Me. (26)

icchā-dveṣa samutthena dvandva mohena bhārata |
sarva bhūtāni saṁmohaṁ sarge yānti paraṅtapa || 27 ||

Bewildered by the pairs of opposites, Arjuna, which arise from desire and aversion, all beings are born into delusion. (27)

yeṣāṁ tvanta-gataṁ pāpaṁ janānāṁ puṇya-karmaṇām |
te dvandva-moha-nirmuktā bhajante māṁ dṛḍha-vratāḥ || 28 ||

But those who perform virtuous deeds, whose sins have ceased, are freed from the illusion of the pairs of opposites. They worship Me, steadfast in their determination. (28)

jarā-maraṇa-mokṣayā mām-āśritya yatanti ye |
te brahma tad viduḥ kṛtsnam adhyātmaṁ karma cākhilam || 29 ||

Those who take refuge in Me and strive for liberation from old age and death, fully understand Brahman, *adhyātma*, and *karma* [2]. (29)

sādhibhūtādhidaivaṁ māṁ sādhi yajñāṁ ca ye viduḥ |
prayāṇa kāle'pi ca māṁ te vidur yukta cetasaḥ || 30 ||

And those who know Me in relation to the *adhibhūta*, *adhidaiva* and the *adhiyajña*, they too with their minds fixed, can know Me even at the hour of death [2]. (30)

'When the Lord manifests Himself in this world, He spreads His *māyā* all over Himself and remains hidden; He covers Himself well with His own *yoga-māyā*, wrapping it around Him like a shawl. However, even if He is covered by His own *yoga-māyā*, He is never touched by *yoga-māyā*.'

'Due to His *yoga-māyā*, the vision of ordinary man cannot pierce this veil, so most people regard Him as just an ordinary human being. Such deluded ones cannot perceive the true identity of the unmanifest. They can only see what He is doing outwardly. The Kauravas said, "Oh, Kṛṣṇa is just a charioteer, sitting there and bringing Arjuna wherever Arjuna wants." They could not see that He is bringing everyone; that it is He, the charioteer, in each one.'

'Due to his faith in Kṛṣṇa, Arjuna could humble himself in front of Him and say, "I take You now as my *guru*. Instruct me. Show me the right way that will free me." It is due to his faith that Kṛṣṇa is there with him. Without this faith, Kṛṣṇa would not be there.'

'Here Bhagavān Kṛṣṇa is saying, "I am the Lord Himself of the past, present and future. Even if I manifested Myself in a human form, even if I have limited Myself in this form in front of you, I am still the Supreme One. I know the past, I know the present and I know what will come, but no one knows Me."'

'Those who are surrendered; the *bhaktas* who have faith; those who are longing to know Him; those who want to get out of ignorance; those who have devotion and love; those who are free from judgement; free from criticising others, free from delusion – such a devotee as this, has a glimpse of Him. Such a devotee knows a little bit of Him. And that little bit itself is everything, because their 'knowing' is not in the mind. That knowing is deep inside of their heart, in their consciousness, in their soul itself.'

[The Lord says:] '"For those blessed souls, who throughout many lives, have done noble deeds, much penance, sacrifice, and charity, and practised devotion, there is no sin. They are guided in this life to have good association, high association. Due to this good association, they are freed. They attain purity of heart. When they worship Me, when they surrender to Me, there is complete eradication of all negativity from all their past lives. They are freed from delusion, from the dualities and from judgement. They are freed from anger. In all circumstances, they stay balanced and ever focused on Me. Their minds never dwell in the world, even while they are doing their daily activities. Their minds are always focused on Me. They have attained the ultimate perfection.'

'They live in Me and I live in them. They become a temple within which I am completely, fully present." They become a movable temple, a portable temple, within which the Lord is moving from one place to another. When you go to a temple, you always profit, isn't it true? Like that, whoever goes to a temple, or whoever meets a temple on the way, gets a blessing, because temples always give this Love of God. Such is the one who has risen above duality, who has completely surrendered to Nārāyaṇa-Kṛṣṇa.'

Chapter Seven Verses: Key Terms

[1] **Jñānī** – the pure devotee who possesses knowledge of who the Lord truly is.

[2] These *Saṅskṛt* terms are defined by Kṛṣṇa in chapter eight.

CHAPTER EIGHT
AKṢARA-BRAHMA-YOGA
THE ETERNAL ABODE

Kṛṣṇa begins by clarifying terms He has used at the end of the previous chapter, and in response to Arjuna's question, explains how He can be known at the time of death. It is our last thought before leaving the body that decides our destination. But this thought is a product of our state of consciousness and therefore Kṛṣṇa urges Arjuna to incessantly fix his mind upon Him. Following on from chapter six, Kṛṣṇa further describes the technique on how to achieve this. By infusing devotion (*bhakti*) into the practise of *yoga* given by Kṛṣṇa thus far, one can control the senses and life breath to reach the Supreme.

This chapter then outlines the cosmology of the universe. Kṛṣṇa states that each life in this world is ultimately suffering since nothing we experience is permanent. The material plane is made up of many realms, the highest of which is where Brahmā [1] resides. But even there one is subject to constant birth and death. Each of Brahmā's Days and Nights lasts thousands of ages (*yugas*), and every time we are helplessly brought out into existence and withdrawn into a dormant state. But beyond his abode there is another realm that is beyond this cosmic cycle and does not decay. Through pure devotion one can reach this highest Abode which is none other than Kṛṣṇa. Hence, Kṛṣṇa's Abode is not the place where Kṛṣṇa resides, but is Kṛṣṇa Himself. This realisation is considered to be the highest realisation one can attain in life, and is also referred to as God-realisation.

Those who know the *Vedas* understand that there are two times to leave the body: one is auspicious and leading to freedom from rebirth, the other brings one back to bondage. But the devotee who is fixed on Kṛṣṇa is not bewildered by these timings. While those who follow the rituals and practise of scripture gain a certain limited reward, the one who practises *bhakti-yoga* [2] attains Kṛṣṇa Himself.

Chapter Eight Intro: Key Terms:

[1] **Brahmā** – deity born from the Supreme Lord responsible for creating within the physical universe.

[2] **Bhakti-yoga** – the path of loving devotion to God.

VERSES 1-4: KṚṢṆA DEFINES DIFFERENT TERMS

arjuna uvāca
kiṁ tad-brahma kim-adhyātma kiṁ karma puruṣottama |
adhi-bhūtaṁ ca kiṁ proktam adhi-daivaṁ kim-ucyate || 1 ||

Arjuna says:
My Supreme Lord, what is that Brahman? What is the *adhyātma*? What is meant by *karma*? What is the *adhibhūta*? And who is said to be the *adhidaiva*? (1)

adhi-yajñāḥ kathaṁ ko'tra dehe'smin madhusūdana |
prayāṇa-kāle ca kathaṁ jñeyo'si niyatātmabhiḥ || 2 ||

Who is the *adhiyajña* and how does He exist in this body, O Kṛṣṇa? And how are You to be known at the time of death by the self-controlled? (2)

śrī bhagavān uvāca
akṣaraṁ brahma paramaṁ svabhāvo'dhyātmam-ucyate |
bhūta-bhāvodbhava-karo visargaḥ karma-saṁjñitaḥ || 3 ||

Lord Kṛṣṇa says:
Brahman is the Supreme that does not change or decay. One's own inherent nature is said to be the *adhyātma*, and the creative force which gives rise to material beings is known as *karma*. (3)

adhibhūtaṁ kṣaro bhāvaḥ puruṣaś-cādhidaivataṁ |
adhiyajño'hamevātra dehe deha-bhṛtāṁ vara || 4 ||

The *adhibhūta* is the material world which perishes, the *adhidaivata* is the cosmic governing deity, and it is I Myself who is the *adhiyajña* present in the body. (4)

'Lord Kṛṣṇa has already spoken about all these terms, but Arjuna is still trying to understand and his mind is getting confused. He says, "You are the Lord of everything. You surpass everything. It would be simpler if You would just tell me, "I am the Lord"! I get confused with all these terms."

'Arjuna didn't really have a confused mind, but a mind that wanted to understand, a scientific, rational mind. But it was good that his mind was in such a state, otherwise he would not have kept Lord Kṛṣṇa talking, giving the *Gītā*, to him and to humanity.'

'This indestructible Self, which is above all the material nature, is the higher nature itself. It is this divinity, Parabrahman, Kṛṣṇa Himself, who is the source and the core of the individual soul.'

'When this higher nature of God manifests and takes form in this lower reality, through His *prakṛti*, through His will, it takes the aspects of the body, the senses, the mind, and the intellect, but it stays completely out of it. The *ātmā* presides over the body, the mind, the senses, and the intellect.'

'When something is limited by matter or by existence and parts of it are taken away, little by little, it reaches a point when every part has been taken away and it's finished! But no matter how many parts of the Lord come out of the Lord, He is still full. He doesn't get diminished! He can manifest Himself many times in this world, yet there's no limit to Him.'

'Lord Kṛṣṇa declares that the supreme reality, the *jīvātmā* [1], and the lower material creation, are three different aspects of the Lord. Even if due to ignorance, the lower material nature affects the body, the mind and the intellect, it doesn't touch the individual soul. Due to ignorance, the people who dwell in the worldly, materialistic reality, completely focused on the outer world, completely focused on the negative qualities, can't perceive the soul, the *ātmā*, inside themselves.

'On the other hand, people who are on the spiritual path, who are dedicated to their *sādhana*, who are calm and stable, can perceive and feel the *ātmā*. Through the knowledge of the Self, through meditating on the *Śrīmad Bhagavad Gītā*, and putting it into practise, one takes the path of *bhakti*. One becomes aware of the *ātmā*. To become spiritual means that you have the awareness that you are not only this body, you are not only this mind: you realise that you are the individual soul, and in that state, you praise the Lord and love the Lord. And then you ascend to such a degree that you perceive the Lord continuously within yourself and have the great joy, the bliss, to serve Him.

'Kṛṣṇa also says that beyond the *ātmā* is "the supreme, indestructible Self (*akṣara*)." The ignorant one can't perceive the Self, but the Self is ever-present. Sometimes It reveals Itself through a certain feeling, through a certain awareness. In the same way, the Supreme soul reveals Himself to the *bhakta* as the Supersoul, the highest of all.'

'When the mind unites with the heart, something else comes out. When the mind is purified to become intellect, that intellect enters the heart. What awakens is the consciousness, the consciousness of the soul... When the consciousness is purified, it reveals the soul. But when that soul is purified, it reveals the Supersoul, the Supreme soul.

'To those who are fully absorbed into the divine bliss, the Lord reveals Himself. He reveals there is no difference between Him and the individual soul. It is the same quality, the only difference is quantity. The Light is the same, but the intensity of that Light differs. When you have a light, you can look at it. But the Light of the Lord you can't look at. The spark taken from the fire you can look at, you can probably put it out with your hand also. But if you have a huge fire and you put your hand in it, you will get burned. Like this, you have different degrees of burning and you have different degrees of light.'

VERSES 5-16: FIXING THE MIND ON KṚṢṆA AT DEATH

antakāle ca mām-eva smaran-muktvā kalevaram |
yaḥ prayāti sa mad-bhāvaṁ yāti nāsty-atra saṁśayaḥ || 5 ||

And the one who leaves his body at the time of death and contemplates upon Me alone, without doubt reaches Me. (5)

yaṁ yaṁ vāpi smaran-bhāvaṁ tyajaty-ante kalevaram |
taṁ tam-evaiti kaunteya sadā tad-bhāva-bhāvitaḥ || 6 ||

Arjuna, whatever state one remembers when leaving the body, that state one will certainly attain after death. For a person's condition is the inevitable result of what has been dwelt upon throughout one's life. (6)

tasmāt sarveṣu kāleṣu mām-anusmara yudhya ca |
mayyarpita mano-buddhir-mām evaiṣyasy-asaṁśayaḥ || 7 ||

Therefore, ever mindful of Me at all times, fight. With your mind and intellect dedicated to Me, you will be free of doubt and shall surely come to Me. (7)

abhyāsa-yoga-yuktena cetasā nānya-gāminā |
paramaṁ puruṣaṁ divyaṁ yāti pārthānucintayan || 8 ||

O Arjuna! With the mind absorbed and constantly engaged in *yoga*, without thinking of anything else, one reaches the Divine Supreme Being. (8)

kaviṁ purāṇam anuśāsitāram
aṇoraṇīyāṁsam anusmared yaḥ |
sarvasya dhātāram acintya-rūpam
āditya varṇaṁ tamasaḥ parastāt || 9 ||

One should meditate on the all-knowing Supreme Person. The one who is the oldest and supreme Controller of all. His form is inconceivable, more subtle than an atom, and the maintainer of everything. He is brilliant like the Sun and beyond all darkness. (9)

prayāṇa-kāle manasācalena
bhaktyā yukto yoga-balena caiva |
bhruvor-madhye prāṇam-āveśya samyak
sa taṁ paraṁ puruṣam upaiti divyam || 10 ||

At the time of death one should dwell in a state of devotion and with the strength of *yoga*, one should maintain an unwavering mind. Keeping the life force between the eyebrows in the proper way, one reaches that Divine Supreme Being. (10)

yad-akṣaraṁ veda-vido vadanti
viśanti yad-yatayo vītarāgāḥ |
yad-icchanto brahmacaryaṁ caranti
tat-te padaṁ saṅgraheṇa pravakṣye || 11 ||

I shall now explain that goal, which the knowers of the *Vedas* call the Imperishable. Those ascetics who are free from desire enter into It, and due to their aspiration for perfection they take vows of celibacy. (11)

sarva-dvārāṇi saṁyamya mano hṛdi nirudhya ca |
mūrdhny-ādhāyātmanaḥ prāṇam-āsthito yoga-dhāraṇām || 12 ||

Having closed all the entrances of the body, focusing the mind within the heart, fixing the life force within the head, one should be engaged in *yoga* practise with steady concentration. (12)

om-ity-ekākṣaraṁ brahma vyāharan mām-anusmaran |
yaḥ prayāti tyajan-dehaṁ sa yāti paramāṁ gatim || 13 ||

Chanting the sacred syllable *oṁ* which embodies the Absolute, thinking of Me constantly one abandons the body and leaves the world, thereby reaching the supreme goal. (13)

ananya-cetāḥ satataṁ yo māṁ smarati nityaśaḥ |
tasyāhaṁ sulabhaḥ pārtha nitya-yuktasya yoginaḥ || 14 ||

O Arjuna, I am easily attainable by that steadfast practicing *yogī* who is constantly mindful of Me, not thinking of anything else. (14)

mām-upetya punar-janma duḥkh-ālayam aśāśvatam |
nāpnuvanti mahātmanaḥ saṁsiddhiṁ paramāṁ gatāḥ || 15 ||

Having reached the highest perfection and attaining Me, the great ones never again take rebirth in this world which is transient and full of misery. (15)

ābrahma bhuvanāllokāḥ punar-āvartino'rjuna |
mām-upetya tu kaunteya punar-janma na vidyate || 16 ||

Rebirth is inevitable right up to the world of Brahmā. But after attaining Me, Arjuna, there is no rebirth. (16)

'Among all the human beings, how many people die with an attitude of leaving the body to attain the Lord? Only very few. After passing through 8.4 million births, and manifesting through the entire chain of creation, the individual soul attains a human body. It's a very rare opportunity to attain the level of a human being who can then strive to attain the Lord. One has to grasp such an opportunity.'

'Bhagavān Kṛṣṇa says to Arjuna, "Fight! But keep your mind focused on Me." This means that one must do one's duty in life. Wherever you are, whatever you are doing in this world, God has placed you there for a reason. So accept it and do your action properly! However, your mind should be fully focused on Him and not only on the outside world.'

'It's very important to control how you breathe. Through control, through *prāṇāyāma*, one learns how to be centred inwardly. People who live a hectic life in the outside world also breathe in a hectic way. They are not just working hard, but they are draining themselves severely...[they] very quickly have heart attacks and die young – the life force is finished.'

'Since time immemorial, the *yogīs* have meditated on the *oṁ* vibration, the primordial cosmic sound, the sound that contains everything and that is beyond the creation, preservation, and destruction of the universe. Lord Kṛṣṇa Himself says, "I am *oṁ*". When the *bhaktas* are fully absorbed in the divine sound, *oṁ*, they become fully immersed in it and go deeper and deeper. At that moment, everything becomes still, the body is still, the mind is still, the consciousness is still: only the cosmic sound, *oṁ*, is vibrating in the third eye. One loses oneself, one loses consciousness of the body, and one perceives the Lord. At that point, it's not only a vibration: the Supreme Lord Nārāyaṇa Himself takes a certain aspect. He manifests Himself, reveals Himself in one's consciousness. The one who has attained that state, "the highest status," becomes a true *bhakta*, who has realised the Absolute.'

'Once one has attained that "highest status," even if one dwells in the outside world, engaging oneself in many activities, one's mind, one's consciousness, is never deviated. The Divine Himself is crystallised into one's mind and then one is free. Whereas the minds of people who have not realised that state, are always busy running towards the outside world. The outside reality is crystallised into their minds and they can never be free. Therefore, *japa-kriyā*, the continuous repetition of the Divine Names, is very important... This leads one to God-realisation; not just to Self-realisation, but to God-realisation. Then one is free from the cycle of birth and death. One perceives the supreme reality, not only in oneself, but everywhere.'

'He reveals Himself to the one who aims for Self-realisation, and to the one who aims to reach even beyond Self-realisation, who aims for God consciousness. In Self-realisation, the Self is revealed to the intellect and the mind, but higher than Self-realisation is God-realisation. Once the Lord has revealed Himself within the core of the Self, one is fully absorbed in His Love and attains Him, the Supreme Puruṣa.'

'When you have this Love for God, He limits Himself and takes an aspect, a form, because as you long for Him, He also longs for you. This is how God manifests in a certain form, making it easy for you to come to Him.

'It's very difficult for those who dwell in the outside world, who have no faith or love, no knowledge of the glory of God, to attain Him. Whereas it becomes easy for a *bhakta*. When people reach the state of entering the heart, what they perceive through that Love miraculously changes their lives. Due to their readiness, they are brought to the spiritual path, they are brought to the spiritual Master, so that they can drink the divine nectar, grow, and perfect themselves. As they have a longing for God, God also has a similar longing for them; the Lord gathers all the people who have this same yearning and brings them together. Then they have the privilege of being in touch with saints and God-realised souls.'

❁ VERSES 17-28: BREAKING FREE OF BRAHMĀ'S CREATION

sahasra-yuga-paryantam aharyad brahmaṇo viduḥ |
rātriṁ yuga sahasrāntāṁ te'horātra-vido janāḥ || 17 ||

Those who know the duration of a cosmic Day and Night understand a Day of Brahmā lasts for a thousand *Mahā-yugas* [1] and a Night of Brahmā lasts for another thousand *Mahā-yugas*. (17)

avyaktād-vyaktayaḥ sarvāḥ prabhavanty-ahar-āgame |
ratry-āgame pralīyante tatraivāvyakta saṁjñake || 18 ||

At the beginning of a Day of Brahmā all beings come forth from the unmanifest, and when the Night comes, they are dissolved back into the unmanifested state. (18)

bhūta-grāmaḥ sa evāyaṁ bhūtvā bhūtvā pralīyate |
ratry-āgame'vaśaḥ pārtha prabhavaty-ahar-āgame || 19 ||

These same beings come forth again and again, and helplessly they are withdrawn at the coming of the Night. When the next Day begins, yet again they manifest. (19)

paras-tasmāt tu bhavo'nyo'vyakto'vyaktāt-sanātanaḥ |
yaḥ sa sarveṣu bhūteṣu naśyatsu na vinaśyati || 20 ||

There is, however, another unmanifest realm which is superior to this unmanifested place of the material world; it is eternal and does not get destroyed when all other living beings pass away. (20)

avyakto'kṣara ity-uktas-tamāhuḥ paramāṁ gatim |
yaṁ prāpya na nivartante tad-dhāma paramaṁ mama || 21 ||

This unmanifest realm is also called 'The Imperishable Realm'. It is the highest goal from which one does not return; it is My Supreme Abode. (21)

puruṣaḥ sa paraḥ pārtha bhaktyā labhyas-tv-ananyayā |
yasyāntaḥ sthāni bhūtāni yena sarvam idaṁ tatam || 22 ||

The Supreme Being is attained by unswerving devotion, Arjuna. He is the One in which all beings exist and by whom this whole universe is pervaded. (22)

yatra kāle tvanāvṛttim āvṛttiṁ caiva yoginaḥ |
prayātā yānti taṁ kālaṁ vakṣyāmi bharatarṣabha || 23 ||

Arjuna, now I will describe to you the different times of leaving this world. One in which the *yogī* does not return and the other in which they do. (23)

agnir-jyotir-ahaḥ śuklaḥ ṣaṇmāsā uttarāyaṇam |
tatra prayātā gacchanti brahma brahma-vido janāḥ || 24 ||

The knowers of Brahman attain that Supreme and leave during the influence of the fire deity (Agni), the day, the bright fortnight, or during the six months of the northern course of the Sun. (24)

dhūmo rātris-tathā kṛṣṇaḥ ṣaṇmāsā dakṣiṇāyanam |
tatra cāndramasaṁ jyotir-yogī prāpya nivartate || 25 ||

But the *yogī* who leaves during the smoke (absence of the fire deity), the night, the dark fortnight, or the six months of the southern course of the Sun, reaches the light of the Moon and then returns. [2] (25)

śukla-kṛṣṇe gatī hyete jagataḥ śāśvate mate |
ekayā yāty-anāvṛtim anyayāvartate punaḥ || 26 ||

Therefore, understand there exist two eternal paths of departure, the light and the dark. By following the path of the light one does not come back, but by following the dark, one returns. (26)

naite sṛtī pārtha jānan yogi muhyati kaścana |
tasmāt sarveṣu kāleṣu yoga-yukto bhavārjuna || 27 ||

But Arjuna, the true *yogī* who knows these two paths is never bewildered. Therefore, O Arjuna, at all times engage yourself in *yoga*. (27)

vedeṣu yajñeṣu tapaḥsu caiva
dāneṣu yat puṇya-phalaṁ pradiṣṭam |
atyeti tat sarvam idaṁ viditvā
yogī paraṁ sthānam upaiti cādyam || 28 ||

Whatever merits are gathered from the study of the *Vedas*, from the performance of sacrifices, or from the practise of austerities and charity, all of it is transcended by the *yogī* who knows this teaching of Mine; he reaches the original, Supreme Abode. (28)

'During the Day and Night of Brahmā, everything is created and everything is destroyed. This also represents the ignorance in man: even if one has this deep, inner wisdom anchored inside, when one has to make a choice between right and wrong, the mind doesn't see clearly enough to make the right decision. Even if one has the feeling, "If I do that, I will suffer. God is guiding me on the way, I know that I have to realise my Self," when one acts, one always does something to make oneself suffer. So one falls again and again into the darkness.'

'It is said that 100 years in the life of Brahmā is equivalent to one breath of Mahā-Viṣṇu [2]. So while Mahā-Viṣṇu is inhaling one time, Brahmā disappears. This means that in just one breath of Mahā-Viṣṇu, the entire collection of countless universes are annihilated and enter into the body of Mahā-Viṣṇu. When Mahā-Viṣṇu exhales, creation happens again. And that takes 311 trillion years!'

'How easy it is to attain the Lord! You don't have to go through all these billions of years. You don't even have to go through one inhaling and exhaling of Mahā-Viṣṇu. You don't have to go through all this, you can just be a *bhakta* and enjoy His Love. Whether He breathes or not, you don't have to bother about it.'

'The ones who are constantly immersed in His Love, the Divine Love within their own Self, realise the essence of God. They realise that God is not just the One they pray to, outside themselves, but He is the essence of their *bhakti*, the essence of what they want to achieve. They realise that He is actually inside them. Those *bhaktas* who have developed such a devotion, who are absorbed in their worship, in their *sādhana*, in their chanting, will quickly reach the state of God-realisation.

'In such a state of *bhakti*, of deep, supreme devotion, one must long for the Lord like a fish which is out of the water longs for water, or like a man who is drowning longs for air. Kṛṣṇa says here that He gives Himself only to a *bhakta* who has such a longing for realisation, who has such a longing for Him. So if you want to reach God-realisation, you have to be very dedicated, you can't be superficial, you can't be insincere, or just a part-time devotee on the spiritual path. To attain the Lord, you have to do everything for the sake of developing that supreme devotion.'

'Death doesn't have any effect on the ones who are completely surrendered to Him [Kṛṣṇa]. Not even Yamarāja, the lord of death, has power over the *bhaktas* of the Lord. They leave this world when He wills them to leave and they come back again when He wills them to come back. A *yogī*, a *bhakta* is fully absorbed into God consciousness, so he will not stay here forever.'

'The *bhaktas* who are surrendered, who have not fully realised themselves before departing this world, go to higher *lokas* to perfect themselves and then they come back again. And when they come back again, they come for the benefit of others. Kṛṣṇa says, "Because they are fully surrendered, I Myself send them down." The saints, who are born again on Earth for the welfare of society, come to remind others about the goal of life.'

Chapter Eight Verses: Key Terms

[1] **Yugas** – defined as an age or epoch in Hindu cosmology. There are four distinct *yugas*: *Satya-yuga*, *Tretā-yuga*, *Dvāpara-yuga* and *Kali-yuga*, each period being shorter, darker, and less righteous than the preceding. Mankind is currently in the age of *Kali-yuga*. In this verse, Kṛṣṇa states that both a Day and a Night of Brahmā lasts a 'thousand *Mahā-yugas*' which is actually a thousand cycles of the four *yugas* mentioned, a period that lasts trillions of years.

[2] Verses 24-25 make reference to the *Vedic Upaniṣads* which describe different ways of leaving the body. The auspicious six months during the light are known as Uttarāyaṇa, and the inauspicious months are known as Dakṣiṇāyana. Both are recognised in the Hindu calendar today.

Chapter Eight Commentary: Key Terms

[1] **Jīvātmā** – term interchanged with *'jīva'*, which refers to the embodied Self.

[2] **Mahā-Viṣṇu** – a cosmic manifestation of the Supreme Lord Nārāyaṇa in which He classically holds the conch, discus, mace, and lotus in each of His four hands.

CHAPTER NINE
RĀJA-VIDYĀ-GUHYA-YOGA
THE SECRET OF DEVOTION

Taking up many of the themes in chapter seven, Kṛṣṇa now explores the way of *bhakti* in more depth. This, He states, is the highest knowledge and the greatest secret. Once again, we learn how the Lord supports and controls the material world, but at the same time is both transcendent and detached from the process. Those great souls who understand this truth engage in acts of devotional worship.

Kṛṣṇa then reiterates His immanence in the world: He Himself is the various aspects of the *yajña*, the sound of *oṁ*, the *Vedas* and the very goal of life. Those who fail to perceive this, carry out the *Vedic* ritual and attempt to enjoy heavenly delights. But once their merit (*puṇya*) is exhausted, they are forced back into this world. They cannot see that it is Kṛṣṇa who is ultimately the enjoyer of all sacrifices and He alone provides prosperity and security. Depending on where we focus our minds (family, spirits, gods or Kṛṣṇa) our destination after death will be decided.

The closing verses describe the power of *bhakti*. Kṛṣṇa states that the simplest of offerings done with love will be accepted by Him, and so He urges Arjuna to make everything in life an offering to Him. Although Kṛṣṇa is equal to all, the devotees are the ones who dwell in the heart of Kṛṣṇa, and He in theirs. He declares that even if one is the worst sinner, *bhakti* to the Lord will transform that person onto the righteous path. Finally, Arjuna is told to fix his mind upon Kṛṣṇa, to bow down and worship Him. If this is done, he is guaranteed to come to the Lord.

VERSES 1-3: KNOWLEDGE OF BHAKTI IS THE HIGHEST

śrī-bhagavān uvāca
idaṁ tu te guhyatamaṁ pravakṣyāmy-anasūyave |
jñānaṁ vijñāna sahitaṁ yat-jñātvā mokṣyase'śubhāt || 1 ||

Lord Kṛṣṇa says:

Arjuna because you are without envy, I shall reveal to you the most secret of all knowledge, along with the process of its immediate realisation, knowing which you shall be freed from the miseries of life. (1)

rāja-vidyā rāja-guhyaṁ pavitram idam uttamam |
pratyakṣāvagamaṁ dharmyaṁ su-sukhaṁ kartum avyayam || 2 ||

This is the king of wisdom, the king of mysteries and the purest of knowledge. It grants direct experience of the Truth, it is based on *dharma*, it is easy to practise and is unfading. (2)

aśraddadhānāḥ puruṣā dharmasyāsya parantapa |
aprāpya māṁ nivartante mṛtyu-saṁsāra vartmani || 3 ||
Those who have no faith in this path, O Arjuna, remain in this cycle of birth and death without ever attaining Me. (3)

'People who are attached to earthly existence, who are attached to the objects of the senses, whose senses and mind revolve around vices, due to their ignorance, are not worthy to receive the Word of God. In the *Bible*, Christ says that we should not cast pearls to pigs. The pigs will trample over them, not knowing their value. Kṛṣṇa says that this deep knowledge is to be given only to the *bhaktas* and should not be given to people who are not ready, because they will not know what to do with it. They will not even understand it.'

'By chanting the Lord's Name and letting your mind be focused on Him, you will get rid of all the vices and evil ways. It will cleanse you of all your past *karmas* and release you from endless suffering. When you are rid of all endless suffering, the *ātmā* reveals Itself.'

'Even when the *ātmā* reveals Itself, that's not everything. You have to attain the supreme bliss. You have to attain the supreme peace. You have to attain God-realisation. God-realisation here means when the Divine reveals Himself. When you realise your Self, you have paved the way towards the divine qualities. This is where all the divine qualities start reflecting through you. You become calm, you become radiant, you become very peaceful, you become non-judgemental. Only then can you do service to society. Only then can you go around and serve freely. The right hand gives and the left hand doesn't know about it. So, you become automatically a great aid for this world. divine virtue starts flowing through you and the way you perceive the world changes.'

'Kṛṣṇa says, "What I am asking of you is not difficult: to surrender your mind to My Feet, to think of Me, place your mind upon My image, My form; nothing can destroy that. Once you build a connection to Me, once you build a relationship to Me, once you attain that Love, there is no going back and it is imperishable because nothing can destroy it." That knowledge of the Self is a secret that has been kept always, and it was given only through Initiation and only when one was ready. But in reality, it's very simple and very easy. Even if it sounds very difficult, it is the easiest thing to do.'

'The soul incarnates in 8.4 million species before attaining a human body. Only through the grace of God, through spiritual advancement, can a soul attain a human body. The ones who surrender to the Divine within themselves, realise how rare it is to get this human existence. When they realise how important this human existence is, they hold on tight to their spiritual path, their meditation, and their Atma Kriya Yoga practice. If they lack faith in the teachings of the Lord, if they are reading or listening to the *Gītā* without faith, they will find it difficult to attain this Love, to surrender and to realise God. Those who find it difficult to realise God, first within the core of themselves, and then everywhere, come back again and again to advance towards unity with the Supreme Divine Being.'

'Without faith, it is impossible to centre the mind. Without faith, it is impossible to love. Without faith, it is not easy to chant. But with faith, it becomes easy.'

VERSES 4-10: KṚṢṆA'S RELATIONSHIP TO THE WORLD

mayā tatam idaṁ sarvaṁ jagad avyakta mūrtinā |
mat-sthāni sarva bhūtāni na cāhaṁ teṣv-avasthitaḥ || 4 ||

This entire universe is pervaded by Me, in My unmanifest form. All beings are in Me, but I am not in them. (4)

na ca mat-sthāni bhūtāni paśya me yogam aiśvaram |
bhūta-bhṛnna ca bhūtastho mamātmā bhūta-bhāvanaḥ || 5 ||

And yet these beings are not in Me, such is My divine mystery! I am the upholder of all beings and yet I am not in them. It is My will alone that causes their existence. (5)

yathākāśa-sthito nityaṁ vāyuḥ sarvatrago mahān |
tathā sarvāṇi bhūtāni mat-sthānīty-upadhāraya || 6 ||

As the mighty wind moves everywhere, but always remains in space, in the same way you should understand how all beings rest in Me. (6)

sarva bhūtāni kaunteya prakṛtiṁ yānti māmikām |
kalpa-kṣaye punas-tāni kalpādau visṛjāmy-aham || 7 ||

All beings, Arjuna, are withdrawn into My *prakṛti* [1] at the end of a cycle of time, and at the beginning of a new cycle, I send them forth again. (7)

prakṛtiṁ svām-avaṣṭabhya visṛjāmi punaḥ punaḥ |
bhūta-grāmam imaṁ kṛtsnam avaśaṁ prakṛter-vaśāt || 8 ||

Using this *prakṛti* of Mine, I repeatedly send forth this multitude of beings. They are helpless, being under the control of *prakṛti*. (8)

na ca māṁ tāni karmāṇi nibadhnanti dhanañjaya |
udāsīnavad-āsīnam asaktaṁ teṣu karmasu || 9 ||

But these actions do not bind Me, Arjuna, for I am detached from them, remaining always indifferent. (9)

mayādhyakṣeṇa prakṛtiḥ sūyate sacarācaram |
hetunānena kaunteya jagad viparivartate || 10 ||

It is because of Me alone that this *prakṛti* produces all the moving and non-moving beings. It works under My direction, hence why the world exists as it does. (10)

'He says, "All existences are situated in Me, but I am not in them." The material, the tangible things exist inside of Kṛṣṇa, but Kṛṣṇa as the Supreme Lord is beyond this material existence and He stays always unconnected. He remains intact, even at the time of *pralaya* [1] when the whole creation is dissolved.

'Imagine a cloudy sky. The sky is completely covered by the clouds, but does this affect the sky? No, it doesn't. When the clouds are dispersed, you see that the sky is still there and that the sky was always there. It's not touched by the clouds at all. In the same way, God is ever-existing. He doesn't cease to exist, even if the whole world disappears, because He existed even before creation.'

'So, He is never touched by anything, even if the world disappears. Even right now, while we are talking, there are universes appearing and disappearing. But the glory of the Lord shines everywhere. There is no place where He is not shining, however, nothing material touches Him.'

'The ego, the pride, the big "I, I, I" are just like clouds in the sky, and when they disappear, only the sky stays. In the same way, the *bhakta* realises that beyond this "I, I, I", there is only One that ever-exists – God. One attains the state where the world stops existing and what exists is only God.'

'In His *nirguṇa* aspect, God is like the ether: uniform, formless, actionless, infinite, unattached and immutable, immune to all changes. Like the wind, like air, all beings spring from God, abide in God and naturally come back into God.

'However, God also has a *saguṇa* aspect. That's why He can conceive the whole creation. Without this, how would He be? He would be complete emptiness. First one has to see that all is present in His cosmic form and that is the Supreme Being. However, He is also the formless, actionless, infinite, unattached. He is beyond everything, yet He pervades everything and infuses energy into everything. When we refer to a small hole saying that it is empty, in reality it's not empty. Air pervades it. There is air in the hole. In the same way, you can take an empty bottle and say that the bottle is empty, yet it's not fully empty, because there is air inside.

'When one rises in awareness, one perceives that every atom, every particle, is pervaded by Bhagavān in His formless state. However, all this drama of countless universes, countless worlds, which are appearing and disappearing, are in His cosmic form, in His *saguṇa* form: beyond that there is nothing else. And when one reaches that state of realisation, and perceives that He is the One who gives the power to the atom, one will see that divine reality; and that's God consciousness. The one who wants to see only the atom, will perceive only the atom and not the power which is behind the atom, giving it the energy to act and manifest.'

'At the end of the dissolution period, another creation manifests. The whole world dissolves into Him and, afterwards, a new world arises from Him. The dissolution period also enables the *ātmā*, the individual soul, to move to a higher level of realisation.'

'*Pralaya* is very long in human years. In this reality, *pralaya* takes trillions of human years, but in the celestial reality, *pralayas* can happen every day. After *pralaya*, the soul comes back to this reality, to this world. As I said before, to advance to God consciousness, one has to be born in this world here, in this reality. That's why all the *avatāras* come to remind people how important it is to realise God in one's life! And this chance is not given in every life, due to the surroundings, the environment, the association, whether it's low or high association. If it's a high association, it's fine. If it is a low association, finish! Nevertheless, whether one takes hundreds of millions of years or hundreds of millions of incarnations, in the end, one will return to where one has come from: to Him. It is Him only.'

'If people have not reached this state of realisation in their lives, due to attachment to the *guṇas* and *karma* created, they are born again and again. They are under the control of *māyā*: they are so attached to the body and to the outside world that it becomes very difficult for them to let go. They don't perceive the cosmic nature of the Lord within their own individual nature. They become blind. They can't perceive that it is the Supreme Lord Himself who is the core of the individual. Here I'm not referring to the individual Self, or to the ego self, but to the Supreme Self, Nārāyaṇa, who is seated deep in the core of one's heart, in the core of one's Self.'

'Bhagavān Kṛṣṇa says that He is the Controller, the Supervisor of this creation; He is the Supervisor behind *prakṛti*. All existences and activities of *prakṛti* derive from Him; but it is His *prakṛti* which carries on all such activities as the creation of the universe.

'Here you can take the example of a farmer. As the supervisor, a farmer plants the seeds in the earth, and then the earth carries on. Even if the farmer has put the seeds in the earth, the earth brings forth a variety of plants according to the kinds of seeds which the farmer planted. Like that, God, Nārāyaṇa, implants the seeds of life in *prakṛti*, and as the supervisor, He then supervises everything. So, *prakṛti* evolves. He plants the seeds of creation inside Her, then *prakṛti* makes the entire creation evolve and all the beings, and species come into existence, into manifestation. Mother Nature carries on doing what She has to do. And the farmer is not attached. The farmer doesn't go around saying, "Grow, grow, grow!" No. He puts the seeds in the earth, but then Mother Nature takes Her course by Herself. The Lord says that by His will He brought forth the creation and then everything was carried on by Nature. It's the same thing when a child is born. You may want to have a child, but if the Supreme Lord Himself doesn't will it, it will not happen. One can say, "There is a tube which is blocked on this side" or "There is no strength in the man", and so on. Science can say many things, but when the Divine wills something, it can happen and then even science gets completely baffled… He can bend His own nature and make things happen that are beyond the limitations of the mind of man to understand.'

VERSES 11-15: RECOGNISING AND WORSHIPPING THE LORD

avajānanti māṁ mūḍhā mānuṣīṁ tanum-āśritam |
paraṁ bhāvam ajānanto mama bhūta-maheśvaram || 11 ||

Fools disregard Me, appearing in a human form, not knowing My divine nature, as the Supreme Lord of all beings. (11)

moghāśā mogha-karmāṇo mogha-jñānā vicetasaḥ |
rākṣasīm-āsurīṁ caiva prakṛtiṁ mohinīṁ śritāḥ || 12 ||

The hopes, the actions and the knowledge of these foolish people are in vain. Being utterly deluded, they take on the nature of *asuras* [2] and Rākṣasas [3]. (12)

mahātmān-astu māṁ pārtha daivīṁ prakṛtim-āśritāḥ |
bhajanty-ananya-manaso jñātvā-bhūtādim-avyayam || 13 ||

But the great souls, O Arjuna, share My divine nature. They adore Me, with a single mind, knowing Me to be the unchanging source of all beings. (13)

satataṁ kīrtayanto māṁ yatantaśca dṛḍha-vratāḥ |
namasyantaśca māṁ bhaktyā nitya-yuktā upāsate || 14 ||

Constantly glorifying Me, taking up vows and bowing down before Me in devotion, they always engage in acts of worship. (14)

jñāna yajñena cāpyanye yajanto mām-upāsate |
ekatvena pṛthaktvena bahudhā viśvato-mukham || 15 ||

There are also others who make offerings in the sacrifice of knowledge. They worship Me as the One Being that has manifested in a variety of forms, with faces in different directions. (15)

'Wise indeed are those who recognise who is in front of them... Those who are detached, those who are free, those whose minds are focused, will see the Divine. But those who are attached and blind, even if the Supreme Lord Himself is in front of them, like the Kauravas, they will not see who He is.'

'Out of compassion for all embodied souls, in order to place them all under His protection, with a view to establish righteousness, to redeem His devotees, His people, the Supreme Lord manifests Himself. He takes various forms and performs various *līlās* [2] in this world to remind mankind of His divinity, to remind mankind of the importance of surrendering to God: "Not my will be done, Thy will be done!"'

'Kṛṣṇa reveals to Arjuna that He is the Supreme Lord who has manifested Himself in various Incarnations, like Matsya, Kūrma, Varāha, Nārasiṁha, Vāmana, Paraśurāma, Rāma and so on. And it is Him now, the same Lord, the same fullness: it is the Supreme Lord fully present in Vāsudeva-Kṛṣṇa.'

'Bhagavān says that the great souls adore Him with a single-pointed mind. Even if they have realised God, even if they see Him inside themselves and know that everything is Him, they never stop adoring Him. These realised souls have exclusive Love for God. Their minds don't feel attracted towards anything other than God. They perceive God within themselves and everywhere, but they don't stop praising and singing the glory of God. These realised souls are never separated from God. As *bhaktas* have this unbearable yearning for Him, the Lord Himself also longs for the *bhaktas* in the same way. As the *bhaktas* perceive the Lord inside themselves, the Lord also perceives the *bhaktas* inside Him. This is the relationship, the connection, that a realised soul has with the Lord. Slowly, slowly the Lord is revealing to Arjuna the essence of *bhakti*.'

'The ones who hear the glory of the Lord with a steadfast mind, the ones whose hearts choke and have tears roll down from their eyes hearing of the divinity of the Lord, are fit for God-realisation. Those devotees who have such longing for the Lord are fit for God-realisation, because they love God for the sake of loving Him. They don't love God just to make a bargain with Him. They love Him because they love Him. That's "Just Love"! The Lord praises these *bhaktas* and He Himself rejoices in the form of a *bhakta*.'

'There may be terrible calamities, the wind can be blowing left and right, a big tsunami can happen, but it doesn't in the slightest affect the true *bhakta*. They are not shaken in their resolution or determination. When the *bhaktas* have this firm resolve, have taken a path and surrendered, nothing which happens in the outside world can shake them. It doesn't matter how much they are criticised or what others say. Nothing can move them. Such *bhaktas* attain the supreme reality. They are fit for God-realisation. But the flickering ones, God discharges them for their next lives.'

VERSES 16-19: THE IMMANENCE OF KṚṢṆA IN THE WORLD

ahaṁ kratur-ahaṁ yajñāḥ svadhāham aham auṣadham |
mantro'ham aham-evājyam aham-agnir-ahaṁ hutam || 16 ||

I am the ritual; I am the sacrifice; I am the offerings made to the ancestors; I am the herbs; I am the *mantra*; I alone am the clarified butter; I am the fire; I am the offering itself. (16)

pitāham-asya jagato mātā dhātā pitāmahaḥ |
vedyaṁ pavitram oṁkāra ṛk-sāma yajur-eva ca || 17 ||

I am the Father, Mother, Support and Grandfather of this universe. I am the object of knowledge; I am the Purifier. I am the syllable *oṁ* and also the *Ṛg Veda*, *Sāma Veda* and the *Yajur Veda*. (17)

gatir-bhartā prabhuḥ sākṣī nivāsaḥ śaraṇaṁ suhṛt |
prabhavaḥ pralayaḥ sthānaṁ nidhānaṁ bījam avyayam || 18 ||

I am the Goal, the Supporter, the Lord, the Witness, the Abode, the Refuge and the Friend of the universe. I am creation, destruction and the basis of everything. I am that which is preserved and the eternal seed. (18)

tapāmyaham ahaṁ varṣaṁ nigṛhṇāmy utsṛjāmi ca |
amṛtaṁ caiva mṛtyuśca sadasac-cāham arjuna || 19 ||

O Arjuna, I am the one who gives heat; I send forth and hold back the rains; I am immortality as well as death; I am the manifest and the unmanifest. (19)

'Lord Kṛṣṇa is explaining to Arjuna about His omnipresence; about how He is in everything. He is gradually guiding Arjuna to perceive that supreme reality. People may say, "Okay, God is everywhere." However, this doesn't mean that they really perceive that God is everywhere.'

'The Lord is taking Arjuna beyond that point to reveal the Truth to him through *bhakti*. When *bhakti* awakens, the *jñāna* is transformed: he not only perceives the formless in everything, but he realises that it's only the Lord who pervades everything, and that everything is just His emanation.'

'He says, "I am the sacred *oṁ*. I am the *praṇava*. I am this life force that sustains everything." Kṛṣṇa is not only talking about the sound itself. Sound is vibration and everything in this world is caused by vibration. The whole universe, everything, is created due to that vibration. He says, "I am the cause of that vibration. I am that *oṁkāra*. I am this sound that vibrates in the whole universe and brings everything into being. I am that vibration itself, and whoever through *sādhana* realises and hears this cosmic sound, attains God-realisation. Through this sound I purify everything"... When one is doing OM Chanting, the *oṁ* vibrates, it purifies.'

'Everything, all beings, emanate from Him alone and He is the "eternal resting place", so everything goes back to Him. Everything comes out of God and everything goes back to God, and everything is happening inside of Him through His *yoga-māyā*.'

'He is the ultimate Truth. He is the One who takes people from the darkness of ignorance and brings them to the Light. He takes people from untruth to Truth. He is the One who leads each person to realise the *ātmā*, releasing them from the cycle of birth and death.'

'Rituals may change, Names may change, everything around may change, but the Lord, the essence that is behind everything is only Him. And those who have the eyes to see, who have the eyes of truth and who have the eyes of wisdom, they will perceive the same Lord that they worship everywhere... Everything becomes an offering, everything is a prayer, because the glories of the Lord are endless and have no limitation. His mercy doesn't have any limitation. His wisdom doesn't have any limitation. His creation is endless.'

VERSES 20-25: THE FATE OF THOSE WHO WORSHIP THE LESSER GODS

traividyā māṁ somapāḥ pūta-pāpa
yajñāir iṣṭvā svargatiṁ prārthayante |
te puṇyam āsādya surendra-lokam
aśnanti divyān divi deva-bhogān || 20 ||

Those who are versed in the three *Vedas*, being purified from sin by drinking the *soma* juice [4], pray for heaven [5] and worship Me with sacrifices. After reaching that place where the king of the demigods [6] resides, they enjoy celestial pleasures. (20)

te taṁ bhuktvā svarga-lokaṁ viśālaṁ
kṣīṇe puṇye martya-lokaṁ viśanti |
evaṁ trayī-dharmam anuprapannā
gatāgataṁ kāmakāmā labhante || 21 ||

Having enjoyed this vast realm of heaven, once their merit is exhausted, they return to the world of mortals. As a result, those who follow the *Vedic* rituals and are motivated by desire, go to heaven temporarily before coming back. (21)

ananyāś-cintayanto māṁ ye janāḥ paryupāsate |
teṣāṁ nityābhiyuktānāṁ yoga-kṣemaṁ vahāmyaham || 22 ||

But then there are those who adore Me alone with undeviating concentration. For those who yearn for Me in this way, I Myself take charge of their prosperity and welfare. (22)

ye'pyanya-devatā-bhaktā yajante śraddhayānvitāḥ |
te'pi mām-eva kaunteya yajanty-avidhi-pūrvakam || 23 ||

Understand, Arjuna, that even those who worship other demigods with faith, actually worship Me alone but in an improper way. (23)

ahaṁ hi sarva-yajñānāṁ bhoktā ca prabhur-eva ca |
na tu mām-abhijānanti tattvenātaś-cyavanti te || 24 ||

For I alone am the enjoyer and the Lord of all sacrifices. But such people do not recognise Me in My true nature, hence they fall from the positions they attain. (24)

yānti deva-vratā devān pitṝn-yānti pitṛ-vratāḥ |
bhūtāni yānti bhūtejyā yānti madyājino'pi mām || 25 ||

Those who worship the demigods, go to the demigods. Those who worship the ancestors will go to the ancestors. Those who worship the spirits will reach them. But My devotees will come to Me. (25)

'Here Bhagavān Kṛṣṇa says that people who don't realise the Truth about the Self and God, but who surrender to the demigods, attain the fruit of transitory pleasures in the celestial *lokas* of the demigods, according to what they did in their lives. However, their good *puṇya* is transitory. It is not permanent. Due to that *puṇya*, they go for instance to *Indraloka* and get entertained a little bit by Indra and company. But later, when their *puṇya* is finished, when "their bank account is empty," Indra will say, "My dear, now you have used up all your money. You don't have anything else to bet with, so you have to leave this casino." Then they have to come back and be born again here on Earth to work towards realisation. If they fail to realise God, if they don't have the chance to surrender to the Feet of the *guru* so that they can be freed in this life, they will return many, many, many, many more times, and keep repeating the same things. Only the ones who surrender attain God-realisation. The ones who surrender to the Feet of the Master are fortunate. The Master will carry them across the ocean of *saṁsāra* [3], lead them out of this delusion of birth and death, and make them realised.'

'People often work with the lower frequencies of nature as they don't have the knowledge of the higher Self. They start doing lots of shamanic rituals without knowing the true knowledge of the Self and this leads them to an inferior state. Then they are never free. Then they are stuck in that reality. They take birth as those animals, because their minds are so focused on them.'

'God has placed men on Earth to advance towards Him and not to please the demigods or the entities of nature that have a low vibration. There was a time when all of you incarnated as animals, but that reality was finished a long time ago. When you grow up, you let go of your childhood, so you don't keep acting like a small kid, do you?

'Due to the faith that those ones have in the demigods or the entities of nature, the merciful Lord Kṛṣṇa says, "Know that they are worshipping Me alone. I am the sole object of all worship." Even if they end up going to the *lokas* of those demigods or incarnate into a lower state, God will give them opportunities to rise higher, towards God-realisation. To have the grace of being on the spiritual path in order to attain the supreme reality is very rare.'

VERSE 26: KṚṢṆA ONLY WANTS THE LOVE OF THE DEVOTEE

patraṁ puṣpaṁ phalaṁ toyaṁ yo me bhaktyā prayacchati |
tad-ahaṁ bhakty-upahṛtam-aśnāmi prayatātmanaḥ || 26 ||

Whoever offers to Me, with devotion, a leaf, a flower, a fruit or some water, I accept this offering made with devotion by one who is pure of heart. (26)

'This is one of the most beautiful verses in the *Gītā* which shows the humility of the Lord.'

'How beautiful this is! In Hindu prayers we always offer flowers, leaves, fruits, and water. These things are easily obtained by everybody. The Lord is not asking for big things. Actually, He doesn't ask for anything! It's not about His expectation! He is referring to *bhakti*: "Whatever people are offering to Me, whatever desire, whatever they have inside their hearts"; the most simple things; the offering of Love itself, the sacrifice of Love itself, is what the Lord takes and that is what He accepts. It's not about the flower. The flower is here and then finish, soon it has disappeared! The water, and the fruits are offered in front of Him, and then after that, we take the offerings as *prasāda*. But, in reality, what the Lord accepts is the Love that is in the heart of the devotee. It's not through knowledge that one conquers the Lord, but through simplicity, through the simplest things done with devotion. If one offers a leaf, a flower, a few drops of water with gratitude, with a mind focused on the Divine, on the Lord Himself, He accepts that offering of Love.'

'That intensity of faith and worship, that intensity of Love and surrender that you have, comes from the individual soul. God can't make you love Him. You love Him as an act of surrender and offering. You choose to love Him. He can't make that for you. That's why He longs for that Love. That's why when one is fully absorbed in devotion, that Love becomes so intensified in oneself that it brings you to the Lord. This intensity of your worship is something that emerges from deep within you, out. This inclination, this power, this truthfulness which emerges from your soul, that's what Bhagavān longs for. He doesn't need anything. He has everything. The whole universe, the entire creation is His.'

'There are so many people who go to temples and do so many offerings, and so many people who go around doing so much service, but they are full of pride. These offerings… don't even reach His shadow, because that intention is devoid of Love, is devoid of surrender.'

'What Bhagavān accepts from the heart of the devotee is this Love and surrender. You think that you are surrendering, but actually He is. By the action of surrendering to Him, He runs and surrenders to you.'

VERSES 27-33: THE POWER OF BHAKTI

yat-karoṣi yad-aśnāsi yaj-juhoṣi dadāsi yat |
yat-tapasyasi kaunteya tat-kuruṣva mad-arpaṇam || 27 ||

Whatever you do, whatever you eat, whatever you offer in sacrifice, whatever you give away, whatever austerity you practise, O Arjuna, do it as an offering to Me. (27)

śubhāśubha phalair-evaṁ mokṣyase karma-bandhanaiḥ |
sannyāsa yoga-yuktātmā vimukto mām-upaiṣyasi || 28 ||

With a steadfast mind, engaged in this *yoga*, you will free yourself from good and bad results which are the bonds of *karma*. As a result, you will be liberated and you will come to Me. (28)

samo'haṁ sarva-bhūteṣu na me dveṣyo'sti na priyaḥ |
ye bhajanti tu māṁ bhaktyā mayi te teṣu cāpyaham || 29 ||

I am the same to all beings; there is no one hated by Me nor is there anyone I am partial to; but those who worship Me with devotion live in Me and I in them. (29)

api-cet sudurācāro bhajate mām-ananyabhāk |
sādhur-eva sa mantavyaḥ samyag-vyavasito hi saḥ || 30 ||

If even the most sinful person worships Me exclusively, with devotion, he must be regarded as a saint, for he has rightly resolved. (30)

kṣipraṁ bhavati dharmātmā śāśvacchāntiṁ nigacchati |
kaunteya prati-jānīhi na me bhaktaḥ praṇaśyati || 31 ||

Quickly such a person becomes righteous and obtains everlasting peace. O Arjuna, let it be declared that My devotee never perishes. (31)

māṁ hi pārtha vyapāśritya ye'pi syuḥ pāpa-yonayaḥ |
striyo vaiśyās-tathā śūdrās-te'pi yānti parāṁ gatim || 32 ||

By surrendering to Me, whatever their birth, race, sex, or caste, even those whom society scorns will attain the supreme state. (32)

kiṁ punar-brāhmaṇāḥ puṇyā bhaktā rājarṣayas-tathā |
anityam asukhaṁ lokam imaṁ prāpya bhajasva mām || 33 ||

How much more, then, the *brāhmaṇas* and royal sages who are pure and devoted to Me! Therefore, having come into this temporary world of suffering, you should worship Me. (33)

'Kṛṣṇa says that whatever you are doing in life, breathing, doing your *sādhana* (spiritual practice), eating, drinking, sitting, or listening, make it an act of offering. Make it an act of surrendering to the Lord. Make it a prayer to the Lord and offer the prayer to Him. Offer all the merit of whatever you do to Him. You will attain Him and He, who is not attainable by any *yogī*, will give Himself to you.'

'When all good actions are offered and dedicated to the Lord, automatically the result is God-realisation. But if one does a practice to gain a certain result, this will create *karma* which will lead one to be born again. Like that, one will be thrown into the bondage and attachment to this world. One will have to come back again. And when one comes back again, bear in mind that you won't know how that life will be. In this life, one may have attained the grace to be on the spiritual path and to associate with people who have a similar aim and goal, so that makes it easy. But one can't know about the next life. Here Bhagavān says, "Do everything as an act of surrender to Me, 'with your soul in union with the Divine through renunciation.'" Don't be attached to anything. Your mind should only be focusing on the Lord within yourself. The heart of a devotee is not stained by anything, apart from Divine Love. Through that Love, "you will become free and attain Me."

'At night, before sleeping, close your eyes, think of Nārāyaṇa-Kṛṣṇa and say, "Lord, I offer You my whole day. I place whatever I have done, 'good' or 'not good', upon Your altar. I surrender every action to you." The Lord Himself will grant you what is needed and will release you from the grip of *māyā*.'

'God doesn't hate anybody. God loves everyone, but hate and love is the choice of men, and they don't go together. Either you love or you don't. Here Bhagavān is equal in all of that. He is like the Sun that doesn't look on whom it is shining. He is like the rain which falls on everybody equally, on the bad and the good. He is the tree which gives shelter to everybody.'

'There are so many saints who were sinners, but through the grace of the Lord, through the association of the right people, they were transformed and changed. Bhagavān says that no matter how big the sins are, if the sinners surrender to Him with love and devotion, if they focus their minds upon Him and make Him their sole refuge, they will become saints. St. Paul is an example, Vālmīki is another example, Mary of Egypt is another example, and like them there are so many others.'

'When one tries to surrender to Him with devotion, all one's evilness, all one's negativity will be overcome. He says, "Don't hang onto this negativity. Don't focus on it. Your aim is to focus on God, not on the negativity." It's of no use beating yourself with a whip saying, "I am a sinner, I am a sinner, I am a sinner." No! Perceive it, but cross over it, go beyond it. Your mind should focus on God, not on your sin. If you are concentrating on your sin, then you become sinful. Then you accumulate more sin. But if you concentrate and focus on the Lord Himself, then you are free.'

VERSE 34: DEVOTION TAKES US TO THE GOAL

manmanā bhāva mad-bhakto mad-yājī māṁ namas-kuru |
māmevaiṣyasi yuktvaivam ātmānaṁ mat parāyaṇam || 34 ||

Focus your mind on Me, be devoted to Me, offer worship to Me, bow down to Me. Engaging your mind in this way, holding Me as the supreme goal, you will surely come to Me. (34)

'Here He says to Arjuna, "Focus your mind on Me, be devoted to Me, offer worship to Me." Can you see the power that is behind this? Kṛṣṇa is not saying this superficially. No! Here is God Himself talking to Arjuna with all power! There is no pride in it. He says, "Here I am, the Supreme Lord Himself. I'm God Himself. I'm the God of which speak the *Vedas*. It is I who am here talking to you and I am telling you how to surrender to Me! Focus your mind on Me. Be devoted to Me. Awake. Let your heart dwell on Me. Offer worship to Me. Serve Me in your worship, in your charity, in your daily chores. Do it as a form of worship. Bow down to Me. Be humble. Engaging your mind in this manner and regarding Me as the supreme goal, you will come to Me." If the mind and the heart are focused on the Lord, and everything one does is done with this attitude of surrender to the Lord, there is no doubt that one will reach Him.'

Chapter Nine Verses: Key Terms

[1] **Prakṛti** – substance from which all material creation manifests. It forms part of Kṛṣṇa's nature and is therefore under His control.

[2] **Asuras** – beings created by Brahmā, who are perpetually at war with their cousins, the *devas* (demigods). *Asuras* are typically associated with negative attributes. Although there are exceptions, they are generally self-centred and refuse to surrender to the Lord. The *devas* on the other hand are generally associated with positive qualities and understand their position in relation to the Lord.

[3] **Rākṣasas** – a race of beings who are generally well known for their aggressive and blood thirsty nature.

[4] **Soma juice** – powerful plant extract that formed a central part of the *Vedic* ritual sacrifice.

[5] **Heaven** – in the context of this verse, heaven is not the Supreme Abode of the Lord, but is considered to be the material realm of the demigods where one can temporarily enjoy celestial pleasures.

[6] **King of the demigods** – also known as Indra, the leader of the *devas* (demigods) and the ruler of the heavens.

Chapter Nine Commentary: Key Terms

[1] **Pralaya** – the periodic dissolution of the material world, in which creation is withdrawn into the body of God.

[2] **Līlā** – when the Lord takes on limitation to uplift and interact with His devotees.

[3] **Saṁsāra** – *karmic* cycle of repeated birth and death.

CHAPTER TEN
VIBHŪTI-YOGA
THE GLORIES OF KṚṢṆA

In this chapter, Kṛṣṇa continues to reveal to Arjuna His endless glories. As the Lord He is the origin of creation. The *ṛṣis*, the gods, and all qualities come from Him. Knowing this truth, the pure devotees worship Him with love. They rejoice in talking and glorifying Him. To such people, Kṛṣṇa Himself gives the knowledge by which they can come to Him. From within their hearts, He destroys the darkness of ignorance and raises the light of realisation.

Thrilled by these statements, Arjuna fully accepts Kṛṣṇa as the Supreme Lord. Eager to taste more of His glory, Arjuna urges Him to describe exactly how His presence can be known in this world. Kṛṣṇa replies that there is no end to His attributes, but in order to appease Arjuna the most prominent will be described.

What follows is a series of poetic descriptions where Kṛṣṇa identifies with various deities, beings, principles and values. The overriding message is that whatever we can perceive with beauty and wonder in this world is simply a manifestation of the Lord's divinity. At the same time, Kṛṣṇa stresses that what has been described is only a small part of His nature. With just a fraction of His being, He sustains all that is.

VERSES 1-7: KṚṢṆA IS THE ORIGIN OF ALL

śrī bhagavān uvāca
bhūya eva mahā-bāho śṛṇu me paramaṁ vacaḥ |
yatte'haṁ prīyamāṇāya vakṣyāmi hita-kāmyayā || 1 ||

Lord Kṛṣṇa says:
O Arjuna, because I desire your welfare and you are My dear friend, listen once more as I deliver this supreme teaching. (1)

na me viduḥ sura-gaṇāḥ prabhavaṁ na maharṣayaḥ |
aham-ādir-hi devānāṁ maharṣīṇāṁ ca sarvaśaḥ || 2 ||

Neither the hosts of demigods nor the great seers know My glory. Indeed, it is Me who is the sole source of the demigods and the great seers. (2)

yo mām ajam anādiṁ ca vetti loka-maheśvaram |
asammūḍhaḥ sa martyeṣu sarva-pāpaiḥ pramucyate || 3 ||

One who knows Me as unborn and without a beginning, the great Lord of the worlds, is undeluded among mortals and is liberated from all negative acts. (3)

buddhir-jñānam asammohaḥ kṣamā satyaṁ damaḥ śamaḥ |
sukhaṁ duḥkhaṁ bhavo'bhāvo bhayaṁ cābhyam-eva ca || 4 ||
ahiṁsā samatā tuṣṭis-tapo dānaṁ yaśo'yaśaḥ |
bhavanti bhāvā bhūtānāṁ matta eva pṛthag-vidhāḥ || 5 ||

Intelligence, knowledge, non-delusion, forbearance, truth, restraint, self-control, pleasure and pain, exaltation and depression, fear and fearlessness; non-violence, equanimity, cheerfulness, austerity, beneficence, fame and infamy — these different qualities arise from Me alone. (4-5)

maharṣayaḥ sapta pūrve catvāro manavas-tathā |
mad-bhāvā mānasā jātā yeṣāṁ loka imāḥ prajāḥ || 6 ||

The seven great seers [1], the four sages before them and the Manus [2], are all My mental expansions empowered by Me. All the creatures of the world are descended from them. (6)

etāṁ vibhūtiṁ yogaṁ ca mama yo vetti tattvataḥ |
so'vikalpena yogena yujyate nātra saṁśayaḥ || 7 ||

He who knows the truth of My glory and power becomes undoubtedly fixed in the unshakeable *yoga* of *bhakti*. (7)

'Bhagavān Kṛṣṇa is saying that even the *ṛṣis*, the sages, the *śāstras*, the holy scriptures don't know anything of Him. They can speak only a little of Him, but they can't speak about the full revelation of Himself. He has assumed various forms, more than it is written in the *śāstras* and the *Vedas*. Whenever His devotees have called upon Him, He has manifested Himself. Even if for a short while, He has taking a form and manifested Himself into this world.'

'He assumes various aspects, various forms, as desired by His devotees. Whoever calls Him, in whatever form they call Him, He will come to the *bhakta* in that aspect. To a worshipper of Lord Śiva, He will appear as Śiva. To a worshipper of Devī, He will appear as Devī. To a worshipper of Nārāyaṇa, He will appear as Nārāyaṇa.'

'If you don't perceive the divinity within yourself, if you don't perceive God inside yourself, you will never find Him outside. This is true knowledge, the knowledge of the Self. When this wisdom arises, when one gets this revelation, and dives into the ocean within oneself, then one perceives God within. The saints perceive the Divine within themselves, and they see the same Lord everywhere. Then they don't judge anyone. Why should they judge someone when they see that what is inside them is also in the other person, who performs a different role? But this is high knowledge.'

'The creation will never understand the Creator. The only thing that the creation can do is to surrender to the Creator, nothing else. That's why He says that even if the *ṛṣis* try to understand, even if the *yogīs* try to understand, even if the demigods try to understand, their knowledge is limited.'

'On the spiritual path, through your *sādhana*, many kinds of gifts, *siddhis*, arise and start to manifest themselves inside of you. But these *siddhis* should not be the aim. The aim should be attaining God-realisation, nothing else. Use these gifts that manifest for the good of others, but keep them to one side, do not give them attention. Very often you see spiritual people who, when they get the gift of clairvoyance or clairaudience, elevate themselves and say, "There's no better than me, everybody has to listen to me!" There are many people like this. They don't realise God has given them these gifts in order to help others. They become deluded, even if they reach this level of spirituality. It actually doesn't represent a very high level of spirituality, but one step. However, as a result of this delusion, they don't advance. Here Bhagavān says, "These are all My qualities, but it's not Me! If you want Me, forget these gifts which arise and aim for the Ultimate!"'

'Nowadays people go around trusting everybody. There is a saying that says, "When traveling by plane, you trust the pilot." But you don't know him. Of course, he introduces himself, but do you know who he is? No, you don't. But yet, when you are sitting on the plane, you trust that he knows what he is doing. When you go on a boat, you trust the captain. When riding on a bus, you trust the driver. But do you know the captain? Do you know the driver? They have a name, but you don't know them. However, very few trust the Controller of life. People go through life, but very few trust in God, truly. He who truly cares for you, He who has brought you here. Your trust should be completely on Him, trusting that He is the Controller. He is the true guide and He is placing you where you have to be.'

VERSES 8-11: KṚṢṆA GIVES KNOWLEDGE TO HIS DEVOTEES

ahaṁ sarvasya prabhavo mattaḥ sarvaṁ pravartate |
iti matvā-bhajante māṁ budhā bhāva-samanvitāḥ || 8 ||

I am the source of all; everything emerges from Me, realising this Truth the enlightened ones worship Me with loving devotion. (8)

mac-cittā mad-gata-prāṇā bodhayantaḥ parasparam |
kathayantaśca māṁ nityaṁ tuṣyanti ca ramanti ca || 9 ||

With their minds focused on Me and their lives centred upon Me, they inspire one another. By always speaking of My glory, they derive bliss and contentment. (9)

teṣāṁ satata-yuktānāṁ bhajatāṁ prīti-pūrvakam |
dadāmi buddhi-yogaṁ taṁ yena mām-upayānti te || 10 ||

To those who are constantly engaged with Me, and who worship Me with intense Love, I give them the realisation by which they can come to Me. (10)

teṣām evānukam pārtham aham ajñānajaṁ tamaḥ |
nāśayāmy-ātmabhāvastho jñāna-dīpena-bhāsvatā || 11 ||

Out of compassion for them, from within their hearts, I lift the lamp of knowledge and dispel the darkness born of ignorance. (11)

'Those who are deluded – the sensually minded people – are engrossed in all kinds of worldly enjoyments, and they find great delight in them. People who work the whole week, and look forward to getting drunk at the weekend, don't realise when the weekend has passed. What have they done? They don't remember. They call this 'life'. I know many of you have gone through this stage, when you were young. Not all of you had the grace to be on the spiritual path as quickly as others. You experienced *māyā*... Now you're drinking the *amṛta*, which in turn helps you to become Divine. The one who drinks the nectar that is derived from hearing the glory of the Lord, is purified. Even just by hearing the glory of the Lord, all the sins of one's past – not only of this life, but also of past lives – are washed away. And *bhakti* awakens in the heart of one who is not deluded by the world. His ultimate reality is revealed only to the one who is ready. Many are not ready, but you experience this in your daily life.'

'One who is fully surrendered in devotion to Him is full of great joy... Through this surrender and this Love, one becomes like a lantern and start to shine the light for others in the darkness. One becomes a beam of light, a supporter. The Lord says that a *bhakta* is one who helps others to come on the way, to find the Divine, to become spiritual. A *bhakta* is not egoistic. You don't keep what you get for yourself; you share it, you spread it.'

'There are saints who don't speak one word. But the *bhaktas* find great delight, and everything else, in silence – just by being around the saints. Mahāvatār Bābājī doesn't speak as I'm speaking right now. Everything is given in silence and a *bhakta* finds great delight in Him.'

VERSES 12-18: ARJUNA ACCEPTS KṚṢṆA'S DIVINITY

arjuna uvāca
paraṁ brahma paraṁ dhāma pavitraṁ paramaṁ bhavān |
puruṣaṁ śāśvataṁ divyam ādidevam ajaṁ vibhum || 12 ||

Arjuna says:
You are the Supreme Brahman, the Supreme Abode, and the Supreme Purifier. You are the eternal, Divine Person, the original Lord, unborn and all-pervading. (12)

ahus-tvām ṛṣayaḥ sarve devarṣir-nāradas -tathā |
asito devalo vyāsaḥ svayaṁ caiva bravīṣi me || 13 ||

All the divine sages, Nārada, Asita, Devala, Vyāsa, and now You, Yourself, declare this to be the Truth. (13)

sarvam etad ṛtaṁ manye yan-māṁ vadasi keśava |
na hi te bhagavan vyaktiṁ vidur-devā na dānavāḥ || 14 ||

O Kṛṣṇa, I am convinced of all that You have said to me. Truly, O Lord, neither the demigods nor the *asuras* know Your identity. (14)

svayam evātmanātmānaṁ vettha tvaṁ puruṣottama |
bhūta-bhāvana bhūteśa deva-deva jagat-pate || 15 ||

O Supreme Being, O Creator of beings, O Lord of beings, O God of gods, O Ruler of the universe, only You Yourself know Yourself by Your own potency. (15)

vaktum arhasy-aśeṣeṇa divyā hyātma vibhūtayaḥ |
yābhir-vibhūtibhir lokān imāṁs tvaṁ vyāpya tiṣṭhasi || 16 ||

Now kindly tell Me in detail Your divine glories. Describe the various qualities by which You pervade this world and reside within it. (16)

katham vidyām ahaṁ yogiṁs tvāṁ sadā paricintayan |
keṣu keṣu ca bhāveṣu cintyo'si bhagavan mayā || 17 ||

O Almighty Lord and *yogī*, tell me how I can know You and fix my mind upon You. What are the forms of existence that can be contemplated on by me? (17)

vistareṇātmano yogaṁ vibhūtiṁ ca janārdana |
bhūyaḥ kathaya tṛptir hi śṛṇvato nāsti me'mṛtam || 18 ||

Tell me again in detail, O Kṛṣṇa, about Your attributes and glories. For I am never fully satisfied when hearing Your nectar-like words. (18)

'Arjuna is fully absorbed in the Love of Kṛṣṇa. His mind is also fully absorbed, so Arjuna is fully convinced about everything that Kṛṣṇa is saying.'

'He realises the supremacy of the Lord, praises the Lord, and bows to Him, saying, "You are the One that all *ṛṣis* and the *devas* have praised. And here, You – the Lord who all have praised – stands in front of me."'

'Kṛṣṇa has given Arjuna one drop of *amṛta*, and once one has had one drop of *amṛta*, one wants more. The Love that is awakening in Arjuna's heart, the longing, is the *amṛta* which will lead him to immortality, from ignorance of the Self to realisation of the Self. Arjuna says, "I am not satisfied with what I have heard, it's not enough, I want more!" This feeling is not from greed. Out of greediness, someone longs for material things; to get more and more for self-enjoyment; to satisfy the senses with objects of the senses; all just to be pleased on the outside. But here, it's *bhakti* itself; it's the awakening of devotion.'

'Now, Arjuna is not thinking of war; he is not thinking of anything. In the first chapter, his mind is completely destroyed. He doesn't want to fight, he is fully absorbed in a state of delusion, and he is deluding himself completely, even thinking about what will happen to his ancestors later on when they die. When Kṛṣṇa tells him to fight, he finds hundreds of excuses not to fight. But here, he finds hundreds of excuses to listen to the glory of the Lord. He doesn't want Him to stop talking. When Kṛṣṇa stops talking, he says, 'Please!' He's finding excuses to ask Kṛṣṇa to reveal more and more of Himself.'

VERSES 19-42: KṚṢṆA DESCRIBES HIS GLORIES

śrī bhagavān uvāca
hanta te kathayiṣyāmi divyā hyātma vibhūtayaḥ |
prādhānyataḥ kuru-śreṣṭha nāsty-anto vistarasya me || 19 ||

Lord Kṛṣṇa says:
I shall gladly relate this to you, O Arjuna. But understand that there is no end to My glories, and so I shall only relate to you the most prominent of them. (19)

aham ātmā guḍākeśa sarva bhūtāśaya sthitaḥ |
aham ādiśca madhyaṁ ca bhūtānām anta eva ca || 20 ||

I am the Self, O Arjuna, dwelling in the hearts of all beings. I am also their beginning, middle and end. (20)

ādityānām ahaṁ viṣṇur jyotiṣāṁ ravir-aṁśumān |
marīcir marutām asmi nakṣatrāṇām ahaṁ śaśī || 21 ||

Among the Ādityas [3], I am Viṣṇu. Of luminous objects, I am the radiant Sun. Of the Maruts [4], I am Marīci, and among the stars, I am the Moon. (21)

vedānāṁ sāma-vedo'smi devānām asmi vāsavaḥ |
indriyāṇāṁ manaścāsmi bhūtānām asmi cetanā || 22 ||

Of the *Vedas*, I am the *Sāma Veda* [5]. I am Indra among the gods. Among the senses, I am the mind, and among living beings, I am consciousness. (22)

rudrāṇāṁ śaṅkaraścāsmi vitteśo yakṣa-rakṣasām |
vasūnāṁ pāvakaścāsmi meruḥ śikhariṇām aham || 23 ||

Of the Rudras [6], I am Śaṅkara. Among the Yakṣas [7] and Rākṣasas, I am Kubera [8]. Of the Vasus [9], I am Agni. Of the peaked mountains, I am Meru [10]. (23)

purodhasāṁ ca mukhyaṁ māṁ viddhi pārtha bṛhaspatim |
senānīnām ahaṁ skandaḥ sarasām asmi sāgaraḥ || 24 ||

Among the priests, O Arjuna, know Me to be the chief: Bṛhaspati [11]. Among army generals, I am Skanda [12]. Among reservoirs of water, I am the ocean. (24)

maharṣīṇāṁ bhṛgur ahaṁ girām-asmy-ekam akṣaram |
yajñānāṁ japa-yajño'smi sthāvarāṇāṁ himālāyaḥ || 25 ||

Among the great sages, I am Bhṛgu [13]. Among words, I am the single syllable *oṁ*. Among sacrifices, I am the sacrifice of *japa* [14]. Among immovable things, I am the Himalayas. (25)

aśvatthaḥ sarva vṛkṣāṇāṁ devarṣīṇāṁ ca nāradaḥ |
gandharvāṇāṁ citrarathaḥ siddhānāṁ kapilo muniḥ || 26 ||

Of trees, I am the Āśvattha [15]. Among celestial seers, I am Nārada [16]. Of the Gandharvas [17], I am Citraratha and among the perfected beings, I am Kapila [18]. (26)

uccaiḥśravasam aśvānāṁ viddhi mām amṛtodbhavam |
airāvataṁ gajendrāṇāṁ narāṇāṁ ca narādhipam || 27 ||

Of horses, know Me to be Uccaiḥśravas [19] born from the Churning of the Ocean of Milk [20]. Among the lords of elephants, I am Airāvata [21], and among humankind, I am the ruler. (27)

āyudhānām ahaṁ vajraṁ dhenūnām asmi kāmadhuk |
prajanaścāsmi kandarpaḥ sarpāṇām asmi vāsukiḥ || 28 ||

Among weapons, I am the *vajra* [22]. Among cows, I am Kāmadhenu [23]. Of the causes of procreation, I am Kandarpa [24]. Among serpents, I am Vāsuki [25]. (28)

anantaścāsmi nāgānāṁ varuṇo yādasām aham |
pitṝṇām aryamā cāsmi yamaḥ saṁyamatām aham || 29 ||

Amongst the Nāgas, I am Ananta [26]. Of those who live in the water, I am Varuṇa [27]. Of the ancestors, I am Aryamā and among those who enforce the law, I am Yama [28]. (29)

prahlādaścāsmi daityānāṁ kālaḥ kalayatām aham |
mṛgāṇāṁ ca mṛgendro'haṁ vainateyaśca pakṣiṇām || 30 ||

Among Daityas [29], I am Prahlāda and among that which controls, I am Time. Of beasts, I am the lion, and of birds, I am Garuḍa [30]. (30)

pavanaḥ pavatām asmi rāmaḥ śastra-bhṛtām aham |
jhaṣāṇāṁ makaraś-cāsmi srotasām-asmi jāhnavī || 31 ||

Of moving things, I am the wind. Among warriors, I am Rāma. Among fishes, I am the shark, and amongst rivers, I am Gaṅgā. (31)

sargāṇām ādir-antaśca madhyaṁ caivāham arjuna |
adhyātma vidyā vidyānāṁ vādaḥ pravadatām aham || 32 ||

O Arjuna, in relation to beings, I am the beginning and the end, and also the middle. Amongst knowledge, I am the knowledge of the Self. In the discipline of debate, I am the ultimate conclusion. (32)

akṣarāṇām akāro'smi dvandavaḥ sāmāsikasya ca |
aham evākṣayaḥ kālo dhātā'haṁ viśvato mukhaḥ || 33 ||

Among the letters of the alphabet, I am 'A'. Among compound words, I am the dual compound; I am Myself everlasting Time, and I am the Creator, facing every direction. (33)

mṛtyuḥ sarva-haraś-cāham udbhavaśca bhaviṣyatām |
kīrtiḥ śrīr-vāk ca nārīṇāṁ smṛtir-medhā dhṛtiḥ kṣamā || 34 ||

I am death who destroys everyone. I am the origin of all that shall be born. Among the feminine qualities, I am fame, prosperity, eloquence, memory, intelligence, endurance and forgiveness. (34)

bṛhatsāma tathā sāmnāṁ gāyatrī chandasām aham |
māsānāṁ mārgaśīrṣo'ham ṛtūnāṁ kusumākaraḥ || 35 ||

Of the *Sāma Veda* hymns, I am the *Bṛhat-sāma* hymn [31] and among *Vedic* metres, I am the Gāyatrī [32]. Of months, I am Mārgaśīrṣa [33]. Of the seasons, I am the season of flowers (spring). (35)

dyūtaṁ chalayatām asmi tejas tejasvinām aham |
jayo'smi vyavasāyo'smi sattvaṁ sattvavatām aham || 36 ||

Of fraudulent activities, I am gambling. I am the brilliance of the brilliant, I am victory, I am effort, I am the strength of the strong. (36)

vṛṣṇīnāṁ vāsudevo'smi pāṇḍavānāṁ dhanañjayaḥ |
munīnām apy-ahaṁ vyāsaḥ kavīnām uśanā kaviḥ || 37 ||

Of the Vṛṣṇi clan [34], I am Vāsudeva. Of the Pāṇḍavas, I am Arjuna. Among sages, I am Vyāsa [35] and among the great thinkers, I am Śukra. (37)

daṇḍo damayatām asmi nītir-asmi jigīṣatām |
maunaṁ caivāsmi guhyānāṁ jñānaṁ jñānavatām aham || 38 ||

Of the means of enforcing law, I am the principle of punishment. Among conquerors, I am diplomacy. Of secrets, I am silence, and of those who are wise, I am wisdom. (38)

yaccāpi sarva bhūtānāṁ bījaṁ tad aham arjuna |
na tadasti vinā yat syān mayā bhūtaṁ carācaram || 39 ||

Know that I am the seed of all living beings. There is nothing moving or unmoving that can exist without Me. (39)

nānto'sti mama divyānāṁ vibhūtīnāṁ parantapa |
eṣa tūddeśataḥ prokto vibhūter vistaro mayā || 40 ||

Understand that I have only briefly described My manifestations, for there is no limit to My divine glories, O Arjuna. (40)

yad yad vibhūtimat sattvaṁ śrīmad ūrjitam eva ca |
tat tad evāvagaccha tvaṁ mama tejo'ṁśa saṁbhavam || 41 ||

Know for certain that whenever something displays its splendour or power, it comes from just a part of My potency. (41)

athavā bahunaitena kiṁ jñānena tavārjuna |
viṣṭabhyāham-idaṁ kṛtsnam ekāṁśena sthito jagat || 42 ||

But of what use to you is all this knowledge, O Arjuna? With just a fraction of Myself I exist, sustaining this whole universe. (42)

'The Lord is not just a normal ordinary person, even if He appears very human. By being among the people on the battlefield in the Kurukṣetra, everybody could see Kṛṣṇa as normal, but in reality, He was God Himself. It is through Him that creation happens. It is through Him that creation is preserved, and it is through Him that dissolution happens.'

'He is revealing to Arjuna His omnipresence and His identity with all. All creatures which have been created, whatever we see around us, the "moving or unmoving", the "animate or inanimate" are all pervaded by Him alone. So nothing is devoid of the presence of God. The one who looks for Him in their own consciousness will find Him. The one who looks for Him in the stone, will find Him. The one who looks for Him in the tree, will find Him. But the true knowledge of this is to long for God only, not to long for the tree or the creatures of the trees. It's to go beyond this! And then with true knowledge, one realises the presence of the Lord, and that everything is pervaded only by Him. All existence is only Him. So when one has this true knowledge, this true wisdom, one should think only of God, in whatever one is doing. Wherever the mind runs, let it come back, and be focused on the Lord Himself.'

'Here Bhagavān says that the glories are endless and countless, they are so numerous, that what He can say about the glories is just a summary. In all universes, there's no limit to His glory. He says, "What I have given you here is just a fraction, a portion, of these glories. And it is very difficult for a normal human mind to understand these small splinters I have given you."'

'The realised soul, the one who has ascended towards God consciousness, who has attained God-realisation, perceives the eternal Supreme Lord with full knowledge and full awareness.'

'So, all these manifestations are sustained by just a fraction of Himself alone, it's not His fullness. But, in that fraction resides the fullness. However, the fullness doesn't reside in that fraction.'

Chapter Ten Verses: Key Terms

[1] **Seven great seers** – created by Brahmā and known as the *Sapta-ṛṣis*, they are responsible for guiding the human race during the four *yugas* (ages). They are in complete communion with the Lord at all times and work towards maintaining a balance on Earth. Before them, and also born from Brahmā, were the four Kumāras: Sanaka, Sanātana, Sanandana, Sanat-kumāra.

[2] **Manu** – title given to the first man of every age (known as a *manvantara*). All humans are believed to have descended from his lineage.

[3] **Ādityas** – these are the twelve deities which take the role of the Sun. Every month these deities change, and out of them, Viṣṇu is the most radiant.

[4] **Maruts** – identified as wind deities, each with a specific function. All of them are presided over by Marīci.

[5] **Sāma Veda** – one of the four *Vedas*. The *Sāma Veda* contains melodies and chants.

[6] **Rudras** – described as loyal companions of Rudra, also identified as Lord Śiva. Rudras are messengers and different aspects of Śiva and are fearsome in nature. Śaṅkara is commonly known as the ascetic form of Śiva who dwells in Mount Kailāśa.

[7] **Yakṣas** – class of nature spirits who serve Kubera (deity responsible for wealth).

[8] **Kubera** – deity responsible for material wealth, and king of the Yakṣas (nature spirits).

[9] **Vasus** – eight elemental deities representing different aspects of nature. The element of fire is presided over by Agni.

[10] **Meru** – the sacred five-peaked mountain, considered to be the centre of the physical, metaphysical and spiritual universe. It resides in the spiritual realm and cannot be perceived with the physical eyes.

[11] **Bṛhaspati** – deity responsible for wisdom and is the preceptor of the *devas* (demigods).

[12] **Skanda** – born from the third eye of Śiva, he is the brother of Gaṇeśa, and leads the celestial armies against the *asuras*.

[13] **Bhṛgu** – one of the seven great *Sapta-ṛṣis* born from Brahmā.

[14] **Japa** – meditative repetition of a *mantra* or a Divine Name.

[15] **Āśvattha tree** – a sacred fig tree mentioned in various Hindu texts.

[16] **Nārada** – a great *Vedic* sage born from Brahmā and one the foremost devotees of the Lord. He wanders the universe imparting the knowledge of devotion.

[17] **Gandharvas** – a group of celestial deities skilled in various arts such as music and dancing. Among the Gandharvas, Citraratha is said to be highly skilled in the art of singing.

[18] **Kapila** – Incarnation of the Lord and a great sage who taught his mother Devahūtī the knowledge of the Self, as mentioned in the *Śrīmad Bhāgavatam*.

[19] **Uccaiḥśravas** – beautiful white horse produced from the Ocean of Milk and claimed by Bali, the leader of the *asuras*.

[20] **Churning of the Ocean of Milk** – one of the central events in the eternal struggle between the *devas* (demigods) and *asuras*. Both groups churned the Ocean of Milk to obtain the nectar of immortality (*amṛta*).

[21] **Airāvata** – considered to be the best among elephants, and the vehicle of the king of the demigods (Indra).

[22] **Vajra** – the main weapon of the king of the demigods (Indra) in the form of a thunderbolt.

[23] **Kāmadhenu** – the mother of all cows who provides her owners with whatever they desire.

[24] **Kandarpa** – deity responsible for human love. Most commonly associated with Cupid in the West.

[25] **Vāsuki** – king of the serpents, who helped in the Churning of the Ocean of Milk.

[26] **Nāgas (Ananta)** – half human/half serpent beings that reside in the netherworld. Ananta is the king of the Nāgas and eternal servant of Viṣṇu. Viṣṇu is often depicted resting on Ananta.

[27] **Varuṇa** – deity responsible for the oceans.

[28] **Yama** – the lord of death who rules the netherworld. For those bound to this material world, he delivers justice for each soul.

[29] **Daityas** – a clan of *asuras* who are eternally engaged in a fight with the *devas* (demigods). Prahlāda was a great king of the *asuras* and devotee of the Lord. He played a central role in the incarnation of the Nārasiṁha-avatāra.

[30] **Garuḍa** – considered to be the best among birds, in the form of an eagle. He is the vehicle and eternal servant of Viṣṇu.

[31] **Bṛhat-sāma** – a hymn which praises the Lord. The *Bṛhat-sāma* is chanted at the conclusion of auspicious *Vedic* ceremonies.

[32] **Gāyatrī-mantra** – highly revered *mantra* from the *Ṛg Veda* dedicated to the Sun deity and is chanted widely by Hindus.

[33] **Mārgaśīrṣa** – the ninth month in the Hindu lunar calendar when grains from agriculture fields are collected by farmers to earn money and make their living in India.

[34] **Vṛṣṇi Clan** – ancient *Vedic* Indian clan which Kṛṣṇa was born into. Vasudeva, who belonged to the Vṛṣṇi clan was the father of Kṛṣṇa.

[35] **Vyāsa** – a great *Vedic* sage who organised and divided the *Vedas*. He authored many of the puranic scriptures, but is perhaps most famous for authoring the *Mahābhārata* and the *Śrīmad Bhāgavatam*.

CHAPTER ELEVEN
VIŚVARŪPA-DARŚANA-YOGA
THE COSMIC FORM

Up until now, Kṛṣṇa has only described His identity as the Supreme Lord. But this description has awakened Arjuna's longing to experience this divinity first-hand. As a result, Arjuna requests Kṛṣṇa to actually show him that which he has heard so much about. But this cosmic form (Viśvarūpa), is beyond the material world. As an act of grace therefore, Kṛṣṇa gifts Arjuna divine vision through which he can behold this inconceivable form.

Because of this grace, Arjuna can suddenly see all creation and all living beings present in this one Person. There are endless faces, weapons and ornaments with unimaginable effulgence. All the *Vedic* gods and *ṛṣis* are glorifying Kṛṣṇa in this infinite space. Amongst the many arms, bellies and mouths, there are gnashing teeth and blazing fires. In front of this terrible form, Arjuna is unable to compose himself. Amongst everything else, he sees the enemies being sucked into the mouths of the Lord. Trembling with fear, Arjuna bows down and begs to know who Kṛṣṇa really is.

Kṛṣṇa replies that He is Time, the great destroyer of worlds. He assures Arjuna that the result of the war has already been decided, and that he is merely an instrument. Overwhelmed with emotion, Arjuna utters prayers to the Lord and begs forgiveness for any offences done out of ignorance. Arjuna asks Kṛṣṇa to relieve him of this experience and show him instead His four-handed form. The Lord explains that this cosmic form which has never been seen before, was given out of grace and cannot be obtained through any ritual or austerity. It is only by devotion that one can know, see and enter into Him.

VERSES 1-4: ARJUNA'S REQUEST TO SEE KṚṢṆA'S COSMIC FORM

śrī arjuna uvāca
mad-anugrahāya paramaṁ guhyam adhyātma saṁjñitam |
yat tvayoktaṁ vacas tena moho 'yaṁ vigato mama || 1 ||

Arjuna says:
Out of compassion for Me, You have revealed the most profound mysteries; this spiritual knowledge has completely removed my delusion. (1)

bhavāpyayau hi bhūtānāṁ śrutau vistaraśo mayā |
tvattaḥ kamala-patrākṣa mahātmyam api cāvyayam || 2 ||

O Kṛṣṇa, I have heard in great detail about the beginning and end of all beings, as well as Your inexhaustible glory. (2)

evam etad yathāttha tvam-ātmānaṁ parameśvara |
draṣṭum icchāmi te rūpam aiśvaraṁ puruṣottama || 3 ||

O Supreme Lord, I know You are everything You have described Yourself to be. Now I actually long to see that glorious form of Yours, O Supreme Person. (3)

manyase yadi tacchakyaṁ mayā draṣṭum iti prabho |
yogeśvara tato me tvaṁ darśayāmānam avyayam || 4 ||

O Lord, if you believe it is possible, then reveal Yourself completely to me, show me Your unlimited universal Self, O Lord of *yoga*. (4)

'Here, Arjuna is expressing his gratitude. As long as a *bhakta*, a devotee, hangs onto his own ideas, and as long as he relies on his own will, or effort or practices, but doesn't count on the divine grace of the Lord, he will not achieve a higher state. By one's own effort one can only reach a certain level. But… when someone has completely surrendered to Him, one counts not on one's own effort but on the grace of the Lord, the grace of Kṛṣṇa, and knows that everything is His grace. Whatever happens, whatever is given, is the grace of God. Life itself is the grace of God. It is the grace of the Lord Himself that brings each *bhakta* on each step of their path, to the point where each *bhakta* has to be.'

'Of course, for a long time he has heard from others – he has heard from Bhīṣma, he has heard from all the sages – how great Kṛṣṇa is. He has heard all the *līlā* of Kṛṣṇa. But at this point, he realises that due to his pride, due to a lack of this true knowledge, he could not perceive this – he used to see Kṛṣṇa only as his friend, his best friend.'

'As Arjuna is asking the Lord to see His divine form, it may appear as if there is still doubt. If somebody asks this, you will say, "You want to see because you don't trust fully in me!" But it's not like this…there is no trace of doubt in him. He had full trust in the virtues of the Lord, full trust in His glory, His reality, His power. But due to this yearning (which the Lord Himself put inside of Arjuna), he asks Him for this.

'Let's say that you know someone who is truthful – he always speaks the truth, nothing else. And you have heard from some friends that this man has a philosopher's stone. You know this person very well, and you know that whatever he says is not untrue. You have full trust in this person. You know his whole life is based on the truth. But you have heard that he has a philosopher's stone. What would your reaction be? First of all, you would not say directly, "Let me see!" Firstly, to be polite, you would say, "I have heard that you have the philosopher's stone?" And the person would say, "Yes, I do." What would be your next question? It would be "Let me see!" You would ask this question because you want to see it – if you didn't want to see it, you would not ask the question. It's not about doubting the person. But this is the curiosity of humans, the excitement. Due to this excitement, you ask to see it. It is the same with Arjuna here. It's not because he doubts the Lord; he has full trust in the

Lord. It is due to this excitement, due to this faith, and the trust that he has in the word of Bhagavān Kṛṣṇa. There is no slight doubt at all. And due to this child-like excitement, he says with folded hands, "I desire to see Your cosmic form!" This is full trust, full love!'

VERSES 5-8: ARJUNA IS GIVEN DIVINE VISION

śrī bhagavān uvāca
paśya me pārtha rūpāṇi śataśo'tha sahasraśaḥ |
nānā vidhāni divyāni nānā varṇā kṛtīni ca || 5 ||

Lord Kṛṣṇa says:
Behold Arjuna, there are hundreds and thousands of My divine forms, of different shapes, colours and sizes. (5)

paśyādityān vasūn rudrān aśvinau marutas tathā |
bahūny-adṛṣṭa-pūrvāṇi paśyāścaryāṇi bhārata || 6 ||

Arjuna, see the Ādityas, the Vasus, the Rudras, the two Aśvin-kumāras [1] and the Maruts. Behold the many wondrous things which have never before been seen. (6)

ihaikasthaṁ jagat kṛtsnaṁ paśyādya sacarācaram |
mama dehe guḍākeśa yac cānyad draṣṭum icchasi || 7 ||

See Arjuna, the whole universe with all the movable and non-moveable things, and indeed whatever else you wish to see, all existing in one place within My body. (7)

na tu māṁ śakyase draṣṭum anenaiva sva-cakṣuṣā |
divyaṁ dadāmi te cakṣuḥ paśya me yogam aiśvaram || 8 ||

But you will not be able to see this with your physical eyes. Therefore, I give you divine eyes. Behold My mystic power. (8)

'The Lord, who is inside the heart of all, the Lord that dwells within the core of the *ātmā* Itself, knew why Arjuna couldn't see. Because Arjuna, even though he had transcended this doubt, is still searching in the outside reality. Even if his mind has no doubt, yet he has this one desire to see Him in His cosmic form. It's not that he doesn't believe what Kṛṣṇa is saying to him. He is drinking it fully. Kṛṣṇa is standing in front of him saying, "This body itself, this body here, has everything here in front of you! All creation, all universes, all the stars, everything 'moving and unmoving', all the Ādityas, Rudras, everything!" And Arjuna is standing there looking at Him. Without any doubt, he is looking at His form that he knows. All this time, Arjuna has known Kṛṣṇa as his dear friend.'

'The physical eyes lack the faculty due to their limitation to seeing only matter. They hang only on matter, only on the limitation, so they can't grasp this reality. For this, other eyes must be given to see and perceive the cosmic form of the Lord. So the Lord endowed Arjuna with the cosmic power, the supernatural power, to have the real vision of the Lord Himself. You need divine eyes to perceive an innermost seeing. With these divine eyes, even if you appear as though you are looking outside, the vision is the inner vision, which projects itself outwardly.'

VERSES 9-14: THE COSMIC FORM OF KṚṢṆA REVEALED

sañjaya uvāca
evam uktvā tato rājan mahāyogeśvaro hariḥ |
darśayāmāsa pārthāya paramaṁ rūpam aiśvaram || 9 ||

Sañjaya says:
Having spoken thus O king, Śrī Kṛṣṇa, the great Lord of *yoga*, then revealed to Arjuna His supreme cosmic form. (9)

aneka vaktra nayanam anekādbhuta darśanam |
aneka divyābharaṇaṁ divyānekodyatāyudham || 10 ||

There were innumerable mouths and eyes and many other astonishing features. There were numerous divine ornaments and scores of divine weapons held aloft. (10)

divya mālyāmbaradharaṁ divya gandhānulepanam |
sarvāścaryam ayaṁ devam anantaṁ viśvato-mukham || 11 ||

He wore celestial garlands and garments, and He was anointed with divine perfumes. Facing all directions, He was full of wonders, resplendent and limitless. (11)

divi sūrya sahasrasya bhaved yugapad utthitā |
yadi bhāḥ sadṛśī sā syād bhāsas tasya mahātmanaḥ || 12 ||

If a thousand suns, each with blazing effulgence, were to rise all at once in the sky, perhaps that magnificence might be something like the radiance of that Supreme Being. (12)

tatraikasthaṁ jagat kṛtsnaṁ pravibhaktam enekadhā |
apaśyad deva-devasya śarīre pāṇḍavas tadā || 13 ||

In that cosmic form, Arjuna saw the entire universe with all its divisions situated in one place, all within the body of the God of gods. (13)

tataḥ sa vismayāviṣṭo hṛṣṭa-romā dhanañjayaḥ |
praṇamya śirasā devaṁ kṛtāñjalir abhāṣata || 14 ||

Then Arjuna, overcome with amazement, his hair standing on end, bowed his head to the Lord, and with palms pressed together, began to speak. (14)

'With this spiritual vision, Arjuna is baffled; he doesn't know what to express, or how to express himself, because he has the ultimate sense of devotion. He just kneels in deep devotion in front of the Lord. And seeing this magnitude aspect, he can't do anything. At that moment he realises how small he is in the universe. He looks at the Lord with His cosmic body in awe, wonder, and amazement.

'He can't say this is beautiful. This is the beauty of beauties, it is beyond beautiful; the greatest of the great; and everything is sublime in itself. He even feels fear looking at this vision, because he realises at that moment how small he is in comparison to the Lord. Arjuna realises, "I, who have been looking at the greatness of the Lord Himself, have realised that I wanted to understand Him, but how could I?" He is trembling, thinking, "He, who I took as my friend, who was related to me, my goodness!" This is when ignorance is removed; one perceives the Lord in His glory everywhere. But this is more than His glory. This is His cosmic form that never, ever, had God manifested and shown to anyone.'

VERSES 15-31: ARJUNA DESCRIBES THE LORD'S FORM

arjuna uvāca
paśyāmi devāṁs tava deva dehe
sarvāṁs tathā bhūta viśeṣa saṅghān |
brahmāṇam īśaṁ kamalāsanastham
ṛṣiṁśca sarvān uragāṁśca divyān || 15 ||

Arjuna says:
I see, O Lord, in Your body all the gods and the whole host of living beings. There is Brahmā sitting on a lotus, Śiva, the sages and the celestial serpents. (15)

aneka bāhūdara vaktra netraṁ
paśyāmi tvāṁ sarvato'nanta rūpam |
nāntaṁ na madhyaṁ na punastavādiṁ
paśyāmi viśveśvara viśvarūpa || 16 ||

With Your innumerable arms, torsos, mouths and eyes, I see Your infinite form on all sides. There is no end, middle or beginning to You, for You are the Lord of the universe, and the universe is Your body. (16)

kirīṭinaṁ gadinaṁ cakriṇaṁ ca
tejorāśiṁ sarvato dīptimantam |
paśyāmi tvāṁ durnirīkṣyaṁ samantād
dīptānalārka-dyutim aprameyam || 17 |

I behold You with crown, mace and discus. Your blazing effulgence radiates in all directions. Even though You are everywhere, You are hard to look at, for Your brilliance is immeasurable like a burning fire or the sun. (17)

tvam akṣaraṁ paramaṁ veditavyaṁ
tvam-asya viśvasya paraṁ nidhānam |
tvam-avyayaḥ śāśvata dharma goptā
sanātanas tvaṁ puruṣo mato me || 18 ||

You are the Imperishable, Supreme One to be realised. You are the Supreme Abode of this universe. You are unchanging; the Guardian of the Eternal Law, I know You are the eternal Supreme Being. (18)

anādi madhyāntam ananta-vīryam
ananta bāhuṁ śaśi-sūrya netram |
paśyami tvāṁ dīpta hutāśa vaktraṁ
sva-tejasā viśvam idaṁ tapantam || 19 ||

I see You without beginning, middle and end. Your creative power is infinite. You have countless arms, the Sun and Moon are Your eyes. Your mouth is blazing with fire, searing the entire universe with Your radiance. (19)

dyāvāpṛthivyor idam antaraṁ hi
vyāptaṁ tvayaikena diśaśca sarvāḥ |
dṛṣṭvādbhutaṁ rūpam idaṁ tavograṁ
loka trayaṁ pravyathitaṁ mahātman || 20 ||

The space between Heaven and Earth, and all the directions, are filled by You alone. Beholding Your awesome, yet terrible form, O Kṛṣṇa, the three worlds [2] are trembling. (20)

amī hi tvāṁ surasaṅghā viśanti
kecid bhītāḥ prāñjalayo gṛṇanti |
svastītyuktvā maharṣi siddha-saṅghāḥ
stuvanti tvāṁ stutibhiḥ puṣkalābhiḥ || 21 ||

The demigods are entering into You, and some out of fear pray to You with palms joined. The different sages and perfected beings cry out, 'Hail to You!', as they glorify You with *Vedic* hymns and words of praise. (21)

rudrādityā vasavo ye ca sādhyā
viśve'śvinau marutaścoṣmapāśca |
gandharva yakṣāsura siddha-saṅghā
vīkṣante tvāṁ vismitāścaiva sarve || 22 ||

The Rudras, the Ādityas, the Vasus, the Sādhyas [3], the Viśvadevas [4], the Aśvin-kumāras, the Maruts, the ancestors, and the hosts of Gandharvas, Yakṣas, *asuras*, and Siddhas — all gaze upon You in amazement. (22)

rūpaṁ mahatte bahu vaktra netraṁ
mahābāho bahu-bāhūru-pādam |
bahūdaraṁ bahu daṁṣṭrā-karālaṁ
dṛṣṭvā lokāḥ pravyathitās tathāham || 23 ||

Your great form has many faces and eyes; there are many arms, thighs, feet. It has many bellies and dreadful fangs. O Kṛṣṇa, beholding this form, all beings are terrified including myself. (23)

nabhaḥ-spṛśaṁ dīptam aneka varṇaṁ
vyāttānanaṁ dīpta viśāla-netram |
dṛṣṭvā hi tvāṁ pravyathitāntarātmā
dhṛtiṁ na vindāmi śamaṁ ca viṣṇo || 24 ||

O Kṛṣṇa, on seeing You radiant and multi-coloured, touching the highest Heaven, with Your gaping mouths and huge glaring eyes, I am shaken to the core. I have lost all composure and peace. (24)

daṁṣṭrā-karālāni ca te mukhāni dṛṣṭvaiva kālānala sannibhāni |
diśo na jāne na labheca śarma prasīda deveśa jagannivāsa || 25 ||

Seeing Your mouths and awesome teeth, which are like the flames of cosmic destruction, I am completely disorientated and confused. Have mercy on me, O Lord of the Devas! O Abode of the universe! (25)

amī ca tvaṁ dhṛtarāṣṭrasya putrāḥ s
arve sahaivāvanipāla saṅghaiḥ |
bhīṣmo droṇaḥ sūta-putras tathāsau
sahāsmadīyairapi yodha-mukhyaiḥ || 26 ||
vaktrāṇi te tvaramāṇā viśanti
daṁṣṭrā-karālāni bhayānakāni |
kecid vilagnā daśanāntareṣu
saṅdṛśyante cūrṇitair-uttamāṅgaiḥ || 27 ||

All the sons of Dhṛtarāṣṭra, the other kings, Bhīṣma, Droṇa and Karṇa, along with the leading warriors of our side, are all rushing into Your fearsome mouths with terrible fangs. Some are even caught between Your teeth and are having their heads crushed. (26-27)

yathā nadīnāṁ bahavo'mbuvegāḥ
samudram evābhimukhā dravanti |
tathā tavāmī naraloka vīrā
viśanti vaktrāṇyabhito vijvalanti || 28 ||

As the many rivers rush towards the ocean, so do these heroes of the world enter Your blazing mouths. (28)

yathā pradīptaṁ jvalanaṁ pataṅgā viśanti nāśāya samṛddha-vegāḥ |
tathaiva nāśāya viśanti lokās tavāpi vaktrāṇi samṛddha-vegāḥ || 29 ||

As moths rush irresistibly into a blazing fire, so too do people of the world madly rush into Your mouths to meet their destruction. (29)

lelihyase grasamānaḥ samantāl
lokān samagrān vadanair jvaladbhiḥ |
tejobhir āpūrya jagat samagraṁ
bhāsas tavogrāḥ pratapanti viṣṇo || 30 ||

O Viṣṇu! Devouring all the worlds on every side, You lick them up with Your flaming mouths. Your brilliant rays scorch the whole universe, filling it with their radiance. (30)

ākhyāhi me ko bhavān-ugra-rūpo
namo'stu te deva-vara prasīda |
vijñātum icchāmi bhavantam-ādyaṁ
na hi prajānāmi tava pravṛttim || 31 ||

O Lord, with this fearsome form. Tell me who You are! Salutations to You, O Supreme God. Be merciful, You are the Original Person and I desire to know You. I cannot comprehend Your actions. (31)

'Here Arjuna is in front of God Himself, shining like 1000 suns all together. What he sees at that moment is incomparable. But yet, due to the divine vision, he could perceive this transient infinite Sun, this effulgence of the Lord as the cosmic Light itself.'

'Arjuna beholds in the person of the Supreme Deity the entire universe: many visions and shapes; each of the gods that Bhagavān Kṛṣṇa has mentioned earlier are inside of Him in their fullness; all the beasts, animals, demigods, plants; all creation – from the smallest one to the biggest one; are all present inside of Him. All the pleasures; all the pains; all the joys appear in His cosmic body.'

'Here, note one thing – this cosmic form of the Lord in front of him on the battlefield, nobody else can see. For those on the outside, the Kauravas and the Pāṇḍavas, they can only see Arjuna standing in front of Kṛṣṇa full of deep emotion. They can feel that something else is happening, but they can't understand what it is. They are wondering, "What is happening?" Because this vision doesn't happen on this field, in this reality; it surpasses this reality. With the divine sight that Arjuna has received, he perceives the Lord in His glory. Everything on the battlefield disappears. He sees only the Lord there in His cosmic form.'

VERSES 32-34: KṚṢṆA IS TIME, THE GREAT DESTROYER

śrī bhagavān uvāca
kālo'smi loka-kṣaya-kṛt pravṛddho
lokān samāhartum iha pravṛttaḥ |
ṛte'pi tvāṁ na bhaviṣyanti sarve
ye'vasthitāḥ pratyanīkeṣu yodhāḥ || 32 ||

Lord Kṛṣṇa says:
I am Time, the mighty force which brings destruction to the world. I have manifested to destroy all these worlds. Even without you, none of the warriors gathered here for battle shall survive. (32)

tasmāt tvam uttiṣṭha yaśo labhasva
jitvā śatrūn bhuṅkṣva rājyaṁ samṛddham |
mayaivaite nihatāḥ pūrvam eva
nimitta-mātraṁ bhava savyasācin || 33 ||

Therefore rise and win glory! Conquer your enemies and enjoy a prosperous kingdom. They have already been slain by Me; therefore, you should act merely as My instrument, O great Archer! (33)

droṇaṁ ca bhīṣmaṁ ca jayadrathaṁ ca
karṇaṁ tathā'nyānapi yodhavīrān |
mayā hatāṁs-tvaṁ jahi mā vyathiṣṭhā
yudhyasva jetāsi raṇe sapatnān || 34 ||

Droṇa, Bhīṣma, Jayadratha, Karṇa, as well as other mighty warriors, have already been destroyed by Me, therefore, kill them without hesitation. You shall surely defeat your enemies in battle. (34)

'Bhagavān again is reminding Arjuna that everything created through *prakṛti* has a certain time. There is a beginning and there is an end. Everything gets destroyed and everything gets dissolved... This body was taken from the five elements and it will go back to the five elements. What stays is the *ātmā*, the soul which is eternal. That's the reality. Everything that is bound by time, everything that is bound by limitation, will disappear.'

'All the galaxies and all the spheres and all the many, many thousands of worlds go into His mouth and dissolve, and then new creation happens. This annihilation and creation happens continuously. So on one side of the Lord all the worlds enter His mouth, disappear, and finish! But on the other side, new worlds come out, new births occur, new creation arises.'

'Bhagavān says to Arjuna, "It is meant for these people to be killed. Whether you want to kill them or not, they will die! I don't need you." What He is showing to Arjuna here is that in His cosmic form they were all dying. Bhagavān is saying, "Arjuna it is not you who will kill them! Are you thinking that you will take your weapon, the Gāṇḍīva, and shoot them, and they will be dead? No, my dear! These mighty heroes can't be killed like that. It is not you who will do this; It is Me, the Supreme Lord, who will do it!"'

'Here the Lord is saying to all, "Everything is in the divine plan."... Nothing can happen without Him willing it, and He plans everything beforehand. He lets Māyā guide everybody, to bring them to a certain place. And then people say, "Yippee, I have made it!"'

'The *bhakta* that is completely surrendered to the Lord – who realises the Lord – knows that the Lord is guiding them in every part of their life. Each part of their life and whatever happens in their life is being guided by the Lord Himself. There is nothing that is not being guided by the Lord. This is all His will. All of you, all creation that we see around us, is Him. You just need to be in tune with it. It is like a radio: the frequencies are in the atmosphere, but for you to hear the beautiful music or the news, you have to tune the radio to the frequency that you want to listen to. So, if your longing is to surrender to the Lord, you have to tune your radio to spirituality; tune your radio to *bhakti*, to Love! And when your radio is at the right frequency, you will hear it clearly.'

'In life, whenever a certain challenge arises, you should not run away. Bear in mind that all comes from God. Even the challenges come from God for you to become stronger. And when you start accepting the challenges, He Himself comes in the form of strength and power. He strengthens you; He gives you the strength to go through it, and to be free from the problem in the challenge.'

'Here again, Kṛṣṇa is reminding Arjuna of his *dharma*. Again, He is reminding everyone of their *dharma* in life. Wherever God has given you a certain duty in life, happily accept it! Do it with loving surrender to the Lord. Even if your mind doesn't like it on the outside, learn to love it. The moment you learn to love what God has given you, it will flow very easily. And even if you have to change, He will make you change. He will put you in a better place. But if you have not been able to handle this place, what better place are you looking for? It will be similar! You will say, "Oh my goodness I have changed my job. I looked for another job, but here I find the same." Do you know the saying, "Jumping from the frying pan into the fire?" However, if you accept your *dharma* and move freely with it, the Lord carries you and makes everything easy.'

VERSES 35-46: ARJUNA IS OVERCOME WITH FEAR

sañjaya uvāca
etacchrutvā vacanaṁ keśavasya
kṛtāñjalir vepamānaḥ kirīṭī |
namaskṛtvā bhūya evāha kṛṣṇaṁ
sagadgadaṁ bhītabhītaḥ praṇamya || 35 ||

Sañjaya says:
Having heard the words of Śrī Kṛṣṇa, Arjuna placed his palms together and bowed down. Trembling with fear and awe, he paid his respects and spoke in a choked voice. (35)

arjuna uvāca
sthāne hṛṣīkeśa tava prakīrtyā
jagat prahṛṣyaty-anurajyate ca |
rakṣāṁsi bhītāni diśo dravanti
sarve namasyanti ca siddha-saṅghāḥ || 36 ||

Arjuna says:
O Kṛṣṇa, it is right that the world is delighted by You and glorifies You. While the terrified demons flee in all directions, the hosts of perfected beings bow down to You. (36)

kasmācca te na nameran mahātman
garīyase brahmaṇo'pyādikartre |
ananta deveśa jagan-nivāsa
tvam akṣaraṁ sadasat tatparaṁ yat || 37 ||

And why should they not bow down to You, for You are greater than even Brahmā. O Infinite One, Lord of gods, O Abode of the universe! You are the Imperishable Brahman, the manifest and the unmanifest, and that which is beyond both. (37)

tvam ādidevaḥ puruṣaḥ purāṇas
tvam asya viśvasya paraṁ nidhānam |
vettāsi vedyaṁ ca paraṁ ca dhāma
tvayā tataṁ viśvam ananta rūpa || 38 ||

You are the Original Godhead and the most Ancient Person. You are the ultimate support of the universe. You are the Knower and the knowable. You are the supreme goal. This whole universe is pervaded by You, O Lord of infinite forms. (38)

vāyur-yamo'gnir-varuṇaḥ śaśāṅkaḥ
prajāpatis-tvaṁ prapitā-mahaśca |
namo namaste'stu sahasra-kṛtvaḥ
punaśca bhūyo'pi namo namaste || 39 ||

You are Vāyu [5], Yama, Agni, Varuṇa, the Moon, Prajāpati [6] and the great-grandsire; I bow down to You, I bow down to You a thousand times! Then I still bow down to You! (39)

namaḥ purastād atha pṛṣṭhas-te
namo'stu te sarvata eva sarva |
ananta-vīryāmita-vikramas-tvaṁ
sarvaṁ samāpnoṣi tato'si sarvaḥ || 40 ||

I bow to You from the front and the back! I bow down to You from all directions, since You are everything. O Lord who has unbounded power and limitless might, You pervade all beings and therefore are all that is. (40)

sakheti matvā prasabhaṁ yaduktaṁ
he kṛṣṇa he yādava he sakheti |
ajānatā mahimānaṁ tavedaṁ
mayā pramādāt praṇayena vāpi || 41 ||
yaccāvahāsārtham asatkṛto 'si
vihāra śayyāsana bhojaneṣu |
eko'thavāpy acyuta tat-samakṣaṁ
tat kṣāmaye tvām aham aprameyam || 42 ||

Either through negligence or affection, I was unaware of Your majesty. Thinking of You as a friend, I spoke rashly and addressed You saying, 'O Kṛṣṇa, O Yādava [7], O friend'. Whatever disrespect I have shown You, while joking, playing, resting, while we were sitting or eating together, while alone or in the presence of others — I beg Your forgiveness, for You are beyond understanding. (41-42)

pitāsi lokasya carācarasya
tvam-asya pūjyaśca gurur garīyān |
na tvat samo'sty abhyadhikaḥ kuto'nyo
lokatraye'py apratima-prabhāva || 43 ||

You are the Father of this world, of all moving and unmoving beings. You are its Teacher and the One most worthy of reverence. There is none equal to You. How then could there be another greater than You in the three realms? Your glory cannot be matched. (43)

tasmāt praṇamya praṇidhāya kāyaṁ
prasādaye tvām aham īśam īḍyam |
piteva putrasya sakheva sakhyuḥ
priyaḥ priyāyārhasi deva soḍhum || 44 ||

Therefore, bowing down and prostrating myself, I beg Your pardon, O adorable Lord. Please tolerate me as a father does his son, a friend does his friend, and a lover his beloved. (44)

adṛṣṭa-pūrvaṁ hṛṣito'smi dṛṣṭvā
bhayena ca pravyathitaṁ mano me |
tadeva me darśaya deva rūpaṁ
prasīda deveśa jagannivāsa || 45 ||

O Lord! I am delighted that I have seen what has never been seen before, but my mind is overwhelmed with anxiety. Be gracious and show me Your other form, O Lord of the gods! Abode of the universe! (45)

kirīṭinaṁ gadinaṁ cakra-hastam
icchāmi tvāṁ draṣṭum ahaṁ tathaiva |
tenaiva rūpeṇa catur-bhujena
sahasra-bāho bhava viśvamūrte || 46 ||

I wish to see You wearing a crown, holding a mace and discus in hand. O Viṣṇu! O Thousand-armed one! Show me once more Your four-armed form. (46)

'Because of all the mixed emotions Arjuna feels, he doesn't know what to do or what to say. He is super-shocked, his heart has shrunk inside him. He feels his body is full of electric currents, flowing everywhere inside his body. All his hairs are standing on end. He doesn't know what to do apart from bowing his head down, and with *śaraṇāgati*, with folded hands, falling at the Feet of the Lord. Overwhelmed with joy and wonder, he has seen that which sages and saints have not perceived. By the grace of the Lord Himself, because of the Love He has for His devotee, He has not denied him the ultimate vision.'

'Arjuna says, "There is nothing which is not You. You surpass the whole universe itself; everything in, out, left, right, up, down, is only You." Wherever Arjuna looks, whatever he does, there is not a small space where he cannot perceive the Lord. He is saying that in every single atom is the manifestation of Nārāyaṇa. And there is nothing other than Him. Although he praises Him, salutation upon salutation, this can't do justice to His greatness. Arjuna is filled with reverence, filled with gratitude that the Lord has permitted him to perceive this cosmic vision.'

'Arjuna asks the Lord for forgiveness for anything he has said to Kṛṣṇa in a certain tone, with arrogance or pride. Due to his ignorance, he has thought of Him as a friend and sometimes as a normal human being, and forgetting who He is, he has said many things. He has never had in mind that He is the Lord of lords, until he has seen this cosmic form of Lord Kṛṣṇa. And due to this intimacy – this thoughtless sense of fun that he had towards his friend – he didn't perceive the reality of who He is.

'It is very important to know where the *guru* stands and where the disciple stands. Even if the *guru* allows the disciple to be close, to be friends and dear, the *guru* always remains the *guru*. One must always know where one stands and not be fooled by the outside.'

'Bhagavān has not withdrawn his mind completely, He is still letting him feel his individual Self. Even if he knew that the Lord is all prevailing, yet the individual Self is separated. There is this intimacy; there is still this separation. This is how one can enjoy the beauty of the Lord. This is how one can drink this nectar! This is how one can enjoy the *līlā* of the Lord, the Love that emanates from God! If one would become fully merged with Him, one couldn't not enjoy that. This is the sweetest thing! This relationship that one can have with Bhagavān, when one can have a personal relationship with God, and can love Him! Then you can say, "Yes, I love God!" And not just by superficially saying,

"I love God, He is everywhere." But this is when you truly love Him; when all the *bhāva* [1] awakens inside of you; when you have this longing; your heart is in pain; you can't breathe; you can't for a single moment divert your mind left or right. Such a *bhāva* when –just by thinking of Him, by chanting His Name, wherever you are in the world – your mind, your heart is always with Him! It always runs to Him, as your heart always runs here, to the *āśrama*. Such devotion! Such surrender! Arjuna is rejoicing inside himself, but it is this separation which allows him to experience this wonder of the cosmic form of the Lord; that is how he could enjoy it. And this is most beautiful! Without this separation, there would not be this enjoyment! And this is the greatness of *bhakti*: you are not completely separated from the Lord but you enjoy the *līlā*, the love, the *bhāva* of serving Him, longing for Him, wanting to be with Him at all times, driving you crazy! That is the sweetness of this.'

'"Be gracious and show me Your other form, O Lord of the gods!" – Here again he is asking for grace, because it is only through grace that everything is possible. Through *kṛpā*, Bhagavān can take people from Hell and put them in Heaven. Through *kṛpā*, He can give Himself fully to His *bhakta* – just through grace, nothing else. This is the power of grace! There is nothing else; everything is His grace.'

VERSES 47-51: THE UNIQUENESS OF THIS COSMIC FORM

śrī bhagavān uvāca
mayā prasannena tavārjunedaṁ
rūpaṁ paraṁ darśitam ātma yogāt |
tejomayaṁ viśvam anantam ādyaṁ
yan me tvad anyena na dṛṣṭa-pūrvam || 47 ||

Lord Kṛṣṇa says:

O Arjuna, by My grace this Supreme Manifestation has been revealed to you through My divine potency. It is filled with energy, it is cosmic, infinite, and primeval. It has never been seen before by anyone apart from you. (47)

na veda yajñādhyayanair na dānair
na ca kriyābhir-na tapobhir-ugraiḥ |
evaṁ rūpaḥ śakya ahaṁ nṛloke
draṣṭuṁ tvadanyena kuru-pravīra || 48 ||

Neither through the study of the *Vedas*, nor by sacrifices, nor by recital of the scriptures, nor by charity, nor by rituals, nor by strict austerities, can I be seen like this by anyone else but you in this material world, O Arjuna! (48)

mā te vyathā mā ca vimūḍha bhāvo
dṛṣṭvā rūpaṁ ghoram īdṛṅ-mamedam |
vyapetabhīḥ prīta-manāḥ punas tvaṁ
tad eva me rūpam idaṁ prapaśya || 49 ||

Do not fear or be confused anymore by looking at this terrifying form of Mine. Let it be finished. Let your anxiety subside and your mind be contented, behold again that other form of Mine. (49)

sañjaya uvāca
ityarjunaṁ vāsudevas tathoktvā
svakaṁ rūpaṁ darśayāmāsa bhūyaḥ |
āśvāsayāmāsa ca bhītam-enaṁ
bhūtvā punaḥ saumya vapur mahātmā || 50 ||

Sañjaya says:
Having spoken in this way to Arjuna, Śrī Kṛṣṇa revealed His four-armed form. That great Being, reassured the frightened Arjuna, and then again Śrī Kṛṣṇa assumed His benign two-handed form. (50)

arjuna uvāca
dṛṣṭvedaṁ mānuṣaṁ rūpaṁ tava saumyaṁ janārdana |
idānīm asmi saṁvṛttaḥ sa cetāḥ prakṛtiṁ gataḥ || 51 ||

Arjuna says:
Seeing this human form of Yours, O Kṛṣṇa, my mind is at peace and I have been restored to my normal state. (51)

'The cosmic form that the Lord took was very terrible for Arjuna to perceive or to understand. Very often people ask for something that they think would be good for them. And when they have it, they don't know how to handle it. When someone doesn't truly know what one is asking for, when one receives it – in whichever form, and however it is given – it is very difficult to deal with. In daily life, when we ask for things without knowing what we are asking for, or how it will come, it's hard to handle.

'I remember once somebody asked me, "I want to realise myself straight away." And I asked this person, "Do you know what you are asking for?" He said, "Yes I know!" I said, "Are you sure that you know what you are asking for?" He said, "Yes, yes", with deep conviction. I said, "Okay." Very often people think of themselves as being very superior but in reality, they are not superior at all. If people think of themselves as superior, they are not superior. Only when one is humble one attains the state of surrender, but not when one is proud. So this person said, "Yes, yes, I know very well what it is." I said, "Okay, fine, you know what you are asking for. So may God bless you for it."

'And at that moment his life turned upside down, everything turned around. He cried, "I didn't ask for this. I am suffering, I have all this suffering." And I replied, "Sure, you did not ask for this suffering but you asked for realisation, for liberation, and this is the cost of it; it comes together with it!" When nature is forced into something, everything gets accelerated. This is why it is not good to ask. If you really want to ask one thing, ask God for His Love. Of this, you are fully guaranteed! He signs and seals all the documents! This is the only thing you can be sure of. Don't ask for something when you don't know what you are asking for.'

'When this Viśvarūpa disappeared, in front of him stood the Caturbhuja – the four-armed Mahā-Viṣṇu with the *Cakra*, the *Śaṅkha*, the *Gadā* and the *Padmā*. And this form is so sweet and calm that the whole atmosphere completely changed. Even the *bhāva* of Arjuna inside himself; he is not trembling, he is not shaking, he is calm, he is at ease, and he can understand. His mind has automatically subdued itself.'

'Here Bhagavān Kṛṣṇa as a great Teacher, as the *guru*, consents to let Arjuna have a glimpse of His cosmic form. He wants him to have this glimpse so that he can put his mind at peace about who is with him, telling him to go and fight. The Lord has a plan for each individual soul. Nothing that you do is really you doing it.'

VERSES 52-55: THE SUPREMACY OF BHAKTI

śrī bhagavān uvāca
sudurdarśam idaṁ rūpaṁ dṛṣṭavān asi yan mama |
devā apy asya rūpasya nityam darśana-kāṅkṣiṇaḥ || 52 ||

Lord Kṛṣṇa says:
It is extremely difficult to behold this form of Mine which you have seen. Even the gods are ever longing to see it. (52)

nāhaṁ vedair na tapasā na dānena na cejyayā |
śakya evaṁ vidho draṣṭuṁ dṛṣṭavān asi yan mama || 53 ||

Not through the *Vedas*, nor by austerities, nor by charity, nor by the performance of sacrifices, can I be seen in the way You have here. (53)

bhaktyā tv-ananyayā śakya aham evaṁ vidho 'rjuna |
jñātuṁ draṣṭuṁ ca tattvena praveṣṭuṁ ca parantapa || 54 ||

Only by single-minded devotion, Arjuna, is it possible to truly know, see and indeed enter into My Abode. (54)

mat karma-kṛn mat-paramo mad-bhaktaḥ saṅga-varjitaḥ |
nivairaḥ sarva bhūteṣu yaḥ sa māmeti pāṇḍava || 55 ||

Whoever serves Me, regards Me as the highest, whoever is devoted to Me, is free from attachment, and shows no malice towards any living being, comes to Me, O Arjuna. (55)

'The fool regards Him [Kṛṣṇa] as just being a normal human being. When they see Him dressed normally, acting normally, eating, drinking, sleeping, having fun, they think that He is just a normal person. But He is not. This is just to bewilder the mind. This is His *māyā*, which He has put over His creation so that no one perceives Him. Only the one who is worthy will perceive this. From time to time He reveals Himself through His *līlā*. From time to time He reveals Himself through the heart of the *bhakta*, through intuition and feeling.'

'Here Bhagavān is saying, "The demigods themselves desire to look upon that cosmic form. All the angels, sages, saints, all the prophets, want to see that cosmic form, but none have ever seen it. They have seen only a partial manifestation of Me. They realised only a part of Me, not the fullness of My manifestation. It is not possible even if one performs austerities. It is not possible even if one studies the *Vedas* and chants all kinds of *mantras*. It is not possible if one is performing every kind of ritual. But to those who have single-pointed devotion towards Me, those who are surrendered to Me completely, I raise them to that state where they come face to face with Me. And I do that due to the Love they have for me. Due to their devotion and surrender, out of grace, I reveal a different aspect of Myself.'"

Chapter Eleven Verses: Key Terms

[1] **Aśvin-kumāras** – twin celestial deities responsible for medicine.

[2] **Three worlds** – referenced in *Vedic* texts as Heaven, Earth and the netherworld.

[3] **Sādhyas** – class of divine beings dwelling in the celestial planets.

[4] **Viśvadevas** – term used to describe all the celestial deities as a whole.

[5] **Vāyu** – deity responsible for the winds.

[6] **Prajāpati** – personification of creative power.

[7] **Yādava** – Kṛṣṇa is a descendant of King Yadu, and is therefore also referred to as Yādava.

Chapter Eleven Commentary: Key Terms

[1] **Bhāva** – an intense feeling of Love and self-surrender directed towards God.

CHAPTER TWELVE
BHAKTI-YOGA
THE YOGA OF LOVE

After the great revelation of the cosmic form, Arjuna poses a question to Kṛṣṇa: Which is the better way to attain Him, as a devotee who is constantly engaged in worship of His personal form, or as one who contemplates upon the formless aspect of the Divine?

Kṛṣṇa's response is clear, the way of devotion is higher. The path of contemplation on the formless aspect of the Divine is filled with difficulty and suffering, whereas those devotees who are constantly absorbed in the Lord are delivered through grace.

Kṛṣṇa then outlines a step-by-step guide as to how one can ceaselessly fix one's minds upon Him. In the beginning, one should develop a mood of detachment through *karma-yoga* described in the earlier chapters. Then this internal renunciation should be suffused with *bhakti*, dedicating all actions to Kṛṣṇa. Finally, one will be in a position to perform a meditation practice which can steady the mind to remain exclusively on the Lord.

In the closing verses we hear about the various qualities of the true devotees. They are beyond the ways of the world, untouched by joy and sorrow, detached from pain and pleasure. At the end of each statement, Kṛṣṇa repeatedly states that such devotees are dear to Him.

VERSES 1-5: WHICH IS SUPERIOR, DEVOTION OR KNOWLEDGE?

arjuna uvāca
evaṁ satata-yuktā ye bhaktās-tvāṁ paryupāsate |
ye cāpyakṣaram-avyaktaṁ teṣāṁ ke yoga-vittamāḥ || 1 ||

Arjuna says:
Between the devotees who worship You, meditating on You in the way described, and those who contemplate on the imperishable, impersonal aspect of You — who is superior? (1)

śrī bhagavān uvāca
mayyāveśya mano ye māṁ nitya-yuktā upāsate |
śraddhayā parayopetās-te me yuktatamā matāḥ || 2 ||

Lord Kṛṣṇa says:
In My opinion, those who are forever absorbed in Me with strong faith and worship My personal form with focussed minds, are on the highest path. (2)

ye tvakṣaram-anirdeśyam-avyaktaṁ paryupāsate |
sarvatragam-acintyaṁ ca kūṭastham acalaṁ dhruvam || 3 ||
saṁniyamyendriya-grāmaṁ sarvatra sama-buddhayaḥ |
te prāpnuvanti mām-eva sarva-bhūta-hite-ratāḥ || 4 ||

But those who contemplate on the imperishable, the indefinable, the unmanifest, omnipresent, inconceivable, transcendent, unchanging, immovable impersonal aspect of the Truth, having subdued all their senses, remaining equal-minded and engaged in the welfare of all beings — they too eventually come to Me. (3-4)

kleśo'dhikataras-teṣām avyaktā-sakta-cetasām |
avyaktā hi gatir-duḥkhaṁ dehavadbhir-avāpyate || 5 ||

But greater is the difficulty of those whose minds are attached to the impersonal Truth. For those who are embodied, that path is filled with suffering. (5)

'Here Arjuna is asking, which one is better? Those devotees who have love and longing and want to have this connection with the Supreme Lord, or those who are meditating upon the formless God?'

'Kṛṣṇa is saying, "Those who surrender to Me, who serve Me, who pray to Me, who long for Me: that is the easiest way."'

'You have a body, a mind, and a brain that acts. All the pictures one sees are just images of things. And every day you build up 100,000 new images and input them into "this computer" inside your head. So, how can you picture the emptiness? That's why certain words don't have an image, like "no" or "emptiness". They are blank. The brain goes into meltdown. But yet, when this mind that is in meltdown perceives the cosmic Lord, it is in awe; it is wonderstruck and shocked. And then the mind will say, "I always thought You were attribute-less; I always thought You were formless. I always thought You were just energy, flying from left to right." No, no, my dear.

'Beyond this energy is someone who controls all this energy. There's a generator that creates this energy. Like the electricity that is everywhere: you touch it there, you will get electricity, you touch it here, you'll get electricity, but the generator that is making this energy is a manifestation. A generator can't be gliding in the air, flying somewhere. Even in an electric eel, the electricity is created inside, it goes through different organs, and then it arises as electricity outside. And this is what one perceives outside as electricity; just a manifestation, just a feeling. This is the same. Who can perceive this? Not everybody, but only the one whose mind is calm and who is surrendered. This is the state of a true *bhakta*.'

'You may take the path of *tapasya*, letting go of the world completely, doing certain hard austerities: torture! God is not a masochist! He says that it is possible to attain the state of the unmanifest, the void, but it takes rigorous, strong effort. And one goes through lots of suffering and pain. It's a big roller coaster, yet one does get there, if one survives!'

'A *bhakta* who worships God with attributes does go through this, but more easily. By worshipping the Lord, the Lord becomes easy relatable and very easy to adapt to. Then the Lord becomes the mother who carries the child, who cares for the child. This is why in other verses Bhagavān praises *bhakti*.'

VERSES 6-7: THE LORD RESCUES HIS DEVOTEES

ye tu sarvāṇi karmāṇi mayi saṁnyasya mat-parāḥ |
ananyenaiva yogena māṁ dhyāyanta upāsate || 6 ||
teṣāṁ ahaṁ samuddhartā mṛtyu-saṁsāra-sāgarāt |
bhavāmi na cirāt-pārtha mayyāveśita-cetasām || 7 ||

But for those who love and surrender all their actions to Me, who worship Me with exclusive devotion and fix their minds on Me alone, for such people, Arjuna, who have their consciousness absorbed in this way, I quickly deliver them from the ocean of birth and death. (6-7)

'Bhagavān Himself is saying that He will deliver those whose minds are still and focused on the different forms of the Lord, surrendered to Him; those who perform all their actions, their duties, but being free from the result don't have any expectation; who don't acknowledge the action as their own and who surrender everything. At night when they go to bed they say, "Kṛṣṇa, it's only You". They say, "*Kṛṣṇa-arpaṇamastu*", offering everything to Him. The Lord says, "To them I give Myself. These who are single-minded in their devotion, who are constantly fixed on Me, I deliver them from the cycle of birth and death." They are the ones who have this exclusive Love inside them and who have cultivated this Love. They recognise that the Lord is everywhere. Through this Love they perceive in each person they meet, they meet the Lord Himself. With such Love they become selfless, free from egoism. There's no trace of selfishness inside of them. There's no pride, because they are not thinking of "I, I, I". They become true *yogīs*, unshakable in their faith. Through this Love that they have constantly, they become like a lover. They are constantly in Love; the mind constantly dwells on Him; "who fix on Me all their consciousness". Their mind is fully absorbed only on Him. It's like you are continuously in Love. Wherever you go, whatever you do, you think of your beloved.

'This was the case of the *gopīs*, the ladies from Vṛndāvana. Their minds, when they were doing their duties – attending to their husbands and children – were always on their beloved Kṛṣṇa. And it was for Kṛṣṇa's sake that they did everything. In their husbands, they didn't see their husbands; they saw Kṛṣṇa. In their children, they didn't see their children; they saw only Kṛṣṇa. All are His manifestation, the manifestation of the Lord Himself. And one who has devotion – who listens to His glory, meditates upon His glory, His virtues, does *bhajana*, *kīrtana*, chants His Name, and does *japa* – the Lord frees. So, it's easy! And this is the key. Love frees oneself. True Love frees oneself.'

VERSES 8-12: THE STEPS TO PERFECT DEVOTION

mayyeva mana ādhatsva mayi buddhiṁ niveśaya |
nivasiṣyasi mayyeva ata ūrdhvaṁ na saṁśayaḥ || 8 ||

Place your mind on Me alone and let all your understanding be absorbed in Me. Then without doubt you will dwell in Me. (8)

atha cittaṁ samādhātuṁ na śaknoṣi mayi sthiram |
abhyāsa-yogena tato mām-icchāptuṁ dhanañjaya || 9 ||

But if you are unable to centre your mind on Me, then seek to reach Me, O Arjuna, by constantly practicing *yoga*. (9)

abhyāse'pyasamartho'si mat-karma paramo bhava |
mad-artham api karmāṇi kurvan siddhim avāpsyasi || 10 ||

But if you are unable to practise this *yoga*, then devote yourself to serving Me. For even by dedicating your actions to Me, you will attain perfection. (10)

athaitad apyaśakto'si kartuṁ mad-yogam āśritaḥ |
sarva karma phala tyāgaṁ tataḥ kuru yatātmavān || 11 ||

But if you are unable to even to act in remembrance of Me, then to gain self-control renounce the fruits of every action. (11)

śreyo hi jñānam abhyāsāt jñānād-dhyānaṁ viśiṣyate |
dhyānāt karma phala tyāgas tyāgāt-chāntir anantaram || 12 ||

Knowledge is far better than simple practice. Meditation is better than knowledge, and renouncing the fruits of action is better than meditation; from such renunciation peace immediately appears. (12)

'Bhagavān is making it easier and easier and easier for the devotee.'

'You have time to "lazy yourself". You have time to do everything which keeps you attached to the world. But to give your time for God? People find many excuses for not doing it… Stop finding excuses that you don't have time, but train your mind to think that whatever you are doing, you are doing it for God.'

'Here He is giving the assurance: "Those who are constantly thinking of Me, those who do everything with Me in their minds, whose meditation is focused upon Me, those with single-minded devotion,…those who are absorbed in Me in their daily work – for them, I make everything easy."'

'Bhagavān is saying that for the ones who recognise God alone as their supreme refuge and constantly bear Him in mind through their speech and controlling of the body; their every action becomes a sacrifice, a charity. All actions become penance. So to the one who can't control sitting in meditation for 5 minutes, Bhagavān says, "Go and do your work! Do charity! Do your daily chores with great love and surrender." Bhagavān is saying that this work is also a form of meditation and if you do it with love, if you enjoy what you are doing, it will become an adoration to the Lord, to Bhagavān Himself. It will become a prayer! This is where the expression "work is worship" comes from. For those who can't sit down to meditate, those that don't have time, due to many other obligations, or for those who are "very hyperactive", He says do your duty properly with a mind of surrender, a mind which is constantly focused on Him. Know that with such faith, whatever you do is a sacrifice, a charity, is penance to Him. All this is transformed into worship. Bhagavān says, "Even to this kind of a *bhakta*, I will also reveal Myself."'

'The ones who are not attached to the fruit of their action perceive Him; the Lord will reveal Himself. He will reveal Himself by His own mercy and Love! But the *bhaktas* who are on the way to the Lord should remove all feelings of doership and not be attached to their action. One should not even consider oneself the instrument of God. Praise the Lord in all His glory. Because, you see, if you start seeing yourself as the instrument, there is a separation. And when there is separation, pride will arise.'

VERSES 13-20: THE QUALITIES OF A DEVOTEE WHO IS DEAR TO KṚṢṆA

adveṣṭā sarva bhūtānāṁ maitraḥ karuṇa eva ca |
nir-mamo nir-ahaṅkāraḥ sama duḥkha sukha kṣamī || 13 ||
santuṣṭaḥ satataṁ yogī yatātmā dṛḍha-niścayaḥ |
mayyarpita mano buddhiḥ yo mad-bhaktaḥ sa me priyaḥ || 14 ||

The person who has no hatred towards any living being, who is friendly and compassionate to all, who is free from the notions of 'I' and 'mine', who regards pain and pleasure with equanimity, who is forbearing; contented, who is constantly contemplating, self-restrained and firm in one's convictions, dedicating his mind and intellect to Me — such a devotee is dear to Me. (13-14)

yasmān no dvijate loko lokān nodvijate ca yaḥ |
harṣāmarṣabhayo-dvegaiḥ mukto yaḥ sa ca me priyaḥ || 15 ||

He who does not disturb the world, and is not disturbed by the world, who is free from joy and sorrow, fear and passion — he is dear to Me. (15)

anapekṣaḥ śucir dakṣaḥ udāsīno gatavyathaḥ |
sarvārambha parityāgī yo mad bhaktaḥ sa me priyaḥ || 16 ||

One who is free from expectations, who is pure, skilled, impartial and free from anxiety and who has renounced material pursuits — he is dear to Me. (16)

yo na hṛṣyati na dveṣṭi na śocati na kāṅkṣati |
śubhāśubha parityāgī bhaktimān yaḥ sa me priyaḥ || 17 ||

One who is full of devotion to Me, who does not rejoice or hate, who does not grieve or desire, who renounces both enjoyable and vile objects — such a devotee is dear to Me. (17)

samaḥ śatrau ca mitre ca tathā mānāpamānayoḥ |
śītoṣṇa sukha duḥkheṣu samaḥ saṅga vivarjitaḥ || 18 ||
tulya nindā stutir maunī santuṣṭo yena kenacit |
aniketaḥ sthira-matiḥ bhaktimān me priyo naraḥ || 19 ||

He who is the same to both enemy and friend, who sees honour and dishonour as equal, who is indifferent to cold and heat, pleasure and pain, who is free from all attachments; who is unaffected by both praise and blame, and content with any condition, who has no home, who is steady in mind, and who is devoted to Me — such a person is dear to Me. (18-19)

ye tu dharmyāmṛtam idaṁ yathoktaṁ paryupāsate |
śraddha-dhānāḥ mat-paramā bhaktāste'tīva me priyāḥ || 20 ||

But those devotees who practise this immortal teaching with full faith as taught by Me, and who regard Me as the Supreme, are exceedingly dear to Me. (20)

'These last seven verses of this chapter are where Bhagavān Kṛṣṇa reveals the qualities of a *bhakta* who is completely surrendered to Him, and who has Him as the supreme aim, the supreme goal. Whatever one does is only for Him. These seven verses are the basis of religion for the upliftment of humanity. The fulfilment of human existence lies in the heart of a *bhakta*. Whosoever follows this ideal – these seven verses that we have just talked about – makes one the ideal *bhakta*, the true *bhakta*. And this *bhakta* attains God-realisation. The ones who have these qualities attain God-realisation and they become immortalised. Due to this realisation they will always have the mark of the Lord on them.'

'The *bhaktas* don't have any egoism. The *bhaktas* are an ocean of mercy and forgiveness. The *bhaktas* always stay in deep connection with the Lord. Nothing can deviate the *bhaktas* who are surrendered to their spiritual path. Those who can be deviated are not *bhaktas*. They will be deviated; they will "fly" somewhere else. They are "shoppers", who like going from one shop to the other. They would say, "I go to this shop to get some sweets." Once they have finished eating the sweets, they will go to another shop to buy other things. They are always "shopping". Or, you can also call it "hopping": *guru* hopping, spiritual hopping or any kind of hopping. They are always "hop on", "hop off". They hop, hop, hop; it is hopeless! A true *bhakta* doesn't have this "hopping-ness", this "hopeless" state. A true *bhakta* has stability and is anchored! Rooted!'

'When one practises spirituality, one has to have a firm faith and firm steadiness. It's of no use "hopping" around, from here to here. You should make one single jump from your head to your heart. I always say that from the head to the heart is only 40 centimetres – a very short way. That's only one hop! A leap of faith, which makes one stronger.'

'If you see someone in front of you with an affliction, automatically you get afflicted also. You feel the pain. But does it change the world if you feel this pain? No, the world doesn't change. If you want to help the world, you have to be strong. If you let the light inside of you dim itself, you can't shine. But by being self-centred, being absorbed in the will of God inside you, this becomes your strength. And by being strong, you shine this Light into the world. This is how peace happens! This is how things change in this world. If you want peace, yet you say, "O my goodness, it's terrible!" What image is in your mind? Which is the more powerful image in your mind? Is it the peaceful image or the terrible image? It's always like this! Because this is the mind of the world. This is how people function: they hang on negativity. However, the outside world should not bother you. This doesn't mean that you don't care. You do care, but you should be focused! Because you have Love inside you, you care, but you don't become weak. And in this way, you can bring forth change.'

'The *bhakta* is open to many possibilities. This is why He says, "Don't be attached to the fruit of your action, because I create the possibilities. If A here doesn't work, I will create B. If B doesn't work, I'll make C, but I'll lead you to perfection. There's always a plan B, and there's always a plan C. And if C doesn't work, I'll create D! If D doesn't work, I'll create E! But if you hang on to one outcome, then you are sitting on A, and A will lead you only to A."'

'One who is surrendered on their spiritual path, and one who has the chance to meet the *satguru*, knows that the *satguru* looks after their welfare as a mother looks after her baby. One tries one's best, though; it doesn't mean that you can sit down and say, "Okay, I won't do anything. Guruji will look after it." No, you have to put in your maximum effort, but be detached from it. You have to try your best. And due to this, when *guru*/God sees that you are making an effort, that you have taken one step – and it is very important that the *guru* sees this in the devotee – then he says, "Ahh, this one is ready! We can help advance him." This is in reality what happens on the spiritual path.'

'The ones whose aim is only God are "the perfect devotees". In this verse He says that this single-pointedness is the mark of a truly surrendered devotee. The devotees who have such focus dwell eternally with the Lord. For the saints who have achieved unity with God, God dwells constantly with them. There's no difference between the saints and God. When a saint touches something, it's purified. The touch of a saint is the same as from the Lord; the Lord touches through the saints.'

'Bhagavān Kṛṣṇa praises His devotees, praises those who are surrendered to Him, showing how dear He is surrendered to them. You think that you are longing for Him? No, He is longing more for you. You think that you love Him? Your love is like a grain of dust, but His Love is like an ocean. You think that you are walking towards Him? He is running towards you. That's the greatness and the humility of the Lord Himself.'

CHAPTER THIRTEEN
KṢETRA-KṢETRAJÑA-YOGA
MATTER AND SPIRIT

At this point, Kṛṣṇa makes another dramatic shift in His teaching. These final six chapters provide supplemental teaching, which connects and expands upon the main discourse already given in the *Gītā*. Arjuna is now given the grounding knowledge needed to walk a spiritual path. Chapter thirteen is a further development on *jñāna-yoga*, and how one can realise oneself as the *ātmā*.

The chapter begins with the Lord elaborating on the relationship between the Field (*kṣetra*) and the Knower of the Field (*Kṣetrajña*). This *kṣetra* is the body made up of material matter. The *Kṣetrajna* is of two types, the inner Self and the Supersoul. The latter is Kṛṣṇa Himself who exists alongside the inner Self as the Witness and Maintainer of life. The Lord then describes the various elements and the different modifications which make up and affect the Field. Next, Kṛṣṇa explains the state of one who has real knowledge. Qualities such as equanimity, detachment and freedom from ego are all symptoms of one who is truly realised.

Having established the different components of the Field, who the Knowers of the Field are, and the nature of one who has knowledge, Kṛṣṇa then describes what we should strive to know: the unfathomable, all-pervasive Lord.

He further points out that both material nature and the Self are beginning-less, and as long as the Self is entangled with it, it undergoes suffering and enjoyment. But the Paramātmā (Supersoul) is also present within. Seekers perceive it in various different ways. Those who have gained this perception behold the Supersoul everywhere and in all living beings. They also recognise that all action is performed within the material world and the inner Self is completely untouched. The one who is able to grasp this truth of the *kṣetra* and *Kṣetrajña* finally becomes liberated.

❁ VERSES 1-7: THE FIELD AND ITS KNOWER

śrī arjuna uvāca
prakṛtiṁ puruṣaṁ caiva kṣetraṁ kṣetrajñam eva ca |
etad veditum icchāmi jñānaṁ jñeyaṁ ca keśava || 1 ||

Arjuna says:
O Kṛṣṇa, I desire to learn about the Self and about material nature, about the Field and its Knower, about knowledge and the goal of knowledge. (1)

śrī Bhagavān uvāca
idaṁ śarīraṁ kaunteya kṣetram ityabhidhīyate |
etad yo vetti taṁ prāhuḥ kṣetrajñā iti tad vidaḥ || 2 ||

Lord Kṛṣṇa says:
This body, O Arjuna, is called the Field (*kṣetra*). One who has knowledge of this is called the 'Knower of the Field' (*Kṣetrajña*), by the enlightened ones. (2)

kṣetrajñaṁ cāpi māṁ viddhi sarva kṣetreṣu bhārata |
kṣetra kṣetrajñayor-jñānaṁ yat tajjñānam mataṁ param || 3 ||

And you should also understand that I am the Knower in all the Fields (as well as the inner Self), O Arjuna. In My view, this knowledge of the Field and (both) its Knowers is the highest knowledge. (3)

tat kṣetraṁ yacca yādṛk ca yad vikāri yataśca yat |
sa ca yo yat prabhāvaśca tat samāsena me śṛṇu || 4 ||

Now, learn briefly from Me about the Field, what its nature is, what changes it undergoes, and which one of these comes from the other; also learn about the Knower of the Field and what His influence is. (4)

ṛṣibhir bahudhā gītaṁ chandobhir vividhaiḥ pṛthak |
brahma-sūtrapadaiścaiva hetumadbhir viniścitaiḥ || 5 ||

This knowledge has been sung about by the sages in different ways, through various distinctive hymns of the *Vedas*. It has also been expressed through conclusive arguments in the *Brahma-sūtra* [1]. (5)

mahā-bhūtāny-ahaṅkāro buddhir-avyaktam eva ca |
indriyāṇi daśaikaṁ ca pañca cendriya gocarāḥ || 6 ||
icchā dveṣaḥ sukhaṁ duḥkhaṁ saṅghātaścetanā dhṛtiḥ |
etat kṣetraṁ samāsena savikāram udāhṛtam || 7 ||

The principle elements, the ego, the intellect, the unmanifested [2], the ten senses [3], the five objects of the senses [4]; attraction, aversion, pleasure and pain, the different faculties of the body, consciousness and one's resolve, is briefly what composes the Field, and the various transformations it undergoes. (6-7)

'Here Bhagavān is saying, "...My dear Arjuna, I know you have been confused with My cosmic form. You have heard Me talking about so many things. I know you are confused, but at the same time you want to know. I will reveal to you in a very simple way, in an easy way, the truth about the purpose of having a human body, the greatness of a human body, and why you have received this human body. I will reveal to you the true identity of the Supersoul, which is unlimited, birthless, eternal, whereas this body and everything which is created is the opposite. The body itself goes through constant changes. At all times you are getting old and at all times this body is moving towards its end."'

'The body is like a field. When a farmer sows seeds with time the seeds start to grow. In this body, the seeds you have sown in your past lives bear fruit in this life. This body is the field where the seeds of *karma* you harvest reap the fruit of your actions in their according time.'

'"*Kṣetra*" means also perishable, so everything that is linked to *kṣetra* is everything that is matter, tangible, everything that decays, impermanent, perishable.'

'The Knower of the Field is the "gardener", the Observer, the *ātmā*, the One who observes life from deep within. When you sit in meditation, who perceives everything? There is an Observer observing how the mind itself is working and observing the body. There is somebody else inside of you. You are not that mind, and you are not the body. The *ātmā*, the Great Observer of life is *Kṣetrajña*. This is the Great Observer that observes the game of life, observes the game where the mind is diverted to the object of senses, observes the senses and so on. But yet it is completely separate from everything it observes; it is not a part of it'.

'The ones who realise this great mystery rise above everything; they rise above gender, and above nature itself. This *ātmā* is not bound by transient limitation; it is not bound by anything that one perceives. It is genderless, changeless, without modification, eternal. When one realises it, one enters the consciousness of this *ātmā*, and the essence of the Divine starts manifesting.'

'Here Bhagavān Kṛṣṇa says to Arjuna, "Understand Me, I am the Great Observer of life, I am this Para-Puruṣa. I am this Paramātmā, the great soul, the Supersoul."'

VERSES 8-12: KṚṢṆA DESCRIBES TRUE KNOWLEDGE

amānitvam adambhitvam ahiṁsā kṣāntir ārjavam |
ācāryopāsanaṁ śaucaṁ sthairyam ātma-vinigrahaḥ || 8 ||
indriyārtheṣu vairāgyam anahaṅkāra eva ca |
janma-mṛtyu-jarā-vyādhi duḥkha doṣānudarśanam || 9 ||
asaktir anabhiṣvaṅgaḥ putra-dāra-gṛhādiṣu |
nityaṁ ca sama-cittatvam iṣṭān-iṣṭopapattiṣu || 10 ||
mayi cānanya-yogena bhaktir-avyabhicāriṇī |
vivikta deśa-sevitvam aratir jana-saṁsadi || 11 ||
adhyātmajñāna nityatvaṁ tattva-jñānārtha darśanam |
etajjñānam iti proktam ajñānaṁ yadato'nyathā || 12 ||

Being free from pride and deceit; having humility; not harming; patience; integrity; serving the Master; purity; steadfastness and self-restraint; being detached from sense objects; rising above the sense of ego; seeing the misery of birth, death, old age and suffering; being without attachment and entanglement for son, wife, home and other such things; being equal-minded; having exclusive undeviating devotion to Me; being in solitude; having aversion to mundane society; having constant dedication to the path of Self-realisation and the goal of Truth – all of this should be considered 'knowledge' and everything else is ignorance. (8-12)

'When one becomes spiritual, one enters the heart, and one perceives the divinity inside. The body becomes a temple, where you come face to face with God. Here, inside you, runs the Gaṅgā, the Yamunā, and the Sarasvatī rivers... your body is this place of solitude; it is this mountain, this wonderful nature that we look at – like when you look outside the *āśrama* here, you see the beautiful valley. When a *bhakta* perceives this beauty inside themselves and enters this calm state within the body, they perceive these three rivers, Gaṅgā, Yamunā, and Sarasvatī, flowing inside them. Even with all the noise outside, they're drawn towards the sound of the water, they are drawn to the cosmic sound inside them, and they enter this deepness residing inside. One achieves an inner peace, an inner tranquillity, a holy atmosphere, and if one enters this state, it has a deep impact on the body. And such is this impact, that it is said that, at that moment, there is such a beam that, in a state of complete focus and *śānti*, peace, there is also a cessation of disease. In the state of complete calmness, all germs, all illnesses, are removed from the body. For some saints, there comes a point that the body itself stops aging. For example, at the time of the war He was partaking in, Bhagavān Kṛṣṇa Himself was a great-grandfather, but yet He appeared only 25 years old. He was not bound by age. He was going through the *līlā*, and when the *līlā* was complete, when the body had reached a certain age, He kept it from changing. So the aging process stopped.'

'With the true knowledge, one knows that this body goes through changes and that one is the *ātmā*. The *ātmā* is eternal and it constantly longs for the Lord. The *ātmā* constantly wants to attain Him, to be with Him, to return home until one enters a deep state of *samādhi*. Then, in this state one enters the universal and eternal presence of the Lord. One attains the inner vision, the *darshan* of the Lord within oneself... In this state all pride, all arrogance, all hypocrisy, everything disappears. And this is the state that the *bhakta* achieves, just by loving the Lord, just by serving Him.'

VERSES 13-19: THE OBJECT OF KNOWLEDGE: THE SUPERSOUL

jñeyaṁ yattat pravakṣyāmi yajjñātvāmṛtam aśnute |
anādi mat-paraṁ brahma na sattannāsad ucyate || 13 ||

I shall now explain what one must strive to know. Once this is realised, one attains immortality. That object of knowledge is beginning-less, it is Brahman [5] which is dependent on Me; it is said to be neither existing nor non-existing. (13)

sarvataḥ pāṇi-pādaṁ tat sarvato' kṣiśiro-mukham |
sarvataḥ śrutimalloke sarvam-āvṛtya tiṣṭhati || 14 ||

Its hands and feet are everywhere; Its eyes, heads and faces are everywhere; Its ears are on all sides; and It exists, pervading all things. (14)

sarvendriya guṇābhāsaṁ sarvendriya vivarjitam |
asaktaṁ sarva bhṛccaiva nirguṇaṁ guṇabhoktṛ ca || 15 ||

It illumines the senses while remaining unconnected with the sense organs; It is detached and yet supports all; It is free from the *guṇas* and yet it experiences the *guṇas*. (15)

bahir-antaśca bhūtānām acaraṁ caram eva ca |
sūkṣmatvāt tad avijñeyaṁ dūrasthaṁ cāntike ca tat || 16 ||

It is inside and outside all beings; It is moving yet unmoving; It is so subtle that no one can comprehend It; It is far away, and yet so very near. (16)

avibhaktaṁ ca bhūteṣu vibhaktam iva ca sthitam |
bhūtabhartṛ ca tajjñeyaṁ grasiṣṇu prabhaviṣṇu ca || 17 ||

It is one and yet appears divided among living beings. That which must be known is the sustainer of all living beings. It devours them and brings them back into existence. (17)

jyotiṣām api tajjyotis tamasaḥ param-ucyate |
jñānaṁ jñeyaṁ jñāna-gamyaṁ hṛdi sarvasya viṣṭhitam || 18 ||

It is the Light of all lights, beyond all darkness. It is knowledge itself, the object of knowledge and it can be attained through knowledge; It is present in the hearts of all beings. (18)

iti kṣetraṁ tathā jñānaṁ jñeyaṁ coktaṁ samāsataḥ |
mad bhakta etad vijñāya mad bhāvāyopapadyate || 19 ||

In this way I have briefly explained the Field, knowledge and the object of knowledge. Upon realising this, My devotee attains that supreme relationship with Me. (19)

'Kṛṣṇa is indicating that even if everything comes out from Him, He is still superior. God (as the Supersoul) is still superior to the soul itself. This is equivalent to the example I gave of the mighty ocean and the droplet. They are the same in their qualities, but in quantity the ocean is far superior to a droplet. The droplet can't claim to be the ocean! The ocean is mighty. Bhagavān says here, "This individual soul is just a spark of Myself. I am superior to this; I am the whole mighty ocean itself."'

'The minds of men think, "I am praying to God. When God has time, He will listen to me," or "When He is not busy, then He will connect and fulfil the prayer." No, through His innumerable ears, He hears all praises. When you pray, when you ask, He can hear everything, because He is seated deep inside everyone.'

'The duty of man is to realise God, to realise the Divine within themselves and to attain Him. He is the Light of all; He is the knowledge itself, and the object of knowledge. So whatever you do in life is only to serve Him, to attain Him. There is not a single moment in your life that He is not present. This is why I said, "Do your *dharma*!" When you do your *dharma* properly, you embrace this knowledge; you're attuned to it. When you learn to accept life, and whatever

God gives you in life, whole-heartedly, this is the object of knowledge that God has given you to attain perfection. Without this, you can't attain perfection. If you fight what He has given you as an object to attain Him, you will not be able to do your *dharma* in life. Then it is far away. Even one who appears the nearest and dearest to you will appear far and very difficult to attain. But when you embrace what He gives you at every moment, you will see how easy it is. He is seated in the hearts of men. That is beautiful!'

'Even though the Lord is present everywhere, in everything – everything is His manifestation – yet the heart of man is a different reality; it is more superior than any other manifestation of Him. Bhagavān is saying that the heart is very special. Your heart is not just a heart. For example, the sun is present everywhere. But when the sun's rays reflect on a mirror, the light is different: it is greatly intensified and it is stronger. Even if the rays of the sun are equally present everywhere, when there is a cloud, the sun pierces through the cloud. However, when the sun's rays hit a mirror or a magnifying glass, the light gets intensified. Normally the sun would not burn anything. But if it reaches a certain angle on a magnifying glass and becomes intensified, then it burns. It is the same with the hearts of men. The Lord is present everywhere, but in the heart of human beings His Light shines more brightly. The heart of man is the seat of the Lord; if He is seated in the heart, He becomes greatly intensified. The heart of man is the manifestation of God. It is there that one can feel Him, meet Him, speak with Him. This heart, which is inside the body, is unique; this is what makes human beings unique.'

VERSES 20-24: THE SELF WITHIN MATERIAL NATURE

prakṛtiṁ puruṣaṁ caiva viddhyanādī ubhāvapi |
vikārāṁśca guṇāṁścaiva viddhi prakṛti saṁbhavān || 20 ||

Know that both material nature and the Self are without beginning, and all the transformations and *guṇas* arise from this material nature. (20)

kārya kāraṇa kartṛtve hetuḥ prakṛtir ucyate |
puruṣaḥ sukha-duḥkhānāṁ bhoktṛtve hetur ucyate || 21 ||

nature is said to be the cause of all material causes and effects. The embodied soul, however, is said to be the cause of the various pleasures and pain experienced. (21)

puruṣaḥ prakṛtistho hi bhuṅkte prakṛtijān guṇān |
kāraṇaṁ guṇa saṅgo'sya sadasad yoni janmasu || 22 ||

The Self which is situated in material nature experiences the effects of the different *guṇas* that arise from it. Entanglement to these *guṇas* is the cause of higher and lower births. (22)

upadṛṣṭānumantā ca bhartā bhoktā maheśvaraḥ |
paramātmeti cāpyukto dehe' smin puruṣaḥ paraḥ || 23 ||

But within the body, supreme to the Self, there is another One that is called the Witness, the One who grants permission, the Supporter, the Enjoyer, the Great Lord, the Supersoul. (23)

ya evaṁ vetti puruṣaṁ prakṛtiṁ ca guṇaiḥ saha |
sarvathā vartamāno'pi na sa bhūyo'bhijāyate || 24 ||

One who understands the spiritual and material nature along with its *guṇas*, is not born again, regardless of their situation. (24)

'People say this world is an illusion, that nothing is existent. This is not true. How can there be no existence when everything here is manifested? With which power does it manifest? With the *māyā* of the Lord Himself, so it is not an illusion. Even the air has molecules. And these molecules are a manifestation; there's a molecule of the Divine Himself in each of them. So, why is the world considered an illusion? It is an illusion because you don't see the divinity. You don't perceive divinity through the mind, in the way you see things. However, behind this "illusion" is the Lord's energy, which pervades everything. This is why it is not an illusion – this "illusion" is filled with the Lord Himself. A realised soul perceives that everything around them is the potency and the manifestation of the Lord. Not just merely an illusion. What would be the use of devotion? What would be the use of going on a spiritual path? It would become useless. But people always say one should see this as an illusion. It is true that it is an illusion, but behind the illusion is the Lord who pervades that illusion. And this is what a *bhakta* who loves the Lord and sees the Lord everywhere will see: that in each atom it is only Him.'

'Due to the *guṇas*, you are born in a certain category. *Bhaktas* are born in high categories. When you are born, the soul has only one aim: to attain the Lord. No matter how the world is, how it rotates, how strong the illusion of the world might be, how strong the surroundings themselves can be, a *bhakta* is born as a *bhakta*. They carry on from their previous life performing their devotional practices. As I said earlier, a saint is born a saint due to his past life. There is evolution, but one attains the state of sainthood in this life due to *bhakti*, and this is through grace. If one is attached to the *guṇas*, due to these *guṇas*, one takes a certain aspect in life and manifests it here. And *prakṛti* makes this manifestation possible so that one can cleanse and evolve towards God-realisation. Even those who are far away from Light, or carry very heavy *karma* with them, or are born in an evil womb, are constantly advancing towards God-realisation.'

'Sometimes you are born due to a certain *karma*, but yet, for you to become a devotee, it's not a coincidence. The Lord placed you where you have to finish certain *karma* with other people. Once you come on the spiritual path, once this love and longing of realising yourself awakens, everything changes. Somebody asked me last time, "Swamiji, why have you waited so long to call me? Why now? I'm old, I can't really serve you. You should have called me earlier." If I had called you earlier, you would not even want to know who I am. Because what makes you a devotee, what called you on the spiritual path, was not yet awakened inside of you. Once that call awakens inside of you, that's when you come on the spiritual path. So, it is always at the right time.'

'The moment one attains realisation, one doesn't have anything to do with *prakṛti*, which means that, at that moment, all creation of *karma* ceases. Due to this divorce from *prakṛti*, such a soul is not bound by ignorance. If one is not bound by the ignorance of separateness, such a realised soul perceives the Supreme Lord everywhere, in everything. *Prakṛti* doesn't have a grip on this person so there is no creation of *karma*. When you do your Atma Kriya Yoga, it makes you dwell in another consciousness, or awareness.'

'The *ātmā* goes through endless births until the *ātmā* realises Itself. But just one realisation can erase all the *karmas* of many lives. This is what Atma Kriya Yoga does! When one practises Atma Kriya Yoga, one cleanses *karmas* that have been created through many, many lives, as well as the *karma* that is being created now – it comes up and Atma Kriya Yoga makes it disappear. Finished! It helps one to free oneself fully from the cycle of birth and death.'"

VERSES 25-35: DIFFERENT WAYS TO PERCEIVE THE SUPERSOUL

dhyānenātmani paśyanti kecid ātmānam ātmanā |
anye sāṅkhyena yogena karma-yogena cāpare || 25 ||

Some perceive the Supersoul within themselves by meditation, others through gaining knowledge, and still others by *karma-yoga*. (25)

anye tvevam ajānantaḥ śrutvānyebhya upāsate |
te'pi cātitarantyeva mṛtyuṁ śruti parāyaṇāḥ || 26 ||

Then there are those who do not follow any of these paths, but having heard teachings from others, they devote themselves to the Supreme and they too pass beyond death. (26)

yāvat sañjāyate kiñcit sattvaṁ sthāvara jaṅgamam |
kṣetra kṣetrajña saṁyogāt tad viddhi bharatarṣabha || 27 ||

O Arjuna, whatever comes into being, be it moving or non-moving, only arises through a combination of the Field and the Knower of the Field. (27)

samaṁ sarveṣu bhūteṣu tiṣṭhantaṁ parameśvaram |
vinaśyatsv-avinaśyantaṁ yaḥ paśyati sa paśyati || 28 ||

Whoever sees the Supreme, dwelling alike in all bodies and never perishing despite the body doing so, truly sees. (28)

samaṁ paśyan hi sarvatra samavasthitam īśvaram |
na hinasty-ātmanātmānam tato yāti parāṁ gatim || 29 ||

One who sees the Supreme as equally existing in every place, does not degrade the Self by the mind. Therefore, they reach the highest goal. (29)

prakṛtyaiva ca karmāṇi kriyamāṇāni sarvaśaḥ |
yaḥ paśyati tathātmānam akartāraṁ sa paśyati || 30 ||

One who sees that the Self does nothing and all action is done by material nature alone, truly sees. (30)

yadā bhūta pṛthag bhāvam ekastham anupaśyati |
tathaiva ca vistāram brahma saṁpadyate tadā || 31 ||

When one understands that the difference and individuality of all beings is rooted and expanded from one Being, he realises Brahman. (31)

anāditvān nirguṇatvāt paramātmāyam avyayaḥ |
śarīrastho'pi kaunteya na karoti na lipyate || 32 ||

O Arjuna, this Supreme Self is without beginning and is unchanging. Though It is in the body, It is free from the *guṇas*; It neither acts nor is It stained by action. (32)

yathā sarvagataṁ saukṣmyād-ākāśaṁ nopalipyate |
sarvatrāvasthito dehe tathātmā nopalipyate || 33 ||

As all-pervading space is never affected by anything because of its subtle nature, so too the Self dwelling in the body is not tainted by the body. (33)

yathā prakāśayatyekaḥ kṛtsnaṁ lokam imaṁ raviḥ |
kṣetraṁ kṣetrī tathā kṛtsnaṁ prakāśayati bhārata || 34 ||

As the Sun alone illumines this whole world, Arjuna, so too does the Knower of the Field illumine the whole Field. (34)

kṣetra kṣetrajñayor-evam antaraṁ jñāna-cakṣuṣā |
bhūta prakṛti-mokṣaṁ ca ye vidur-yānti te param || 35 ||

Those with the eye of wisdom, who can perceive the difference between the Field and the Knowers of the Field, and how beings can be liberated from material nature — they attain the Supreme. (35)

'Those who don't have time to sit and do *japa*, their *sādhana*, their *yoga*, their meditation, yet they hear the glories of the Lord, hear of His *līlā*, hear about the greatness of the *bhaktas* of the Lord - with faith and concentration, not superficially but with the absorption of a "sponge" - will also be free. See how merciful He is?'

'The heart of the *bhakta* is like the sun shining on a clear mirror, reflecting the light onto others. The Lord is seated equally inside all hearts, yet not everyone perceives this. However, the realised soul, the one who has attained God-realisation, perceives the same Lord everywhere, even in the one who is not realised. This is why the saintly evolved beings, who have attained God-realisation, don't judge anybody.'

'Those who have this knowledge of the Self, those who have this knowledge to move towards God consciousness, are free; they will achieve this state. And those who do not have this knowledge or lack this equal vision are constantly in judgement; they constantly criticise each other. They are very friendly to somebody who does good towards them, and they reject those and are unfriendly to those who are mean to them. Such people have to undergo this repetition of birth and death. Bhagavān is saying to everyone, "Don't! Break through! See this unity! Awaken this universal Love! Love how I love you! And do everything in this attitude as a service to the Lord, remembering God at all times." This will free oneself. Especially when you take a spiritual path, one has to love.'

'When one starts saying, "I did this! I did that!", this big "I" arises, and at that moment there is creation of *karma*; the mind becomes very active, alert and very possessive.'

'The ones who have realised themselves are detached from *prakṛti*. You walk, but it's not you who is walking. You have the awareness that it is the body that is walking. When you die, it's not you who dies. It is the *ātmā* that leaves the body. You don't die. In every act and every move done with such a realisation, you are always in connection with the supreme reality. You are always swimming in the ocean of that bliss. Everything that you do will be infused with that bliss, infused with that knowledge of the Self, infused with that Love. Here Bhagavān is saying, "Enter into that supreme reality within yourself. Meet Me there. Know that everything else is just an act"...like the light, the bulb is just *prakṛti*, the light is the reality. You can feel the light – you can feel the electricity even without the light. You touch, you put your little finger in the socket, you will feel it. You don't need to see if the light is on or not.'

'So, when that truth shines, the seers start to see. That's why when people are around a Self-realised person, their *karma* starts to activate very quickly, because that 'observer' that is inside of them also wants to reach that same level. That's what purification is. Association with those who love God will purify others. This is the duty of the *bhaktas* of the Lord: to let the Light of the Lord shine through them to this world.'

Chapter Thirteen Verses: Key Terms

[1] **Brahma-sūtra** – a philosophical scripture that summarises the spiritual ideas of the *Upaniṣads*.

[2] **Unmanifested** – the dormant state of matter not yet differentiated into the various forms of material nature.

[3] **Ten senses** – the *jñānendriyas*, which are the five modes of perception (sight, hearing, touch, taste, smell), and the *karmendriyas*, which are the five organs of action (hands, feet, voice, anus, and genitals).

[4] **Five objects of the senses** – form/colour, sound, touch sensations, flavour and aroma

[5] **Brahman** – although Brahman has been used to denote the Supreme Lord throughout the *Gītā*, here Kṛṣṇa says that Brahman is dependent on Him, which means He is referring to the all-pervasive aspect of Himself as the Supersoul.

CHAPTER FOURTEEN
GUṆATRAYA-VIBHĀGA-YOGA
THE THREE MODES OF NATURE

In the opening verses, Kṛṣṇa states that He is the one who gives life to the unconscious *prakṛti* (material world) which then gives birth to all things. Out of this *prakṛti* comes the different *guṇas* (qualities) known as *sattva*, *rajas* and *tamas*. These *guṇas* bind the Self to this material body.

Sattva is goodness which brings wisdom, purity, detachment and kindness. *Rajas* is passion that encourages activity, restlessness and attachment. *Tamas* is ignorance that brings negligence, lethargy and sleep. At various times and situations, one *guṇa* will predominate over the others, influencing our state and experience of life.

Kṛṣṇa tells Arjuna that those who exist in *sattva* at death will be in true knowledge and attain higher realms. Those in *rajas* will come back to a life of action in this world, and those who dwell in *tamas* will be dragged down to be born amongst the deluded. But real eternal freedom is gained by one who rises beyond all three of the *guṇas*. Such a person is not swayed by this material world and is unaffected by pain, pleasure, joy and sorrow. In conclusion, Kṛṣṇa reminds Arjuna that it is through *bhakti* that one can cross over the bondage of the *guṇas* to realise the supreme state.

❁ VERSES 1-4: KṚṢṆA GIVES LIFE TO THIS MATERIAL WORLD

śri bhagavān uvāca
paraṁ bhūyaḥ pravakṣyāmi jñānānāṁ jñānam uttamam |
yaj-jñātvā munayaḥ sarve parāṁ siddhim ito gatāḥ || 1 ||

Lord Kṛṣṇa says:
I shall speak to you again of another kind of knowledge; this is the best of all forms of knowledge. By knowing this, all the sages have attained the highest perfection beyond this world. (1)

idaṁ jñānam upāśritya mama sadharmyam āgatāḥ |
sarge'pi nopajāyante pralaye na vyathanti ca || 2 ||

Dedicating themselves to this knowledge, they attain the same nature and quality as Me. As a result, they are not born at the time of creation, and are unaffected at the time of its dissolution. (2)

mama yonir mahad-brahma tasmin garbham dadhāmyaham |
saṁbhavaḥ sarva bhūtānāṁ tato bhavati bhārata || 3 ||

My womb is the totality of material existence, within which I place the seed of life. From that, O Arjuna, all beings are born. (3)

sarva yoniṣu kaunteya mūrtayaḥ sambhavanti yāḥ |
tāsāṁ brahma mahad-yonir ahaṁ bīja-pradaḥ pitā || 4 ||

Different beings come from various wombs, O Arjuna, but this material nature is the womb for all of them and I am the seed-giving Father. (4)

'Bhagavān says that all creation is His womb, and is where He places the seed. He places each spirit according to their qualities, their *dharma*, and certain things that they have to do; like seeds that sprout into various forms.'

'He also says that your spirit is free, it is never touched by these qualities. But *karma* – the qualities – that roams around the spirit determines the form of creation. If they are good qualities, one is born as a human being, with good nature and manners; you are brought on your spiritual path, finding your spiritual way.'

'When the *ātmā* starts to manifest into this world, it utilises matter – *prakṛti* – to manifest. From the subtle state it manifests into the gross state, which implies all forms, including not only all the species in this world, but also of the different spheres in the celestial worlds. He is also referring to the *devas*, like Indra, and to the Rākṣasas, the demons, the lower beings, spirits, and ghosts, which symbolise the *tamasic* lower qualities.'

'It's through *prakṛti* that His will is manifested, but He's ever-free from it. Everything and everybody is under His influence and supervision. Wherever He has placed each one and however He is guiding each one, is perfect. And one has to learn to accept this.'

VERSES 5-18: HOW THE GUṆAS INFLUENCE OUR EXPERIENCE

sattvaṁ-rajas-tama iti guṇāḥ prakṛti saṁbhavāḥ |
nibadhnanti mahābāho dehe dehinam avyayam || 5 ||

***Sattva*, *rajas* and *tamas* are the *guṇas* that arise from *prakṛti*. They are responsible for the bondage of the unchanging Self to the body, O Arjuna. (5)**

tatra sattvaṁ nirmalatvāt prakāśakam anāmayam |
sukha-saṅgena badhnāti jñāna-saṅgena cānagha || 6 ||

Of these, because *sattva* is pure, it is illuminating and free from contamination. It causes bondage, O Arjuna, through attachment to happiness and to learning. (6)

rajo rāgātmakaṁ viddhi tṛṣṇā-saṅga samudbhavam |
tan nibadhnāti kaunteya karma-saṅgena dehinam || 7 ||

O Arjuna, understand that *rajas* is the nature of passion and arises from craving and attachment, it causes bondage through attachment to action. (7)

tamas tvajñānajaṁ viddhi mohanaṁ sarva dehinām |
pramād-ālasya nidrābhis-tan nibadhnāti bhārata || 8 ||

Arjuna, know that *tamas* is born of ignorance and causes the delusion of all embodied souls. It creates bondage, through negligence, laziness and sleep. (8)

sattvaṁ sukhe sañjayati rajaḥ karmaṇi bhārata |
jñānam āvṛtya tu tamaḥ pramāde sañjayaty-uta || 9 ||

The mode of *sattva* generates attachment to pleasure and *rajas* to action, O Arjuna. But the mode of *tamas*, obscuring wisdom, creates attachment to negligence. (9)

rajas tamaścābhibhūya sattvaṁ bhavati bhārata |
rajas sattvaṁ tamaścaiva tamas sattvaṁ rajas-tathā || 10 ||

Sometimes *sattva* prevails by subduing *rajas* and *tamas*, O Arjuna. Sometimes *rajas* prevails by subduing *tamas* and *sattva*, and other times *tamas* prevails by subduing *rajas* and *sattva*. (10)

sarva dvāreṣu dehe'smin prakāśa upajāyate |
jñānaṁ yadā tadā vidyād vivṛddhaṁ sattvam ityuta || 11 ||

When the light of wisdom radiates in all the doorways (senses) of the body, then one should know that *sattva* prevails. (11)

lobhaḥ pravṛttir ārambhaḥ karmaṇām aśamaḥ spṛhā |
rajasyetāni jāyante vivṛddhe bharatarṣabha || 12 ||

Greed, intense endeavour, the undertaking of different tasks, restlessness and craving, arise, O Arjuna, when *rajas* is dominant. (12)

aprakāśo'pravṛttiśca pramādo moha eva ca |
tamasyetāni jāyante vivṛddhe kuru-nandana || 13 ||

Dullness, stagnation, negligence and even delusion arise, O Arjuna, when *tamas* dominates. (13)

yadā sattve pravṛddhe tu pralayaṁ yāti deha-bhṛt |
tadottama vidāṁ lokān amalān pratipadyate || 14 ||

If the embodied Self meets death when *sattva* predominates, then It proceeds to the pure realms of those who know the highest Truth. (14)

rajasi pralayaṁ gatvā karma saṅgiṣu jāyate |
tathā pralīnas tamasi mūḍha-yoniṣu jāyate || 15 ||

Meeting death when *rajas* predominates, one is born among those attached to action. Similarly, one who meets death when *tamas* prevails is born among beings in delusion. (15)

karmaṇaḥ sukṛtasyāhuḥ sāttvikaṁ nirmalaṁ phalam |
rajas-astu phalaṁ duḥkham ajñānaṁ tamasaḥ phalam || 16 ||

The result of *sattvic* action is a pure good deed; the result of *rajasic* action is suffering; the result of *tamasic* action is ignorance. (16)

sattvāt sañjāyate jñānaṁ rajaso lobha eva ca |
pramāda-mohau tamaso bhavato'jñānam eva ca || 17 ||

From *sattva* arises wisdom, from *rajas* comes greed, and from *tamas* comes negligence, delusion, as well as ignorance. (17)

ūrdhvaṁ gacchanti sattvasthā madhye tiṣṭhanti rājasāḥ |
jaghanya guṇa vṛttisthā adho gacchanti tāmasāḥ || 18 ||

Those who are established in *sattva* rise upwards; those who dwell in *rajas* remain in the middle; and those who adhere to *tamas*, influenced by the lowest tendencies, go downwards. (18)

'Bhagavān is describing here the qualities of the three *guṇas*: how they manifest and what qualities one perceives. This is not about judging others. It's not about seeing these qualities in other people. Be careful! These qualities are not in other people; they are in you, in each individual. You have this human body due to these three *guṇas*. Bhagavān has previously said that this world is created due to these three *guṇas*. And these three *guṇas* include also your physical body and the mind. It's not about pointing a finger at others. It's about looking at yourself – which *guṇa* predominates inside of you. This is also not about judging yourself. Of course, if you are fully *tamasic* you will start judging. But be aware what you have to change and what you have to transcend to purify yourself.'

Qualities of *sattva-guṇa* – 'The *sattvic guṇa* is a touch of the divine positive nature. This *guṇa* guides one in doing all good actions… one is not attached to power, name, fame, glamour, or wealth. Everything becomes balanced. The mind, the mental state, is always at peace, even if everything else is busy, one's mind is calm and serene.'

'Someone who has *sattvic* qualities focuses their enjoyment on the Lord. Whatever one does is to achieve God-realisation. Everything they do is with purity. Everything is bound by a great knowledge of the Lord, a great knowledge of the Self, and someone who has these *sattvic* qualities is happy; they are in bliss. They are not worried about how and what. They are not worried about what they have. They know that the Lord will take care of them and they long for their spiritual advancement.'

Qualities of *rajo-guṇa* – 'For one who has *rajasic* qualities, the mind always dwells on external enjoyment or desires, greed, envy, lust and many activities where the mind is in a permanent state of restlessness, constantly moving left, right, left, right, left, right; so, one becomes miserable. Due to this state of mind, one is dragged into the cycle, the whirlpool, of birth and death. Constantly coming out and in, in and out, one remains a slave. One would say, "When will I be free?" But to be free one has to transcend these qualities.

'Bhagavān says here that one with *rajasic* qualities does not learn to attain the grace of God, to attain the Lord through devotion and Love. How many people really understand Love? Not many. How many people really live this Love? Not many. People whose minds always dwell on outside things don't know about this Love; they have a certain image of love. They create a certain reality and they call it love, when in reality it's not love at all. It is attachment and this type of love falls into this category. Whereas true Love frees oneself, and true Love is the core of what one has to attain.'

Qualities of *tamo-guṇa* – 'Bhagavān says the roots of *tamasic* qualities arise due to ignorance. You can see this in the world nowadays, when people are not aware that they have a life. They walk like zombies in the street, not present. They are completely deluded by these qualities.'

'The different activities that reflect these qualities include sleeping, lazing around and so on, always playing computer games non-stop. Even when they go away from the computer, the mind is drawn back to the computer game.'

'With these *tamasic* qualities, this attachment to these lower frequencies, to lower manifestations, one becomes a slave to them. They can't be free. And such is the deluded mind: the mind is so active that it doesn't want them to realise themselves, and so the soul goes dormant. The mind that is focused on *tamasic* qualities and has these tendencies is blind; one with such a mind doesn't want to hear about God at all! They don't want to hear about anything that is positive, just like the Rākṣasas, demons, and *asuras*. Their minds are constantly drawn to harming and to hurting. This *tamasic* mind doesn't know anything else. Such people are kept in the cycle of birth and death. They can't be free from this cycle.'

VERSES 19-20: TRANSCENDING THE GUṆAS

nānyaṁ guṇebhyaḥ kartāraṁ yadā draṣṭānupaśyati |
guṇebhyaśca paraṁ vetti madbhāvaṁ so'dhigacchati || 19 ||

When the enlightened one sees that nothing acts other than the *guṇas*, and when he realises what lies beyond the *guṇas*, then he attains My divine nature. (19)

guṇān etān atītya trīn dehī deha samudbhavān |
janma mṛtyu jarā duḥkhair vimukto'mṛtam aśnute || 20 ||

By transcending these three *guṇas* from which the body arises, the embodied Self is freed from birth, death, old age and suffering, and thereby attains immortality. (20)

'When the mind, senses and the vital air are diverted from the normal activities or functions like hearing, seeing, eating, drinking, reflecting, sleeping, sitting and so on – when one attains true knowledge, which one gets on the spiritual path – and one is absorbed through meditation on the Self...the mind runs inwardly.'

'One doesn't go on an outside journey, but an inner journey. When one follows this inner journey, automatically one rises – due to the *sāttvic bhāva* – and the state of mind at that moment changes. The state of mind is not to focus on the outside reality. Due to these *sattvic* qualities inside of you, one makes one's journey inside. When one follows the inside journey, one perceives that there's another reality – the Great Observer – and one perceives that it is the Self that observes the reality of life, and that all this drama of the *sattvic*, *rajasic*, and *tamasic* qualities is just outside. These qualities are not related to the *ātmā*. They are related only to the body. At this moment, true consciousness awakens. In this state, one rises above the *guṇas* and one perceives God within oneself, the Supersoul, the Lord of all.

'One who recognises God within oneself is not connected to the three *guṇas*. One who perceives God in everything is not bound by the three *guṇas* and automatically, one who is absorbed in such a state of divine consciousness, doesn't identify with the outside reality. One perceives that beyond these *guṇas* is only Bhagavān Himself who is the absolute form and that it is Him only in His formless aspect (*nirguṇa* state), that manifests everything.'

VERSES 21-25: QUALITIES OF THOSE ABOVE THE GUṆAS

arjuna uvāca
kair-liṅgais trīn guṇān etān atīto bhavati prabho |
kim ācāraḥ kathaṁ caitāṁs trīn guṇān ativartate || 21 ||

Arjuna says:
What are the indications of one who has transcended the three *guṇas*? How does one behave? And how does one overcome the three *guṇas*? (21)

śrī bhagavān uvāca
prakāśaṁ ca pravṛttiṁ ca moham-eva ca pāṇḍava |
na dveṣṭi sampravṛttāni na nivṛttāni kāṅkṣati || 22 ||

Lord Kṛṣṇa says:
O Arjuna, he does not resent illumination, activity or delusion when they appear, nor does he long for them when they are absent. (22)

udāsīnavad āsīno guṇair yo na vicālyate |
guṇā vartanta ityeva yo'vatiṣṭhati neṅgate || 23 ||

He remains indifferent and undisturbed by the *guṇas*. He knows it is the *guṇas* alone that are active, and so he remains stable and unwavering. (23)

sama duḥkha sukhaḥ svasthaḥ sama loṣṭāśma kāñcanaḥ |
tulya priyāpriyo dhīras-tulya nindātma saṁstutiḥ || 24 ||
mānāpamānayos tulyas tulyo mitrāri pakṣayoḥ |
sarvārambha parityāgī guṇātītaḥ sa ucyate || 25 ||

He is equal in pleasure and pain; he is focused within; he sees a lump of earth, a stone and a piece of gold as the same; he is firmly resolved; he is equal to those who are dear to him and those who are not; he regards praise and blame equally; he is indifferent to honour and dishonour, he is equal to friends and enemies; and he has abandoned all worldly ambitions — such a person is said to have transcended the *guṇas*. (24-25)

'Bhagavān is revealing the qualities of those who are above the *guṇas*. They are not touched by blame or by honour. A mind which is completely under control exhibits the highest degree of calmness, serenity, tranquillity. That mind is not touched by any turmoil. It remains equal under all circumstances.'

'One who has become completely absorbed in the cosmic body of the Lord, whose mind has transformed and become light, is above the game of the three *guṇas*. They observe only... They are not bound by judgement. Their eyes still see, but there's no judgement of what they see. Their nose still smells, but there's no good or bad. Even if they do something that for the mind of men appears crazy, they are not bound by prejudice. They stay always free. Honour and dishonour is the same to them.'

'As long as you entertain these three *guṇas*, you are in the grip of Māyā and you are dancing to Her tune. As I always say, Māyā puts on the music, and you dance like a puppet. Like a tamed animal in a circus, kept in a cage. When the circus man throws his whip, the animal starts dancing, like the tamed monkey that turns and jumps around. This is similar to what Bhagavān Kṛṣṇa is saying: the circus of life. As long as one doesn't break through and rise above this, one remains in this circus. And as long as you stay in the game of this circus, there is judgement. But with the disappearance of all these *guṇas*, when you are above, looking from the *ātmā*'s point of view, when you sit in meditation, you perceive there is no judgement!'

'Bhagavān Kṛṣṇa Himself is saying, 'Be in this state! Don't be in a state of judgement. And don't entertain the game of the *guṇas*, which means, don't say, 'I am *rajasic* or *sattvic* or *tamasic*.'" Also don't look for this in others, because it's easy to see. Now that you have heard about these three *guṇas* you could start saying, "Ah, that person was *rajasic*, that person was *tamasic*. And that person was *sattvic*." Three *guṇas* fever! Move away from this fever, and you'll be healthy!'

'When you are fully absorbed in the Divine within you, you become a '*guṇātīta*', you go above the three *guṇas*. In such a state you are in complete bliss. That's why bliss can't be explained. You can't say bliss is happiness or bliss is sadness. You can't say that this person who is jumping around and happy is in a very blissful state. No! Because bliss is a state when you are fully absorbed in your Self.'

VERSES 26-27: BY DEVOTION WE RISE ABOVE THE GUṆAS

māṁ ca yo'vyabhicāreṇa bhakti yogena sevate |
sa guṇān samatītyaitān brahma-bhūyāya kalpate || 26 ||

And by serving Me with unswerving devotion, one transcends the *guṇas* and becomes fit to attain one's true relationship with Me. (26)

brahmaṇo hi pratiṣṭhā'ham amṛtasyāvyayasya ca |
śāśvatasya ca dharmasya sukhasyaikāntikasya ca || 27 ||

For I am the foundation for the immortal, unchanging Brahman [1]. I am also the basis for this eternal *dharma* and for perfect happiness. (27)

'Bhagavān Kṛṣṇa says, "I am this eternal God Himself who is formless and pervades over this whole universe. I am the One who sustains; I am the One who creates; I am the One who destroys. I am the Supreme, unmanifest and formless God. I am Śiva. I am Viṣṇu. I am Rāma. I am Kṛṣṇa. I am Jesus. I am Allah. I am Yahweh. I am all these Names. Here I am in front of you as Vāsudeva-Kṛṣṇa." All these forms and aspects of the Divine have been manifested throughout time to remind people of their real *dharma*; of why they have come here; why they are here; of how to free themselves; of how to attain their cosmic body and how to rise above this duality; how to rise above the game of *māyā* and how to rise above these three *guṇas*. And only through this will one attain supreme bliss, will one attain this blissful state, will one become blissful. Kṛṣṇa Himself says here, "It's easy to attain this state. Just surrender to Me! If you love Me, if you serve Me, if you hear My glory, I shall reveal this supreme bliss to you. Not outside, but within yourself and from within yourself you will beam this out to all." This is God-realisation. This is surrender and this is true happiness.'

Chapter Fourteen Verses: Key Terms

[1] **Brahman** – this term is used here to refer to the impersonal conception of the supreme reality. Its abstract features (immortal, unchanging, eternal, blissful, etc.) have a concrete existence in the Supreme Lord.

CHAPTER FIFTEEN
PURUṢOTTAMA-YOGA
KNOWING THE SUPREME PERSON

The last two chapters have primarily explained the nature of the material world in relation to the *ātmā*. Now Kṛṣṇa will focus on the Supreme Lord who is beyond both matter and the soul.

The opening verses compare bondage to the material world to being entangled in an upside down banyan tree. With the weapon of detachment, one has to cut through the endless branches, roots and leaves, and only then can we reach the Lord's Abode. Kṛṣṇa states that the soul is an eternal fragment of Himself that enters creation. It moves from body to body, carrying with it the five senses and the mind. Only those with true knowledge are able to perceive it within.

Having described the soul's position, Kṛṣṇa explains how He as the Lord sustains creation in various ways. He is the energy of the Moon, the fire that digests food. He is the one who resides in the hearts of all beings and is the knower of the *Vedas*.

The individual soul has two states: one that is in bondage (*kṣara*) and one that has risen above the material world (*akṣara*), considered to be a state of Self-realisation; but Kṛṣṇa is beyond both. He is known as the Paramātmā, the Lord who pervades creation and sustains it. The *Vedas* also celebrate Him as Puruṣottama, the highest Personality. Those who understand Kṛṣṇa as such, knowing all there is to know, have reached a state of God-realisation. They worship Him with their entire being.

VERSES 1-3: THE TREE OF LIFE

śrī bhagavān uvāca
ūrdhva mūlam adhaḥ śākham aśvatthaṁ prāhur-avyayam |
chandāṁsi yasya parṇāni yastaṁ veda sa vedavit || 1 ||

Lord Kṛṣṇa says:
They [the *Vedas*] speak of an indestructible Āśvattha tree with its roots above and branches below, the leaves of which are the *Vedic* hymns. The one who knows this tree knows the *Vedas*. (1)

adhaścordhvaṁ prasṛtās tasya śākhāḥ
guṇa-pravṛddhā viṣaya pravālāḥ |
adhaśca mūlāny-anusantatāni
karmānubandhīni manuṣya-loke || 2 ||

Its branches are spread out both above and below, nourished by the *guṇas*. The objects of the senses are the shoots. The roots extend downward into this material world where they combine with action that gives results. (2)

na rūpam asyeha tathopalabhyate
nānto na cādir naca saṁpratiṣṭhā |
aśvattham enaṁ suvirūḍha-mūlam
asaṅga śastreṇa dṛḍheṇa chitvā || 3 ||

Its form cannot be fully perceived for it has no end, beginning or foundation. But using the strong weapon of detachment, one should cut down this firmly-rooted Āśvattha tree. (3)

'Here Bhagavān says that as long as this tree of creation which is firmly rooted, very strong and very powerful – is not destroyed, if it is not cut down with the sword of detachment, dispassion, one will never be free. One will never seek the highest goal; one stays blind. Until one develops detachment, one will always remain blind. Bhagavān is saying, "Awake!"

'If we dwell only in the outside world, it is useless; it doesn't bring anything. Someone who doesn't have any knowledge of spirituality, who is not longing for the Divine, is rooted completely in the world outside, and they become like the trees that have a beginning and an end. They identify themselves with the body! They identify themselves with the *guṇas*! They don't think that what one goes through is only short-term happiness, and everlasting suffering. You are happy for a maximum of an hour, and then, it's over! Bhagavān said, "Find eternal happiness!" And this eternal happiness is not outside everywhere, in the things outside, it is inside you. And when you are fully attached to the Divine, even this one hour can become very long; you enjoy the Supreme Lord at all times; you are not attached to outside things only, but are fully focused, fully rooted in divine consciousness; then the outside doesn't matter.'

'Through dispassion one advances towards God-realisation. These qualities that awaken, that one attains, through devotion and surrender, cause one not to return into this world. Who else can give this supreme blissful state to you? Can another human being give this to you? No, they can't!

'The human being varies. You see this in your life: when you're freshly in love, love is sublime; you're so blind that you don't see anything else. But after a month, when you start to see again, it's not the same. At the beginning it's beautiful! But after a month, two months, three months, a year, you only need one little thing to happen to make you go crazy. And with that little thing, all the love you have disappears.

'Bhagavān doesn't tell you that you should not live your life on the outer world. You can live your life, with your husband, wife, children, and so on, but be in a state of God consciousness. Be aware of God in your life. Know where you stand and what your goal is – this is very important! If being in this world you don't know the goal you want to reach, it's impossible to be happy. You will be like these ignorant people who go through life like animals. They don't even know there is a life inside them. And they don't know there is life after death! But one day they will come back again and realise it.'

❁ VERSES 4-6: REACHING THE HIGHEST REALM

tataḥ padaṁ tat parimārgitavyaṁ
yasmin gatā na nivartanti bhūyaḥ |
tameva cādyaṁ puruṣaṁ prapadye
yataḥ pravṛttiḥ prasṛtā purāṇī || 4 ||

One should then seek that realm, which once attained, one never comes back from; there he should surrender to the Supreme Lord from where this whole process emanated. (4)

nirmāna mohā jita saṅga doṣā
adhyātma nityā vinivṛtta kāmāḥ |
dvandvair vimuktāḥ sukha-duḥkha saṁjñāir
gacchanty-amūḍhāḥ padam-avyayam tat || 5 ||

Free from pride and foolishness, having conquered the obstacle of attachment, in constant pursuit of the spiritual goal, having rejected material desire and been liberated from the pairs of opposites known as pleasure and pain, the undeluded one attains that Supreme Abode. (5)

na tad bhāsayate sūryo na śaśāṅko na pāvakaḥ |
yad gatvā na nivartante taddhāma paramaṁ mama || 6 ||

That supreme realm of Mine, is not illumined by the Sun or the Moon, nor by fire. After reaching this place one does not return again. (6)

'To be free from this *aparā-prakṛti*, this lower nature, one has to detach oneself and be free from egoism. One has to be free from attachment, free from all kinds of desires, free from "the duality of joy and grief", the pairs of opposites: agreeable or disagreeable; honour or dishonour; praise or blame; joy or sorrow; these qualities have many names. Those who transcend these are not enslaved by this attraction and aversion, and so they are free. They attain Enlightenment.'

'When a *sādhu*, a saint, touches someone, they are transformed. The saint becomes like the philosopher's stone, which by touching metal, transforms it into gold. People become like this when they are free. They radiate light; wherever they go, they disperse darkness.'

❁ VERSES 7-15: THE SOUL IS AN ETERNAL FRAGMENT OF KṚṢṆA

mamaivāṁśo jīva-loke jīva-bhūtas sanātanaḥ |
manaṣ ṣaṣṭhān-īndriyāṇi prakṛtisthāni karṣati || 7 ||

An eternal fragment of Myself becomes embodied as the living beings – *jīvas* [1] – within this mortal world. It acquires the five senses, and the mind, which is the sixth, all of which reside in this material nature. (7)

śarīraṁ yad avāpnoti yaccāpy-utkrāmat-īśvaraḥ |
gṛhītvaitāni saṁyāti vāyur-gandhān ivāśayāt || 8 ||

Whatever body the Self acquires or departs from, It proceeds, taking with It these six sense-faculties, just as the wind carries a fragrance from place to place. (8)

śrotraṁ cakṣuḥ sparśanaṁ ca rasanaṁ ghrāṇam eva ca |
adhiṣṭhāya manaścāyaṁ viṣayān upasevate || 9 ||

Presiding over the ear, the eye, the sense of touch, the tongue, the nose, and the mind, the Self experiences the objects of the senses. (9)

utkrāmantaṁ sthitaṁ vāpi bhuñjānaṁ vā guṇān-vitam |
vimūḍhā nānupaśyanti paśyanti jñāna-cakṣuṣaḥ || 10 ||

Joined with the *guṇas*, when departing, staying or experiencing, the deluded persons cannot perceive the Self. But those who possess the eye of knowledge can. (10)

yatanto yoginaścainaṁ paśyanty-ātmany-avasthitam |
yatanto'pyakṛtātmāno nainaṁ paśyantyacetasaḥ || 11 ||

The practitioners of *yoga* are able to see the Self abiding within themselves, but those who lack intelligence and have not mastered themselves cannot behold It even if they strive for It. (11)

yadādityagataṁ tejo jagad bhāsayate'khilam |
yaccandramasi yaccāgnau tat tejo viddhi māmakam || 12 ||

You should know that the energy of the Sun, which illumines the whole universe, and the energy of the Moon and fire, are Mine alone. (12)

gām āviśya ca bhūtāni dhārayāmy-aham ojasā |
puṣṇāmi cauṣadhīḥ sarvāḥ somo bhūtvā rasātmakaḥ || 13 ||

Pervading the Earth, I support all beings with My power. I nourish all herbs by becoming the Moon, full of potency. (13)

ahaṁ vaiśvānaro bhūtvā prāṇināṁ deham āśritaḥ |
prāṇāpāna samāyuktaḥ pacāmyannaṁ caturvidham || 14 ||

Becoming the digestive fire, I function within the bodies of all living beings. By joining with the *prāṇa* and the *apāna* [2] air breaths, I digest the four kinds of food [3]. (14)

sarvasya cāhaṁ hṛdi sanniviṣṭo
mattaḥ smṛtir jñānam apohanaṁ ca |
vedaiśca sarvair aham eva vedyo
vedānta-kṛd vedavid eva cāham || 15 ||

And I dwell in the hearts of all. From Me comes knowledge, memory and loss of memory. Indeed, I alone am that which is to be known from all the *Vedas*. I am the creator of *Vedānta* [4] and I alone am the knower of the *Vedas*. (15)

'Kṛṣṇa is saying that it is Him who gives the energy to act. Every action is only Him. The Lord seated in the heart pervades everything and observes the great activities of the body, mind and intellect. Without Him giving that energy, nothing is possible. You are thinking, "I am doing this, I am doing that", just pleasing that petty self, looking for acknowledgement, and forgetting that if God hadn't given you that energy to act, you would not be able to act... It is by His will that every action is happening, every movement is happening. Everything works through His energy, each part of the body.

'When you are so attached to your pride and ego, you are drained of that energy. It doesn't mean that the energy is not there. It is there, but you are focusing that energy in the wrong place, and pride and ego consume lots of energy. It takes lots of energy to think about yourself.'

'The realised ones perceive only the Divine. Everywhere they look, everything they hear, everything they do, is an engagement of realisation. They perceive the Lord within themselves and in all creation. For those who have true knowledge, who have wisdom, who meditate, contemplate, and do their *sādhana*, the Lord is ever-present; there is not a single moment that He is not present.'

'But the ignorant are not drawn towards spirituality; they are far away. For those whose mind is impure, unsteady, always flickering – a mind that is constantly moving, jumping from one thing to the other – it's very difficult to purify themselves. For those with a mind filled with impurities of many kinds, it is very difficult to detach, but not impossible.'

'They perceive that this happiness reflecting from you is not artificial happiness! It's not superficial! It emanates from deep within you and they want it! They perceive it, it reacts on their mind, it reacts on them, and they see there is something different in you. But due to their ignorance, pride, and fear, they judge. However, this is a good sign. Just by this, you know you have had an effect on them. And to have an effect, whether it appears positive or not, when you beam this light and happiness, it is really always positive.'

'The ultimate aim of all the knowledge, the rituals, the worship, and the spiritual practices is to attach one to the Lord Himself, to realise the Lord, to realise God, to attain the qualification of God-realisation. Bhagavān says here that those who attain God-realisation fulfil all that is written in the *Vedas* – not a part of what is written, but all. The ones who are completely surrendered to Him and realise Him – the Lord inside their own Self – go above the *Vedas*.'

'People can read the *Vedas*, they can chant many *mantras*, but if this has not led them to God-realisation, to seeing the Lord, it's useless.'

❁ VERSES 16-20: KṚṢṆA IS THE PURUṢOTTAMA BEYOND THE SELF

dvāvimau puruṣau loke kṣarāścākṣara eva ca |
kṣaraḥ sarvāṇi bhūtāni kūṭastho'kṣara ucyate || 16 ||

Beings exists in two distinct forms: perishable and imperishable. The material body bound to the material world is perishable, while the immutable Self is imperishable. (16)

uttamaḥ puruṣas-tvanyaḥ paramātmety-udāhṛtaḥ |
yo loka-trayam-āviśya bibharty-avyaya īśvaraḥ || 17 ||

But different and beyond these two forms, is the highest Puruṣa, described as the Supreme Self or Supersoul (Paramātmā), He is the unchanging Lord who pervades the three worlds and supports it. (17)

yasmāt-kṣaram-atīto'ham akṣarād-api cottamaḥ |
ato'smi loke vede ca prathitaḥ puruṣottamaḥ || 18 ||

Because I transcend the perishable and am also higher than the imperishable, I am declared in the world and by the *Vedas* as the Supreme Being (Puruṣottama). (18)

yo mām-evam asammūḍho jānāti puruṣottamam |
sa sarva-vid bhajati māṁ sarva bhāvena bhārata || 19 ||

Whoever is not deluded and understands Me as the highest Puruṣa, knows all. He worships Me with his whole being. (19)

iti guhyatamaṁ śāstram idam uktaṁ mayā'nagha |
etad buddhvā buddhimān syāt kṛtakṛtyaśca bhārata || 20 ||

O sinless one, I have now revealed the most mysterious doctrine. By understanding this, O Arjuna, one will become truly wise and would have fulfilled all duties. (20)

'Whoever rises above the threefold universe, the three *guṇas*, perceives that everywhere only the Supersoul pervades. This is the all-pervading God, who has entered the whole universe, who has manifested the whole universe, who upholds the whole universe. It is Him who is all-supporting; this cosmic energy enables both the mutable and the immutable to function, to act, to manifest.

'He who is unaffected, unchanged, who controls and rules over all, is the Almighty God. He is Kṛṣṇa Himself. Bhagavān says that when one rises above this, one perceives only Him within the core of oneself. And when one perceives Him within the core of oneself, one becomes immortalised. One sees the Truth and then one can really enjoy life – this you can call "enjoying life"! When you have risen above this, then you can enjoy life. There's nothing to worry about! Others who have said that they are enjoying life are full of misery and pain. They are happy only for a short time, and then – misery. But the realised soul, one who perceives the Lord everywhere, is ever free! They truly enjoy life because they are not bound by any *karma*. Wherever they go, whatever they do, is in a state of complete freedom.'

'The *guṇas* and the mode of *prakṛti*, are perishable, by nature. Everything that is manifested has an end. Whatever appears through the elements has an end. Bhagavān says, "I transcend the perishable. I transcend *prakṛti*, I transcend material nature itself." But here He doesn't say just this! He says, "I am higher than the imperishable... I am above the soul. I am the Supersoul, the soul of the souls." By saying that He is superior, by claiming superiority over the imperishable, over the soul itself, it means that He is different... He says the imperishable soul, the individual soul itself, is part of Him. It is also eternal, immortal, beyond the perishable.'

'The soul is the controlled, God is the Controller, and the body is the vehicle. The Lord is the worshipped, the praised one, and the soul, with the true knowledge, becomes the worshipper.'

'The *bhakta* who recognises the Lord to be the Almighty, universal, all-powerful, Supreme and Beloved of all, automatically develops faith in the Divine, in the virtues, in the glory, in the Truth, in the essence, in the greatness of God. Through *bhakti*, his mind is absorbed in the Lord. The ears hear only the glory of the Lord, the chanting of the Name of the Lord; the speech is only focused on singing the praises of the Lord, and the eyes see only the "good" the Lord in everything. Such are the minds of the *bhaktas*: they serve Him, they long for Him, they recognise that everything around is from Him. Such *bhaktas* are absorbed in so much Love and attachment to the Supreme Lord, they will perform all their duties, carrying out the daily routine of their work, but absorbed in the Love for God. Everything they touch, everything they do, everything they hear, everyone who is in front of them – everything becomes an act of worship.'

'Here Bhagavān says that whoever has surrendered perceives Him everywhere, and He is the one that takes full control of the *bhakta*. And through different *līlās*, the different pastimes, He acts specifically for each individual; each one has their own personal relationship with Him. He manifests in a certain aspect for that person, and this is how He makes love grow – love for God, and love for all! Because one who loves God truly, perceives the Lord everywhere.'

Chapter Fifteen Verses: Key Terms

[1] **Jīva** – the embodied Self.

[2] **Prāṇa and apāna** – vital life force connected with the breath.

[3] **Four kinds of food** – classified as being eaten, sucked, drunk or licked which leads to an increase in digestive fire. When the digestive fire is in balance with the *prāṇa* and *apāna*, the body is able to digest food properly, which has a positive impact on our mind and body.

[4] **Vedānta** – one of the six schools of Hindu philosophy. Based on *Vedic* knowledge, it focuses on describing the relationship between God, the Self, and material world.

CHAPTER SIXTEEN
DAIVĀSURA-SAMPAD-VIBHĀGA-YOGA
THE DIVINE AND DEMONIC QUALITIES

In this chapter, the *Gītā* moves away from explanations about the soul and the Lord and instead outlines the various qualities and virtues that make up one's character. The '*daivi-sampad*' or the way of the gods, is all about fostering noble and righteous values. Truthfulness, renunciation, not harming, and kindness all fall into this category. The '*asuri-sampad*' is the way of the *asuras* or unrighteous persons. Qualities such as deceit, arrogance and ignorance belong to this path.

Those who have an *asuric* nature are devoid of wisdom and refuse to acknowledge the Lord. They engage in cruel acts that bring destruction to the world. They are enslaved by material desires and endlessly try to gather wealth and kill their enemies. They arrogantly enjoy life whilst performing empty rituals. Such people ignore Kṛṣṇa within and resign themselves to lower realms after death.

Caught in the cycle of rebirth, they fail to attain Kṛṣṇa. Greed, anger and desire are the three gateways which lead to this path. One must overcome them to attain higher levels of realisation.

VERSES 1-6: QUALITIES OF THE RIGHTEOUS

śrī bhagavān uvāca
abhayaṁ sattva saṁśuddhiḥ jñāna yoga vyavasthitiḥ |
dānaṁ damaśca yajñāśca svādhyāyas tapa ārjavam || 1 ||
ahiṁsā satyam akrodhas tyāgaḥ śāntir apaiśunam |
dayā bhūteṣv-aloluptvaṁ mārdavaṁ hrīr acāpalam || 2 ||
tejaḥ kṣamā dhṛtiḥ śaucam adroho nātimānitā |
bhavanti sampadaṁ daivīṁ abhijātasya bhārata || 3 ||

Lord Kṛṣṇa says:

Fearlessness, purity of heart, the steadfast pursuit of knowledge, charity, self-control, worship, study of *Vedas*; austerity, honesty, refraining from harm, truthfulness, freedom from anger, renunciation; tranquillity, freedom from fault finding, compassion to all beings, freedom from greed, kindness, modesty, never wavering; energy, patience, fortitude, purity, freedom from malice and humility – these qualities, O Arjuna, belong to saintly men endowed with a divine nature. (1-3)

dambho darpo'bhimānaśca krodhaḥ pāruṣyam eva ca |
ajñānaṁ cābhijātasya pārtha sampadam āsurīm || 4 ||

Hypocrisy, pride, anger, rudeness and ignorance, O Arjuna, belong to one who possesses a demonic nature. (4)

daivī sampad vimokṣāya nibandhāyāsurī matā |
mā śucaḥ sampadaṁ daivīm abhijāto'si pāṇḍava || 5 ||

Those who have these divine qualities attain liberation, whereas those demonic qualities are a source of bondage. Do not worry, O Arjuna, for you have been born with divine qualities. (5)

dvau bhūta sargau loke 'smin daiva āsura eva ca |
daivo vistaraśaḥ proktaḥ āsuraṁ pārtha me śṛṇu || 6 ||

There are two types of beings that have been produced in this world — the divine and the demonic. So far, the qualities of the divine have been described at length, now hear from Me, O Arjuna, about the demonic. (6)

'The *bhaktas* who are surrendered are standing in the Lord. It doesn't matter what happens on the outside, they are not touched by it; not by the calamities, by the sorrow, by the danger, by what is right or what is wrong. Nothing. They are just absorbed into the Divine inside of them. They don't have any grudge towards anyone, especially not to the ones who are ill-treating them. *Bhaktas* also don't consider themselves superior to others. They are humble. They don't run after fame, name, prestige, or whether somebody gives them respect or not; they don't care. Whether or not somebody praises them, they don't bother about it. They are not running after that. Because people who run after that, they are into it – they want to be praised, they want to get the glory, the glory of "I, I, I". But Bhagavān says that a *bhakta* doesn't have all this and doesn't long for all this.

'A *bhakta* is humble! Humility is the greatest treasure for the *bhaktas*. And due to that humility, they don't judge or criticise anyone. They accept everything coming from the Lord Himself. So, this is one of the most important noble virtues of a *bhakta*: to be humble. If one takes a spiritual path, one must be humble to accept what the Master says. Only due to that humbleness, one will rise above the duality and attain the divine nature.'

'Whatever path you go on which is good, which leads you to God-realisation, surrender to that path with all humbleness. For the ones who have surrendered with all humbleness, all the other negative qualities disappear from them, little by little. The deeper they go into spirituality, the more they are surrendered, their own will disappears more and more. Only the will of the Master and the will of God will pervade them.

'So this is the awakening of the divine characteristics. All the characteristics, which were mentioned here earlier, all these divine qualities awake in a *bhakta* who is truly surrendered. The mind doesn't dwell on the outside but it dwells on advancing deeper and deeper. And that brings one to God-realisation.'

'Those who concentrate upon the negativity, the harshness, pride and arrogance and sing the glory of '*mea culpa, mea culpa*", will never be free. You see, if you take a rope and beat yourself a million times and say, "I am a sinner, I am a sinner, I am a sinner", constantly reminding yourself that you are a sinner, you will become a sinner. But if you say you are humble and you remind yourself of the Love of God, you will be free.'

VERSES 7-20: QUALITIES OF THE UNRIGHTEOUS

pravṛttiṁ ca nivṛttiṁ ca janā na vidurāsurāḥ |
na śaucaṁ nāpi cācāro na satyaṁ teṣu vidyate || 7 ||

***Asuric* individuals know nothing about right action nor what to refrain from. Neither purity, truthfulness, nor right conduct can be found in them. (7)**

asatyam apratiṣṭhaṁ te jagad-āhur anīśvaram |
aparaspara sambhūtaṁ kim anyat kāma haitukam || 8 ||

Such people say that this universe is unreal, without any foundation and without any Lord. They say this has all come into being without any cause. It has simply been brought about by sexual desire, with sensual gratification being the only reason for it. (8)

etāṁ dṛṣṭim avaṣṭabhya naṣṭātmāno'lpa buddhayaḥ |
prabhavanty-ugra karmāṇaḥ kṣayāya jagato'hitāḥ || 9 ||

Those who have ruined themselves, and have little intelligence, hold these views. Hostile to all, they perform cruel deeds and bring destruction to the world. (9)

kāmam āśritya duṣpūraṁ dambha māna madānvitāḥ |
mohād gṛhītvāsadgrahān pravartante 'śuci-vratāḥ || 10 ||

Filled with insatiable desires, due to delusion, they stubbornly hold to false ideas. They act with insincere intentions based on deceit, pride and passion. (10)

cintām aparimeyāṁ ca pralayāntām upāśritāḥ |
kāmopabhoga paramā etāvad iti niścitāḥ || 11 ||

They chase limitless desires thinking that this is all there is, as a result they face endless anxieties right up to the point of death. (11)

āśā-pāśa śatair baddhāḥ kāma krodha parāyaṇāḥ |
īhante kāma bhogārtham anyāyenārtha sañcayān || 12 ||

Bound by hundreds of worries and a mesh of illusion, ruled by desire and anger, they gather wealth through unjust means to fulfil their desires. (12)

idam-adya mayā labdham imaṁ prāpsyase manoratham |
idam astīdam api me bhaviṣyati punar dhanam || 13 ||
asau mayā hataḥ śatrur haniṣye cāparān api |
īśvaro'ham ahaṁ bhogī siddho'haṁ balavān sukhī || 14 ||
āḍhyo'bhijanavān asmi ko'nyosti sadṛśo mayā |
yakṣye dāsyāmi modiṣya ityajñāna vimohitāḥ || 15 ||

Deluded by ignorance, such people declare, 'I have gained this today, and I will gain more to meet my desires. This wealth is mine, and much more will be mine in the future. This enemy is slain by me, and I shall kill the others. I am the lord, I am the enjoyer, I am successful, powerful and happy.

I am wealthy and of noble birth; who else can equal me? I will perform sacrifices, I will give charity, I will rejoice!' (13-15)

anekacitta vibhrāntāḥ moha-jāla-samāvṛtāḥ |
prasaktāḥ kāma bhogeṣu patanti narake'śucau || 16 ||

Bewildered by so many fantasies, caught by the net of delusion and addicted to sensual enjoyments, they fall down into hell. (16)

ātma-saṁbhāvitāḥ stabdhā dhana-māna-madānvitāḥ |
yajante nāma yajñāis-te daṁbhenāvidhi pūrvakam || 17 ||

Being utterly self-centred, stubborn, intoxicated with pride, wealth and passion, they insincerely perform sacrifices in name only, deviating from the prescribed way. (17)

ahaṅkāraṁ balaṁ darpaṁ kāmaṁ krodhaṁ ca saṁśritāḥ |
mām-ātma para-deheṣu pradviṣanto'bhyasūyakāḥ || 18 ||

Overcome with ego, power, pride, desire and anger, these demonic people hate and envy Me, the one who is present in their own bodies and those of others. (18)

tān ahaṁ dviṣataḥ krūrān saṁsāreṣu narādhamān |
kṣipāmy-ajasram aśubhān āsurīṣveva yoniṣu || 19 ||

These wicked people are filled with hatred and are the worst of humankind. Within this cycle of birth and death, I continuously cast them into the wombs of demonic beings. (19)

āsurīṁ yonim āpannā mūḍhā janmani janmani |
mām aprāpyaiva kaunteya tato yānty-adhamāṁ gatim || 20 ||

Life after life, these fools exist among demonic beings and never attain Me, O Arjuna, and so they attain the lowest state of existence. (20)

'When you are born on Earth, when the *ātmā* enters the foetus in a womb of a mother, it's very powerful energy. This energy is like an atomic bomb, or even more powerful than an atomic bomb. So, imagine somebody who is fully negative. Each atom inside of them beams just negativity, they are like "a power of destruction" for this world. They destroy. Here it doesn't mean the world as we see it, but they infuse the negativity into the minds of others, destroying the world of other people, destroying the path of other people. They become "a fount of injury", they become an instrument "of injury and evil". This is where evilness come from; this is where the demons and all the negative qualities come from. They are not out there, they are inside the people themselves. And sometimes, due to that negativity, they want many people to become negative. They have a big agenda: whatever people do, they are doing wrong. That's their constant judgement of the world and for that, they try to get more and more people into their boat, which will sink them all together.'

'They live a miserable life, a life of debauchery, self-enjoyment. They appear to care for people, but in reality, they don't care at all for anybody. People with such a mind full of arrogance and pride carry on like that their whole life. Until they have life inside of them, they carry on with the same kind of behaviour, attachment, longing, enjoyment of all various kinds of luxurious things, and thinking that this is the sole aim of life.'

'They perform sacrifices, they perform charities, they do good work just to show off. Because in reality they don't care. They don't have this love in sharing, they don't have the love when they go and do charitable work, service, or prayer to the Lord. To do something really worthy, you have to have this Love inside of you. When one is devoid of this Love, one can't really do anything good; even if one is appearing to do it, it is not from the heart.'

'It's very good to do charity! But do it full-heartedly. And when you do it, put yourself always down, hidden in the corner. I tell you frankly, I know people who do charity and you don't even know that they have done this charity. Here Bhagavān Kṛṣṇa says that people who act sincerely don't need to be known. They don't need any publicity or any award given to them. Because God sees. They don't need the gratification of the outside.'

'Of course, the Love of God awakens in everybody's life once. You can't say that someone who is living in a 'hellish way' has never experienced the Love of God. Impossible! God is merciful. He reveals throughout and He gives experiences to people. But when people are so much into *māyā*, so much into the negative qualities, so much into this *asuric* nature, they don't perceive it. It passes and goes unnoticed.

'That's how people get into habits, putting themselves into all kind of desires and enjoyments. When one has imprinted this in themselves, and solidified in the mind such a reality, they can't perceive the goodness. It's not that it's not possible to help them. It is very possible to help them. But are they willing to listen? No. Are they willing to change their life? No, they are not. But in that case, when you go towards them, you yourself have to be strong in your qualities. You have to be strong on your path. You have to be like a pillar, a house which is built on a rock. Your faith should not be flickering, because if your faith is flickering, you'll go to people who have these *asuric* qualities and get contaminated. Whereas if your faith is strong and you are well-rooted in your faith and in your inner strength, you can go to them. Then they will not affect you; nothing will touch you. But until you are strong, don't venture into that. Make yourself strong in your path! Make yourself strong in your belief! Awaken all these divine qualities inside of you! And let these divine qualities reflect through you. Then you will be a light in this world of darkness.'

VERSE 21: THE THREE GATEWAYS TO HELL

trividhaṁ narakasyedaṁ dvāraṁ nāśanam ātmanaḥ |
kāmaḥ krodhas tathā lobhas tasmād etat trayaṁ tyajet || 21 ||

There are three gateways to this Hell: desire, anger and greed. Therefore, one should abandon them as they bring ruin to the soul. (21)

'There are three qualities that represent the doors of Hell. These doors are desire, anger and greed.'

'When these three drive man to action, one starts to ruin oneself, ruin the body, ruin the mind. The mind becomes filled with negative evil thoughts, all kinds of duality and judgement. Then, when there are evil thoughts, the evil qualities arise. So all this appears in people's life when they take the path of *tamasic* qualities. When they take the demonic path, they are robbed of joy, peace, purity. Their life becomes hell, and life after life they will have similar pattern.'

'These three qualities – desire, anger and greed – are due to ignorance. Without knowledge of the Self, without any knowledge of the Divine, one ventures downward, pulled to the lower entities and the lower incarnations.'

VERSES 22-24: THE IMPORTANCE OF SCRIPTURE

etair vimuktaḥ kaunteya tamo dvārais tribhir naraḥ |
ācaraty-ātmanaḥ śreyas tato yāti parāṁ gatim || 22 ||

One who has been liberated from these three gates of darkness, O Arjuna, will do what is beneficial to the Self and hence one reaches that Supreme Abode. (22)

yaḥ śāstra vidhim utsṛjya vartate kāma kārataḥ |
na sa siddhim avāpnoti na sukhaṁ na parāṁ gatim || 23 ||

Whoever disregards the principles of the scriptures and acts under the influence of their personal desire, can never attain perfection, happiness, or the Supreme Abode. (23)

tasmāt śāstraṁ pramāṇaṁ te kāryākārya vyavasthitau |
jñātvā śāstra vidhān-oktaṁ karma kartum ihārhasi || 24 ||

Therefore, let the scriptures be your authority for determining what should and should not be done. Having learnt what they have instructed, you can perform your duty. (24)

'They [righteous persons] don't let themselves be filled with other things of this world. They drink the nectar of the *Vedas* and meditate upon the essence of the *Vedas*. They do everything to realise the Lord. Studying the *Vedas* is also about chanting, about reciting different hymns in the praise of the Lord and about reflection upon them; not just about chant and finish, but about going into the deepness of it.'

'The holy scriptures were laid out to perfect yourself, to awaken the divine qualities. But following one's own reason, following the mind, one can't think. Following the mind, people will be tempted to desire, and they start to follow all the desires, and through that, the desire wins. When the desire wins, one loses perfection. One loses happiness and one dwells into the lowest spheres. Bhagavān Kṛṣṇa says that one doesn't attain the *sattvic* qualities.

'However, those who are not ruled by their own reason or pride, who take the shelter of the Master, seek His advice and blessing, then due to this humbleness, due to this humility, all these other qualities disappear. Then they are following their heart, not their reason, not their mind. When the Master, or the Lord Himself, reveals Himself within their heart, they become humble. Only a humble soul, with a humble quality, can surrender to the Master.'

'Taking the shelter of the Master, following the scriptures, following what the Master says, should be done in a selfless spirit, with a humble heart. This must be done with a heart full of Love. And that's what will bring the grace upon oneself. It is through this that one attains God-realisation.'

CHAPTER SEVENTEEN
ŚRADDHĀTRAYA-VIBHĀGA-YOGA
THE THREE DIVISIONS OF FAITH

In the previous chapter, Kṛṣṇa warns Arjuna about abandoning the rules of scripture, for it is through scripture that one can understand one's duty. Prompted by Kṛṣṇa's statements on the authority of scripture, Arjuna asks about those who act with faith but ignore scriptural rules. Kṛṣṇa replies that our faith is not necessarily reliable since it is dictated by the three *guṇas*. This answer initiates a new line of discourse where different aspects of life are analysed through the lens of *sattva*, *rajas* and *tamas*.

Kṛṣṇa begins by discussing the different types of food. Then He explains the various ways of performing ritual (*yajña*). He describes the austerity (*tapas*) of the body, speech and mind and how these also fall under the influence of the *guṇas*. Then finally, the different ways of giving charity (*dāna*) are outlined. Kṛṣṇa stresses that these actions (*yajña, tapas, dāna*) when done under the influence of *sattva-guṇa*, are performed with detachment, free from any desire.

In the closing few verses, the Lord speaks about the sacred words *oṁ tat sat*. This *mantra* has been chanted during the *Vedic* sacrifice since ancient times. Each syllable and its relevance to ritual is explained. But simply following rules is not enough. Kṛṣṇa emphasises once again the importance of sincere faith when carrying out any action such as ritual, charity or austerity. Without it, one cannot obtain any benefit in this world or the next.

VERSES 1-6: FAITH AND THE GUṆAS

arjuna uvāca
ye śāstra vidhim utsṛjya yajante śraddhayānvitāḥ |
teṣāṁ niṣṭhā tu kā kṛṣṇa sattvam āho rajas tamaḥ || 1 ||

Arjuna says:
Kṛṣṇa, what is the position of those who disregard the rules of scripture, but still worship with faith? Is it *sattva*, *rajas* or *tamas*'? (1)

śrī bhagavān uvāca
trividhā bhavati śraddhā dehināṁ sā svabhāvajā |
sāttvikī rājasī caiva tāmasī ceti tāṁ śṛṇu || 2 ||

Lord Kṛṣṇa says:
The faith of embodied beings comes from their inherent nature, and is of three types *sattvic*, *rajasic* and *tamasic*. Now listen while I describe them. (2)

sattvānurūpā sarvasya śraddhā bhavati bhārata |
śraddhāmayo'yaṁ puruṣo yo yacchraddhaḥ sa eva saḥ || 3 ||

O Arjuna, the faith of each person is in accordance with their nature. Whatever is the nature of that faith, that is what they become. (3)

yajante sātvikā devān yakṣa rakṣāṁsi rājasāḥ |
pretān bhūtagaṇāṁścānye yajante tāmasā janāḥ || 4 ||

Those of *sattvic* faith make offerings to the gods. The *rajasic* type worship Yakṣas and Rākṣasas, and the others, who are *tamasic* in faith, worship ghosts and spirits. (4)

aśāstra vihitaṁ ghoraṁ tapyante ye tapo janāḥ |
dambhāhaṅkāra saṁyuktāḥ kāma rāga balānvitāḥ || 5 ||

Those who practise torturous self-discipline (*tapas*), not approved of by scripture, are filled with hypocrisy and egoism, compelled by desire and attachment. (5)

karṣayantaḥ śarīrasthaṁ bhūta-grāmam acetasaḥ |
māṁ caivāntaḥ śarīrasthaṁ tān viddhyāsura niścayān || 6 ||

These foolish people simply torture the elements of their material bodies. They also harm Me who dwells within their body. Such people are demonic by nature. (6)

'Like Bhagavān has explained, there are two kinds of people: people who have divine qualities and people who have demonic qualities. Now, Bhagavān continues explaining how one achieves those qualities. Here you will see that it's very much about how our faith and how the food that we eat affects ourselves and our minds. The surroundings, the companionship, and with whom you associate is very important. In this chapter Bhagavān explains the three types of faith. People who have *sattvic* qualities, people who have *rajasic* qualities and people who have *tamasic* qualities.'

'*Bhaktas* with *sattvic* qualities turn their minds towards godly things, towards the Divine, towards enlightenment, towards awakening. They worship the Lord with faith, with love and dedication. All they do is for the Lord, nothing is for their self-interest or gain.'

'They don't build their friendship, relationship or prayer expecting something in return. They will not even ask God, "Lord, give me this", or, "Give me that. Lord, I love You, reveal Yourself to me." As if God doesn't know when one is ready. They will not even say, "God, give me Your Love." Those devotees who are surrendered to God, pray only for the sake and pleasure of the Lord Himself.'

'Those who are *rajasic* and who pray to the demigods, pray because they are greedy. Due to their pride and arrogance, due to always wanting more and more, they worship and praise people, always befriending people for their own selfish motives. They are always trying to gain something from people.'

'The ones with *tamasic* qualities pray to the ghosts. They like to abuse the power of nature. They utilise the force of nature to do their own dirty job through black magic, through voodoo and working with spirits of lower forces... When they die, they also become like the ones they have been worshipping.

'Because their mind is fully absorbed into that, they have conditioned themselves and programmed themselves so that they are in darkness continuously due to their aspect of always wanting to harm others. So, automatically that becomes their nature. And when they die, they also become like the ones they have been worshipping. And if they come on Earth, they become wicked people.'

VERSES 7-10: TYPES OF FOOD AND THE GUṆAS

āhāras-tvapi sarvasya trividho bhavati priyaḥ |
yajñās tapas tathā dānaṁ teṣāṁ bhedam imaṁ śṛṇu || 7 ||

The food which is enjoyed by all is also of three types, as are sacrifices, austerity and charity. Listen to the distinctions between them. (7)

āyuḥ sattva balārogya sukha prīti vivardhanāḥ |
rasyāḥ snigdhāḥ sthirā hṛdyā āhārāḥ sāttvika priyāḥ || 8 ||

Foods which are liked by *sattvic* people bring longevity, alertness, energy, health, pleasure and delight. Such foods are tasty, juicy, crisp, and pleasant. (8)

kaṭvamla lavaṇāty-uṣṇa tīkṣṇa rūkṣa vidāhinaḥ |
āhārāḥ rājasasyeṣṭā duḥkha śokāmaya pradāḥ || 9 ||

Those dominated by *rajas* like foods which are bitter, sour, very salty, very hot, strong tasting, pungent and burning. Such foods produce pain, sorrow and disease. (9)

yāta-yāmaṁ gata-rasaṁ pūti paryuṣitaṁ ca yat |
ucchiṣṭam api cāmedhyaṁ bhojanaṁ tāmasa priyam || 10 ||

Foods which are stale, tasteless, foul, putrid, left-over and impure, are loved by *tamasic* people. (10)

'The effect of the *guṇas* is also present in the food that we take. So, what we eat is very important, because the food that we eat acts on the brain. And you see that in life itself. People who are aggressive and short-tempered have so many *tamasic* qualities. The meat eaters are always nervous and aggressive because, although you can boil the meat, can you transform the energy in it? You can't. You can cook it, but the energy doesn't change while cooking. The sadness of the animal, the *karma* of that animal from previous lives, and also what they did to be incarnated as an animal is also put into that.'

'Bhagavān gives these explanations to Arjuna, even though Arjuna has not mentioned food. He hasn't asked which kinds of food we should eat. Bhagavān explains that, for faith, it is also important what one puts into one's body. Besides worshiping the Lord, having the faith in the practices that one is doing, and the *sādhana* that one is doing, food is also very important. The *sādhana* also depends on the food. If you sit in your *sādhana* and you have heavy things inside of you, it pulls you down. You can't sit meditating, you feel drowsy."'

'There is a saying that says, "By looking at the food people eat, you can tell how they are." Just by the food. Because people eat certain kinds of food according to their tendencies. Taste is the tendency, but in reality what is behind that taste will also determine the type of food people eat. So, somebody who has *sattvic* qualities will be eating vegetarian food. That helps one's mind to be more calm and peaceful, and so it also helps one on the spiritual path.'

'*Sattvic* qualities act on the intellect, they make the intellect pure, transparent, accurate. It gives one the mental stability so that one doesn't fall into depression. When the mind is stable, you are strong in your will. So, it gives you both inner strength and outer strength. Inner strength is the will. You don't get unbalanced. However, you also become stronger in the body, because *sattvic* food builds up the immune system in the body.'

VERSES 11-13: TYPES OF SACRIFICE AND THE GUṆAS

aphalā-kāṅkṣibhir yajño vidhi dṛṣṭo ya ijyate |
yaṣṭavyam eveti manaḥ samādhāma sa sāttvikaḥ || 11 ||

The *sattvic* sacrifice is one that is performed in strict accordance with scripture, without any desire for reward and is motivated by a sense of duty. (11)

abhisandhāya tu phalaṁ dambhārtham api caiva yat |
ijyate bharata-śreṣṭha taṁ yajñāṁ viddhi rājasam || 12 ||

But Arjuna, the sacrifice which is performed with an expectation of reward, and for the praise of others, is in the nature of *rajas*. (12)

vidhi hīnam asṛṣṭānnaṁ mantra-hīnam adakṣiṇam |
śraddhā virahitaṁ yajñāṁ tāmasaṁ paricakṣate || 13 ||

That sacrifice, which is not based on scriptural authority, which is without proper offerings or recitation of *mantras*, which does not have offerings to *brāhmaṇas* [1] or any sincere faith, is considered to be *tamasic* in nature. (13)

'People who have *sattvic* qualities, the devotees, they give from the heart. Whereas, somebody who has *tamasic* qualities, whatever they give has this arrogance inside of it: "I have done this, I have done that. I have given this." These are hypocrites; they are full of ego.'

'There are different kind of sacrifices. Charity is even considered a sacrifice like the *yajña*, the fire ceremony. When you do a *yajña*, it is a sacrifice. When you do a prayer, it is a sacrifice. When you chant the Name of the Lord, it is a sacrifice. Here Bhagavān says that whatever kind of sacrifice is offered by someone "...

without desire for personal rewards, which is executed according to the right principle of the *śāstras*, and with concentrated mind, that is *sattvic*.'"

'The one who knows the true knowledge of the Self and what one wants to achieve – the Lord Himself – surrenders; one wants to achieve this Love for God. Because, like I said, in the *śāstras* it's only about that: how to attain the Love of God. Nothing else! The ones who have this deep longing inside of them, whatever they do in life they will do only to please the Lord.'

'Of course, you have to work. You have to do your duty. Bhagavān has not said that you have to run away from your duty. But with what mindset are you doing it? This is very important. With what aim are you doing it? This is also very important. So here He also defines the mindset of what you do. If it is *sattvic*, then everything you do will bring you closer and closer to your inner Self. You will be closer and closer to the supreme reality. Enlightenment! Then, you are free.'

'When one is doing something for personal gain like, "O, God, please give me a car!" "O, God, please give me a husband!" "God, please give me a wife!" "God, give me wealth!" "O God, give me a house!" "O God, give me fame, give me prestige, give me victory, give me health, give me bliss, give me joy", it's only about "give me, give me, give me, give me". So, Bhagavān says that this falls into the *rajasic* qualities which are always connected to personal gain and motive. So, one is never free.'

'So, it's also very important how we pray and what we are praying for. Praying is not to ask and ask and ask, because this is the mind. I remember that once I told someone, "Pray to God!" Then the person said, "But, I don't need to ask Him anything." No. God doesn't want anything from you, and also truly inside of yourself you don't want anything from Him except Himself. And for that, even if you ask Him or not, He will give Himself to you the moment you long for Him. Longing is not about asking. It's a feeling which awakens inside, which draws Him. It's a magnet. It is small, but it grows. The more there is Love and longing for Him, the more that magnet grows and becomes big. And wherever He is, He is attracted to you and comes to you. Imagine that this magnet is so big that even attracts the Lord who is in Heaven, and pulls Him towards you.'

'In the *Vedas* there are certain *mantras*: the hymns which bring one closer to the Lord. But, there are other rituals which are not in the *Vedas*, in the *śāstras* and the holy scriptures, and they are used for personal gain. Bhagavān says that these rituals don't reach the Lord. They reach only the Yakṣas, the demons and entities which fulfil only the lower wishes of people.'

'Bhagavān reminds us that one should balance what one receives. But these people do everything only due to expectations. When they do their sacrifices, they don't even bother to feed anybody or to give anything to anyone. They don't even offer *prasāda*.'

'Here Bhagavān reminds you that when you receive, you should always give something in return, a *dakṣiṇā*. This is very important… People without faith don't give *dakṣiṇā*. They don't have any gratitude. They do everything out of expectation; they lack reverence due to their arrogance, self-conceit, delusion, hypocrisy, egoism. They lack understanding. They lack knowledge. Bhagavān says that is *tamasic*.'

VERSES 14-19: TYPES OF AUSTERITIES AND THE GUṆAS

deva dvija guru prājñā pūjanaṁ śaucam ārjavam |
brahmacaryam ahiṁsā ca śārīraṁ tapa ucyate || 14 ||

Austerity of the body is about worship of the gods, *brāhmaṇas*, teachers and enlightened beings. It involves being clean, honest, celibate and refraining from violence. (14)

anudvega-karaṁ vākyaṁ satyaṁ priya-hitaṁ ca yat |
svādhyāyābhyasanaṁ caiva vāṅmayaṁ tapa ucyate || 15 ||

Austerity of speech means not causing distress to others, stating the truth, speaking lovingly and what is beneficial, and also reciting the *Vedas*. (15)

manaḥ prasādaḥ saumyatvaṁ maunam ātma vinigrahaḥ |
bhāva saṁśuddhir ityetat tapo mānasam ucyate || 16 ||

Austerity of the mind means being peaceful, benevolent, silent and self-controlled, with pure thoughts. (16)

śraddhayā parayā taptaṁ tapas tat trividhaṁ naraiḥ |
aphalākāṅkṣibhir yuktaiḥ sāttvikaṁ paricakṣate || 17 ||

When these three forms of austerity are practised with firm faith, and without any desire for reward, they are of the *sattvic* nature. (17)

satkāra māna pūjārthaṁ tapo dambhena caiva yat |
kriyate tad iha proktaṁ rājasaṁ calam adhruvam || 18 ||

Austerity practised with vanity, for the sake of honour, praise and good reputation, is *rajasic*. Such practise is unstable and impermanent. (18)

mūḍha-grāheṇātmano yat pīḍayā kriyate tapaḥ |
parasyotsādanārthaṁ vā tat tāmasam udāhṛtam || 19 ||

And the austerity practised with foolishness, which tortures oneself or inflicts harm to others is considered *tamasic*. (19)

'One has to be aware of the tongue, and control what one says, for not causing any harm. It is said that it's easy if you beat somebody up; the wound will get healed and they will forget about it. But, the wound which you inflict to others caused by the tongue is more painful, because that wound hurts the heart directly, and when it hurts the heart, it hurts Bhagavān Himself.'

'Here Bhagavān talks about the discipline of the mind where all propensities, evil tendencies and evil qualities have been eliminated; all the prejudice, anger, greed, infatuation, lust, arrogance, jealousy and all other kinds of negative things have been removed from the mind. You don't have any grudge towards anybody, you don't have any enmity, envy or intolerance. Then one's mind attains a calm, gentle state of silence and self-control.'

'Purifying everything that comes out of the mind happens through *sādhana*. When you sit for meditation, entering the deep silence within yourself, it also reflects on the outside reality.'

'When one does something in a calm state and with a calm mind, it bears positiveness. But, if somebody does something in a restless way, in an agitated way, it always goes wrong. You see it in your life itself. When you take a decision very quickly, without even considering it, you always take the wrong decision. Even if the right decision was so clear in front of you, you blind yourself. The mind becomes blind so that you don't even perceive. You can't make the distinction between what is right and what is wrong. Then you always tend to take the wrong decision and afterwards you say, "Oh I knew it! I should have listened to the first intuitive feeling that arose." But that's how you have to learn to listen to your intuition. When the mind is calm and gentle, when the mind is silenced through meditation, when you are absorbed in that, you learn to control it and then you also learn to take the right decision. So, the mind is tamed. It's not running very quickly.'

'People who are always looking on the outside, who are doing all these big, big shows – it's only for a short-time glory, a short-time name, short-time fame. You see that in the world nowadays. One year you have a new actor or new actress who is famous. How long? They will be famous for three years and after that you don't even know where they have gone. They have come with a big "Ta-Da!" They have gone and you never hear about them again. And then one day you say, "Is she still alive? Have you ever heard about her again?" No, you don't know where she is. You don't even know when she comes and when she goes.'

'These are *rajasic* qualities and *rajasic* qualities don't last for long. The moment the beauty is gone, the fame, the name, then everything will disappear with it. Here, Bhagavān says, "Keep away from this kind of association also! Keep away from this kind of honour! Keep away from this kind of glory." Because, if you invite all these qualities inside of you, you will have only short-term happiness. And a *bhakta* doesn't long for short-term happiness. A *bhakta* longs for long-term happiness. And that long-term happiness is given to you only by God.'

VERSES 20-22: TYPES OF CHARITY AND THE GUṆAS

dātavyam iti yad-dānaṁ dīyate'anupakāriṇe |
deśe kāle ca pātre ca tad-dānaṁ sāttvikaṁ smṛtam || 20 ||

Charity that is done from a sense of duty, to a deserving person, without expectation, at the proper place and time, is said to be *sattvic* in nature. (20)

yattu pratyupakārārthaṁ phalam uddiśya vā punaḥ |
dīyate ca parikliṣṭaṁ tad-dānaṁ rājasaṁ smṛtam || 21 ||

But charity which is given with the expectation of receiving, in the hope of some future reward, or which is done grudgingly, is considered *rajasic*. (21)

adeśakāle yad-dānam apātrebhyaśca dīyate |
asat-kṛtam avajñātaṁ tat-tāmasam udāhṛtam || 22 ||

That gift which is given at the wrong place and wrong time, to an unworthy person, with neglect and without due respect, is considered *tamasic*. (22)

'"Charity that is done from a sense of duty", here Bhagavān refers to the ones who do charity, like helping people, with the true sense of serving, which is not just for a show, but truly from the heart. It is when you give and forget about it, not even expecting anything, any gratification nor even a "thank you". This is the sense of duty. People with *sattvic* qualities don't even expect the blessing of the Lord.'

'Whoever needs help and goes to a person who is *sattvic* is welcomed at any time. And here Bhagavān says that such a person who has the openness to welcome anybody at any time, any place and doesn't expect anything in return, is fixed in the *sattvic* qualities. They are always overwhelmed with gratitude themselves. They don't expect anything from anybody else outside because they feel that they are full!'

'The mind should be free when you serve. When you are doing service, when you are doing *sevā*, you have to have a mind which is calm and enjoys the *sevā*. Let that joy of service arise through you. When you have that joy of service inside of you, that arises from the *sattvic* quality. So, serve without expecting.'

'The Supreme Lord is watching everything. His eyes are everywhere. And all that you are doing, if you do it with love, will reach Him.'

'If somebody is begging on the road...if somebody is asking, "Oh, I am very hungry, give me food" and you see that they are sincere and they are really longing for food, give. But if you see that the people will indulge themselves, they are begging for drugs and you knowingly give alms, you are participating in harming them. So, their *tamasic* quality will also reflect upon you. That's why it is very important to be watchful.'

'You don't need to judge anyone, but see how you can make that person's life better. Otherwise, instead of making their life better, what is happening? You are making their life worse and that will not profit them or you.'

'There are all these big, big charities who have big, big names; in reality even if your intention is right, by giving gifts to these places, you are participating in all their wrongdoing.'

VERSES 23-27: THE SACRED MANTRA 'OṀ TAT SAT'

oṁ tat sad iti nirdeśo brahmaṇas trividhaḥ smṛtaḥ |
brāhmaṇās tena vedāśca yajñaśca vihitāḥ purā || 23 ||

From the very beginning, the three syllables '*oṁ tat sat*' have personified Brahman. It was with this sacred *mantra*, that the *brāhmaṇas*, the *Vedas*, and sacrifices, were established. (23)

tasmād om-ity-udāhṛtya yajña dāna tapaḥ kriyāḥ |
pravartante vidhān-oktāḥ satataṁ brahmavādinam || 24 ||

Therefore, in accordance with the *Vedas*, the saintly persons always chanted the syllable *oṁ* before all acts of worship, charity and austerity. (24)

tad-ity-anabhisandhāya phalaṁ yajña-tapaḥ kriyāḥ |
dāna kriyāśca vividhāḥ kriyante mokṣa-kāṅkṣibhiḥ || 25 ||

Without expecting the fruits of their action, those who seek liberation from rebirth chant the syllable '*tat*', when they perform acts of sacrifice, austerity and charity. (25)

sad-bhāve sādhu-bhāve ca sad-ity-etat prayujyate |
praśaste karmaṇi tathā sacchabdaḥ pārtha yujyate || 26 ||

Arjuna, the term '*sat*' means existence and virtue and is also used to describe any righteous action. (26)

yajñe tapasi dāne ca sthitiḥ sad-iti cocyate |
karma caiva tadarthīyaṁ sad-ityevābhidhīyate || 27 ||

Because of this, dedication to sacrifice, austerity and charity, is called '*sat*'; and also any action done for the sake of these is termed '*sat*'. (27)

'The three syllables *oṁ, tat, sat* are Bhagavān Himself. It is the Lord, together with this entire creation, consisting of the act of sacrifice and performance of the sacrifice.'

'If ever you do your prayer, your *mantra*, yet you are not sure about it, at the end of the prayer, think of the Lord, think of Bhagavān Kṛṣṇa and just say, "*oṁ, tat, sat*". By doing that, if you made a mistake by pronouncing any *mantra*, a mistake in performing any *mantra* with whatever attitude or with whatever aim that arose during that time, you will be free from the consequences, because you have offered it to Him.'

OṀ – 'The pronunciation of *oṁ* is Bhagavān Himself, the manifestation of the cosmic sound, the word incarnated, the awakening. When people attain realisation, they start to vibrate the cosmic sound of *oṁ*. When you do your Atma Kriya Yoga, when you are inhaling, you are always concentrating on it, infusing yourself with it, reminding yourself continuously of *oṁ*, not outside of you, but inwardly. You are purifying each channel, each chamber, each energy point inside your body and you rise.'

'Everything comes from *oṁ* and everything will go back into *oṁ*. There is nothing else. That's why the *brāhmaṇas*, the great sages start all the *mantras* with *oṁ*. When compiling all the *mantras*, Veda-vyāsa put *oṁ* at the beginning of all *mantras*. He said, "The benefit of *oṁ* is that it's a reminder of God". That's why when we start with *oṁ*, it reminds us that it is *sattvic* in itself. It is directed towards the Divine. It's not in vain. It's not for self-gratification, but it's for pleasing the Lord. It is Him.'

TAT – 'The self-discipline helps one to free oneself from all forms of expectations. *Tat* stands for that: the one who is doing all actions in a state of disinterest, but full of *bhāva* for the Lord, full of Love for the Lord, full of surrender to the Lord. There's not a moment, wherever they are, whatever they are doing, when they are not in constant remembrance that their life is for the Lord Himself. That's what a *bhakta* should attain when they say, "*hari oṁ tat sat*". When you say, "*tat*", it's desireless, free and the mind is focused on the Lord Himself.'

SAT – 'Here *sat* stands for that freedom, that everything is the Lord and that one is not the doer. One perceives that God is doing all. Here Bhagavān says that using the word *sat* means that one does all in the state of divine awareness, full of Love, disinterested about the fruit of their action, not attached to any fruit of the action, lives freely in a state of service to the Lord, perceiving the Lord all the time, loving Him in all His creation.'

'Here Bhagavān says that *sat*, in this quality, purifies the heart of *bhaktas* and makes them realise that He is seated inside of them. This realisation that God is the doer of all, and whatever we do is for His sake, knowing deeply that it is only Him that is doing all, that's *sat*. That's the Truth. Here it is not *satya* (truth), it is *sat* referring to the Almighty, everything.'

VERSE 28: ACTION WITHOUT FAITH IS USELESS

aśraddhayā hutaṁ dattaṁ tapas taptaṁ kṛtaṁ ca yat |
asad ity-ucyate pārtha na ca tat pretya no iha || 28 ||

But Arjuna, whatever is offered without faith, be it sacrifice, austerity or charity, is called '*asat*'. It is worthless in this world and the next. (28)

'If one is performing any action without faith, it's of no use doing it. Because that action which is performed without faith it is a forbidden act. This action will ruin oneself, this action brings sinful qualities to one and the fruit of it is also very destructive. People doing such actions without faith, doing all the service, all the charities, performing all the prayers, practising all the *sādhana* in a hypocrite way, here Bhagavān says that it's called *asat*. As this *asat* is just a show, people have to bear the fruit, people have to reap the painful consequences of their acts.

'Whatever one does, one has to bear the fruit. If you have planted a seed which is not good, it will grow, but don't expect the tree to bear sweet fruits, even if you water it with sweet water. It will bear fruits according to the seed that you planted. If you plant a good seed, it shall grow and multiply a thousand-fold.

When one does a sinful act, or act with a selfish motive, even if it appears very nice on the outside, one will bear the consequence of that. It all depends on how much faith people have. If they have faith in what they are doing, it's good, they will also bear that kind of things in their life. If they have faith in the Lord and completely surrender to the Lord, their faith will also grow and bring them towards the Lord, and their faith will also bring the Lord to them.'

Chapter Seventeen Verses: Key Terms

[1] **Brāhmaṇas** – one of the four classes within the *varṇa* system. *Brāhmaṇas* specialise as priests and teachers, and are responsible for preserving the sacred scriptures of Hinduism.

CHAPTER EIGHTEEN
MOKṢA-SANNYĀSA-YOGA
THE PATH TO LIBERATION

This is the final chapter of the *Bhagavad Gītā* and it is the longest. It begins with Arjuna seeking clarification between two terms '*sannyāsa*' and '*tyāga*'. Kṛṣṇa defines '*sannyāsa*' as the complete giving up of all external duties, while '*tyāga*' on the other hand is the internal detachment from the fruits of one's actions. He insists that acts such as ritual, austerity and charity must always be performed and so naturally *tyāga* is judged as superior to *sannyāsa*.

Carrying on the theme of the previous chapter, Kṛṣṇa delves into a number of aspects in relation to the *guṇas*. The different kinds of renunciation, the different types of knowledge, the nature of action, the performer of action, the different levels of intelligence, the types of determination, and the kinds of happiness one experiences; all of these are discussed in relation to *sattva*, *rajas* and *tamas*.

We find Kṛṣṇa once again returning to *karma-yoga* which dominated the opening chapters. But this time, Kṛṣṇa connects *karma-yoga* with *bhakti*. Previously in the earlier chapters, *karma-yoga* was advocated because it changed the motive behind action, from selfish gain to the detached performance of social duty. Now however, Kṛṣṇa states that action should be performed as a selfless act of worship.

He also reiterates how the perfection of this path brings one to the highest realisation. By carrying out our duties whilst depending entirely on the Lord, we gain full mastery over the mind. Established within, beyond the ways of material existence, we attain God-realisation, the highest state of devotion, where we receive the knowledge of who Kṛṣṇa truly is.

Drawing His teaching to a close, Kṛṣṇa emphasises the path of devotion (*bhakti*), stating it is the easiest and best way to realise true wisdom. Kṛṣṇa advises Arjuna to dedicate all actions to Him and not give into his pride. Even if he refuses to fight, his nature is that of a warrior and so he will be compelled to fight. With that in mind, the Lord advises him to think carefully over everything that has been said and decide for himself what is best. In one last grand declaration, Kṛṣṇa tells Arjuna:

'Fix your mind on Me, be devoted to Me, worship Me, bow down before Me and you shall come to Me. I promise you this for certain, for you are dear to Me. Abandoning all *dharmas*, surrender to Me alone. I will take care of all your sins; I will liberate you. Have no fear.' 18.65-66

After listening intently for eighteen chapters, Arjuna finally tells Kṛṣṇa that his doubts have vanished. His confusion has gone and now he is filled with the determination to carry out the Lord's instruction.

The concluding verses return to Sañjaya as the narrator. Thrilled at the divine words of Kṛṣṇa, and recalling with ecstasy the cosmic form of the Lord, he tells the blind King Dhṛtarāṣṭra:

'It is my firm conviction that wherever there is Śrī Kṛṣṇa, the Lord of *yoga*, and Arjuna who bears the bow, there will always be victory, wealth, success and good judgement.' 18.78

VERSES 1-6: SANNYĀSA OR TYĀGA, WHICH IS BETTER?

arjuna uvāca
saṁnyāsasya mahābāho tattvam icchāmi veditum |
tyāgasya ca hṛṣīkeśa pṛthak keśiniṣūdanam || 1 ||

Arjuna says:
O Kṛṣṇa, I wish to know about *sannyāsa* and the difference between *sannyāsa* and *tyāga*. (1)

śrī bhagavān uvāca
kāmyānāṁ karmaṇāṁ nyāsaṁ saṁnyāsaṁ kavayo viduḥ |
sarva karma phala tyāgaṁ prāhus tyāgaṁ vicakṣaṇāḥ || 2 ||

Lord Kṛṣṇa says:
Learned men understand that *sannyāsa* means the giving up of all works which are motivated by desire, and they declare *tyāga* to be renouncing the fruits of all action. (2)

tyājyaṁ doṣavad ityeke karma prāhur manīṣiṇaḥ |
yajñā dāna tapaḥ karma na tyājyam iti cāpare || 3 ||

Some wise persons say that all actions should be given up as they are inherently defective; others declare that actions such as sacrifice, charity and austerity should not be given up. (3)

niścayaṁ śṛṇu me tatra tyāge bharata sattama |
tyāgo hi puruṣa-vyāghra tri-vidhaḥ saṁprakīrtitaḥ || 4 ||

Now Arjuna, listen to My verdict, regarding *tyāga*, for this can be of three kinds. (4)

yajñā dāna tapaḥ karma na tyājyaṁ kāryam eva tat |
yajño dānaṁ tapaścaiva pāvanāni manīṣiṇām || 5 ||

The acts of sacrifice, charity and austerity should not be given up, but should be performed. For these acts purify even the wise. (5)

etānyapi tu karmāṇi saṅgaṁ tvyaktvā phalāni ca |
kartavyānīti me pārthas niścitaṁ matam uttamam || 6 ||

But Arjuna, even these three practices should be performed giving up all attachment and the desire for reward. (6)

'Bhagavān is saying that these are the two kinds of renunciates: the "*sannyāsin*" and the "*tyāgī*"; the ones who have let go. But if one takes the path of "*sannyāsa*", and yet has not let go of the outside from deep within the heart itself, then one has not let go of anything.'

'Whereas the true sages, whose minds are fully absorbed into the Lord, even if they renounce the world outside, for them there is no difference between "*sannyāsa*" and "*tyāga*". This is why I said that for an enlightened one, it doesn't matter where they are, what they do. They are free, they are ever-free.'

'A "*tyāgī*" is somebody who works in the outside world, yet is not attached to the fruit of their action. Whatever they do, their mind is so focused on the Lord, they are so absorbed in the *sāttvic bhāva* inside of them, that they don't get drawn into any external objectives or aims in life, apart from serving the Lord. They do their *karma-yoga*, with their determination fixed only on serving. They have *bhakti*, devotion.'

'You don't need to let go of everything and run into a cave, but you have to do your duty. The wise seekers of God-realisation, the ones who seek the Lord truly, do their duty in a very joyous way. They do their duty with much Love, with a spirit of disinterest, non-attached to the fruit of the action. They always do it for the benefit of society, for the benefit of others. They do it with an attitude of detachment, without creating any bondage. They do their prayers, their sacrifices, their charity, their penance, but with a pure heart.

'Bhagavān says that one must perform one's duty in this way, because it purifies oneself, it purifies the wise. And one has to get purified, because without being purified, one can't advance on the spiritual path. By doing one's duty in such a way, as Bhagavān said, one cleanses the karma of the past; one purifies not only this life, but past lives also.'

'Bhagavān says to people – to all of you who live in the outside world, "Do your duty full-heartedly!" Do your duty as a husband, a wife, a child, in your job. Whatever you do, do it with full love. And do it with an attitude of surrendering to the Lord. Make your work your prayer, your worship. Make your work your meditation, your *sādhana*, by doing it properly. Bhagavān says that when you have such an attitude, when you have such enthusiasm, it helps to purify you. Then the result doesn't matter; you don't have to worry about the result, because if you surrender to the Lord, He will take care of everything.'

VERSES 7-12: DIFFERENT KINDS OF RENUNCIATION

niyatasya tu saṁnyāsaḥ karmaṇo nopapadyate |
mohāt tasya parityāgas tāmasaḥ parikīrtitaḥ || 7 ||

Actions that have been prescribed should never be given up. Renouncing such actions through ignorance is *tamasic* in nature. (7)

duḥkham ityeva yat karma kāya kleśa-bhayāt tyajet |
sa kṛtvā rājasaṁ tyāgaṁ naiva tyāga phalaṁ labhet || 8 ||

If one renounces action because it is painful, or brings suffering to the body, it is born of *rajas* and does not yield the fruit of renunciation. (8)

kāryam ityeva yat karma niyataṁ kriyate'rjuna |
saṅgaṁ tyaktvā phalaṁ caiva sa tyāgaḥ sāttviko mataḥ || 9 ||

But when prescribed action is performed as a matter of duty, giving up attachment to it as well as its fruits, such renunciation is regarded as *sattvic*. (9)

na dveṣṭy-akuśalaṁ karma kuśale nānuṣajjate |
tyāgī sattva samāviṣṭo medhāvī chinna saṁśayaḥ || 10 ||

The one who is established in *sattva* is wise and free from doubts. He neither hates unpleasant work nor does he become attached to work which is pleasant. (10)

na hi deha-bhṛtā śakyaṁ tyaktuṁ karmāṇy-aśeṣataḥ |
yastu karma-phala-tyāgī sa tyāgīty-abhidhīyate || 11 ||

It is impossible for an embodied being to abandon action entirely. But one who gives up the rewards of action is a true renunciate. (11)

aniṣṭam iṣṭaṁ miśraṁ ca trividhaṁ karmaṇaḥ phalam |
bhavaty-atyāgināṁ pretya na tu saṁnyāsināṁ kvacit || 12 ||

Undesirable, desirable and mixed are the three kinds of results from action. After death, these results affect one who has not renounced, but never those who have. (12)

'Due to this ignorance, one does not perceive that every duty that is allocated to one is very important; it contributes to the advancement of one towards liberation itself. Because every duty that is given is given as a test, to see whether you are ready for something greater or not. If you are not ready, why should God give you realisation, why should God give you liberation? If you can't handle what He has given you in your daily life and you try to run away from it, forget about liberation.'

'Even a hermit sitting in a forest or a cave is doing a lot of work. Maybe one doesn't see this from the outside, but they are actually doing a great deal: they pray, they do their duty.'

'These kind of hermits commit themselves to a certain responsibility in life. They give themselves fully to that duty, because they know that it's the only thing that connects them to God; and they have great joy in serving the Lord – they always put God first. They don't bother about themselves; they don't think, "This will pollute me. I won't touch this. I will not do this job, because this job is not my kind of job. I only want a proper job that will be profitable for realisation only." No, whatever God gives, to the one who is surrendered, one shall accept it! Whatever duty has been given, one should take it with great gratitude and do it! That's a life towards God! That's a life towards God-realisation!'

'The ones who are fully-realised, the *bhaktas*, do not judge the action that has been given to them. Whether they like it or not, they find the same happiness in doing it, because it has been given by God. They accept it – even if it is "unpleasant" – even if they have to clean toilets, they will find great joy in taking on that duty, because they do it for God. It's not for themselves but for God. Even if the duty that is given to them is very easy, very nice, very beautiful, their attitude is the same.

'If they have a certain duty which is not according to what they want, they don't feel, "Oh no, I can't do this. This has to be done only by certain other people – it's their duty, not my duty". They don't say, "This is not my duty, I won't do this". No. Whatever is asked, if it has been given as a duty to perform, one should find great joy in it, whether one wants to do it or not. And that's what Bhagavān says is the sign of a true renunciate; someone with a truly *sattvic* mind.'

VERSES 13-19: THE FIVE CAUSES OF ACTION

pañcaitāni mahābāho kāraṇāni nibodha me |
sāṅkhye kṛtānte proktāni siddhaye sarva karmaṇām || 13 ||

Now learn from Me, Arjuna, about the five factors, established by the Sāṅkhya system, which bring about the results of action. (13)

adhiṣṭhānaṁ tathā kartā karaṇaṁ ca pṛthag vidham |
vividhāśca pṛthak-ceṣṭā daivaṁ caivātra pañcamam || 14 ||

The five factors of action are: the seat of action (the body), the actual performer, the various sense organs, the different kinds of effort, and the Lord Himself, who is the fifth cause. (14)

śarīra vāṅg-manobhir yat karma prārabhate naraḥ |
nyāyyaṁ vā viparītaṁ vā pañcaite tasya hetavaḥ || 15 ||

Whatever work one undertakes with body, speech and mind, whether right or wrong, these five are its cause. (15)

tatraivaṁ sati kartāram ātmānaṁ kevalaṁ tu yaḥ |
paśyaty-akṛta buddhitvān na sa paśyati durmatiḥ || 16 ||

This being the case, the fool with an underdeveloped intelligence, who sees only himself as the agent, does not see at all. (16)

yasya nāhaṅkṛto bhāvo buddhir yasya na lipyate |
hatvāpi sa imāṁ-llokān ah anti na nibadhyate || 17 ||

Even though one slays all these men, if one's understanding is not tainted by action and one is free from any notion of being the doer, one does not kill, nor is one bound. (17)

jñānaṁ jñeyaṁ pari-jñātā trividhā karma codanā |
karaṇaṁ karma karteti trividhaḥ karma saṅgrahaḥ || 18 ||

The act of knowing, the object of knowledge and the knower, are the three things that stimulate action. And the instrument, the act itself, and the performer, are the three components of action. (18)

jñānaṁ karma ca kartā ca tridhaiva guṇa-bhedataḥ |
procyate guṇa saṅkhyāne yathāvac-chṛṇu tāny-api || 19 ||

Based on the three *guṇas*, there are three ways of seeing knowledge, action, and the performer of action. Now listen as I describe them for you. (19)

'Bhagavān says that whatever one does, whether it's good or evil; whatever sacrifices, charity, austerities, study; whatever work...; is due to these five causes [the body, the performer, the sense organs, the different kinds of effort, and the Lord Himself]. Whatever binds one, according to what one has to do, what kind of category one falls into, what stage of life one is in, whatever temperament, whatever manners, whatever character one has, is due to these five causes. Whatever duty has been given, wherever you are, whatever religion you follow, whatever morality you have, whatever action you perform, is due to these five causes.'

'The ones who are ignorant don't see that these qualities of the body are just the game of *prakṛti*. They don't see that all these qualities are not eternal. Life will carry on again, in another body and so on. They don't realise that the *ātmā* that is inside of them is eternal. Due to their false identification with the body; due to their claiming that they are doing this, doing that; dancing in this game of good and evil, and evil and good, and so on, they will remain attached to *karma*, and *karma* attached to them. And due to this *karma*, they can't be free; they don't see this. Whereas those who have the eyes of true knowledge, will see with the eyes of the heart. And when they see with the eyes of the heart, they perceive the supreme reality of the Self. They perceive that human beings are created to be free, not to be attached to themselves. And automatically they will change, they will become humble! So when one is surrendered to the spiritual path, this is what happens – humbleness awakens.'

VERSES 20-22: KNOWLEDGE AND THE GUṆAS

sarva-bhūteṣu yenaikaṁ bhāvam avyayam īkṣate |
avibhaktaṁ vibhakteṣu taj-jñānaṁ viddhi sāttvikam || 20 ||

That knowledge which reveals one changeless reality in all beings, undivided in different bodies, is *sattvic* in nature. (20)

pṛthaktvena tu yaj-jñānaṁ nānā bhāvān pṛthag-vidhān |
vetti sarveṣu bhūteṣu taj-jñānaṁ viddhi rājasam || 21 ||

That knowledge which is based on distinction and which sees different entities, in varying physical forms, is *rajasic* in nature. (21)

yat tu kṛtsnavad ekasmin kārye saktam ahaitukam |
atattvārthavad alpaṁ ca tat tāmasam udāhṛtam || 22 ||

But that knowledge which is not based on reason, which clings to one single idea as if it were everything, which is oblivious to Truth and therefore limited, that knowledge is declared to be *tamasic*. (22)

'In this verse, Bhagavān says that those realised souls who have true knowledge of the Self, perceive the Lord everywhere... Even though the bodies are separated, there are diversities, there are dualities; the one with *sattvic* knowledge, with true knowledge, perceives that *vasudhaiva-kuṭumbakaṁ* – there's only one family. They perceive the Lord inside themselves and in everything; not only in human beings, but also in animals, in plants and in the entire creation.'

VERSES 23-25: ACTION AND THE GUṆAS

niyataṁ saṅga rahitam arāga-dveṣataḥ kṛtam |
aphala prepsunā karma yat tat sāttvikam ucyate || 23 ||

Prescribed work which is done without attachment, without desire or hatred, by one who does not look for any reward, is said to be *sattvic*. (23)

yat tu kamepsunā karma sāhaṅkāreṇa vā punaḥ |
kriyate bahulāyāsaṁ tad rājasam-udāhṛtam || 24 ||

Action performed with a longing to fulfil desires, and which is motivated by ego or excessive endeavour, is said to be *rajasic*. (24)

anubandhaṁ kṣayaṁ hiṁsām anavekṣya ca pauruṣam |
mohād ārabhyate karma yat tat tāmasam ucyate || 25 ||

And that work which is done under delusion, which does not consider one's ability, and does not care about the consequences, loss or injury involved, is said to be *tamasic*. (25)

'Here Bhagavān is again and again reminding Arjuna that one has to do one's duty without any attachment, without any expectation, even without the mind thinking that one is doing something good to please the Lord.'

'If people are fully absorbed in the Divine, in God consciousness, it doesn't matter what the work is, whatever they do – in the eyes of the outside it can be a very terrible work or terrible things – Bhagavān says they are the dearest ones to the Lord. They have this *sattvic* quality.

'It doesn't matter where they come from; what background they have; what predominant qualities they had – whether before they had *rajasic*, *tamasic* or even *sattvic* qualities – they rise above these qualities. A *bhakta* who is fully surrendered rises above even *sattvic* qualities.'

'That's why it is said that when you are spiritual, you have to learn to accept what God has given you – whatever your job is, whatever duty has been given to you. A Self-realised person doesn't question, because who knows best? The Lord knows best what is good for you. A Self-realised person has trust in the Supreme that the duty granted to them is right for them, whatever it is. So here Bhagavān is saying that this is a person with *sattvic* qualities. They don't have any selfish motives, no negativity is cherished in their heart. Everything gets purified.'

VERSES 26-28: THE PERFORMER OF ACTION AND THE GUṆAS

mukta saṅgo'nahaṁvādī dhṛty-utsāha-samanvitaḥ |
siddhy-asiddhyor nirvikāraḥ kartā sātvika ucyate || 26 ||

The performer of action who is free from attachment and self-centredness, who is endowed with determination and enthusiasm and is unaffected by success and failure, is said to be *sattvic*. (26)

rāgī karma phala prepsur-lubdho hiṁsātmako'śuciḥ |
harṣa śokānvitaḥ kartā rājasaḥ parikīrtitaḥ || 27 ||

That performer of action who desires the fruits of his actions, who is greedy, envious, impure and always overwhelmed by delight and grief, is said to be in the mode of *rajas*. (27)

ayuktaḥ prākṛtaḥ stabdhaḥ śaṭho naiṣkṛtiko'lasaḥ |
viṣādī dīrgha-sūtrī ca kartā tāmasa ucyate || 28 ||

And that person who is unqualified, vulgar, stubborn, vicious, dishonest, lazy, morose and a procrastinator, is said to be *tamasic*. (28)

'Those who are non-attached, who are free, who don't lose balance even when they face all kinds of problems, worries, or tests, will take everything as a sacred obligation; they are surrendered to it. They have a mind which is calm and steady; a mind which is still; which is not engaged in any action that harms others or in seeking reward. Bhagavān says that these people have virtue, they have firmness, they have zeal. They love their duty and will not fail to do it, however hard it is. Whatever has been given to them, they will happily do it; they will do it with great joy, with great enthusiasm. So they don't worry about whether they succeed in what they do, or if they fail. Bhagavān says that these are the qualities of a *sattvic* person, somebody who is endowed with *sattvic* qualities and virtues.

'These people, Bhagavān says, receive the Light of God. This Light is hidden, deep inside the heart, hidden from the eyes of everyone. But for the true seeker of God, who loves God and serves Him, for them, the hidden Light is made manifest. Here Bhagavān says that for people with these qualities, nothing is impossible. Because it's not about them, it's about thinking that everything revolves around God. For a *bhakta*, the mind of the *bhakta* focuses on Kṛṣṇa all the time. The *bhakta* perceives Kṛṣṇa in whatever they do. They perceive the same in everybody: the Supreme Nārāyaṇa, sitting in everyone, whoever they meet. Because they have perceived the supreme Light within themselves, they have perceived Nārāyaṇa within themselves.'

VERSES 29-32: INTELLIGENCE AND THE GUṆAS

buddher bhedaṁ dhṛteścaiva guṇatas trividhaṁ śṛṇu |
procyamānam aśeṣeṇa pṛthaktvena dhanañjaya || 29 ||

Now hear Arjuna, as I explain the difference between the three types of intelligence and determination, according to the *guṇas*. (29)

pravṛtiṁ ca nivṛttiṁ ca kāryākārye bhayābhaye |
bandhaṁ mokṣaṁ ca yā vetti buddhiḥ sā pārtha sāttvakī || 30 ||

That intelligence, Arjuna, which understands prescribed action and renunciation of action, which can discern what ought to be done and what ought not to be done, what should be feared and what should not, what brings bondage and what brings liberation, is in the mode of *sattva*. (30)

yayā dharmam adharmaṁ ca kāryaṁ cākāryam eva ca |
ayathāvat prajānāti buddhiḥ sā pārtha rājasī || 31 ||

The intelligence which brings confusion about what is right and what is wrong, and about what should or should not be done, is under the influence of *rajas*. (31)

adharmaṁ dharmam iti yā manyate tamasāvṛtā |
sarvārthān viparītāṁśca buddhiḥ sā pārtha tāmasī || 32 ||

The intelligence, Arjuna, which is covered in darkness, and regards unrighteousness as righteousness and righteousness as unrighteousness, has the wrong idea on all things and is considered *tamasic*. (32)

'People who discriminate are always in peace. They just know what is wrong and what is right, and this decisiveness inside of them enlightens themselves. They have this sense of discrimination which will reveal to them what they have to do and what not to do. They know what to do to not get bound into this external reality and they know how to free themselves. Such an intellect of a devotee who is surrendered to the Lord has no fear. They don't have any cowardice. They are not expecting anything. They are introverted. They are absorbed into their divine Self through *japa*, through their noble acts, through their noble sacrifices, penance, through singing of the Divine Name, and through singing glory of the Lord, in everything they do.'

VERSES 33-35: DETERMINATION AND THE GUṆAS

dhṛtyā yayā dhārayate manaḥ prāṇendriya kriyāḥ | yogenāvyabhicāriṇyā dhṛtiḥ sā pārtha sāttvikī || 33 ||

That determination by which one can steady the mind, breath and senses, in undeviating *yoga* practise, is of the nature of *sattva*. (33)

yayā tu dharma kāmārthān dhṛtyā dhārayate'rjuna |
prasaṅgena phalākāṅkṣī dhṛtiḥ sā pārtha rājasī || 34 ||

That determination, Arjuna, which causes one to seek rewards from the pursuit of righteousness, desire and wealth, is of the nature of *rajas*. (34)

yayā svapnaṁ bhayaṁ śokaṁ viṣādaṁ madam eva ca |
na vimuñcati durmedhā dhṛtiḥ sā pārtha tāmasī || 35 ||

And that determination by which a foolish person is unable to go beyond sleep, fear, grief, depression and egotism, O Arjuna, is of the nature of *tamas*. (35)

'If people have this determination, this motivation to achieve their goal, they don't waver or deviate left or right. They are so focused on their goal; they are fixed on their goal like the lion. When the lion fixes its gaze on a certain prey, there may be hundreds dancing around, but the lion is not distracted; the lion is focused, thinking, "I will have this delicacy today." And the lion will go only for the one it has fixed its attention on. To its left or right might be a weak prey – dancing, tumbling around – but it would not bother about that. That's the aim! To put the ball in the goal! When you watch the World Cup, you watch all the players running; they are determined, they know their aim, they know their goal! They fix their minds towards that the goal. Their vision becomes focused and constant.

'When one has this one objective, which is God-realisation, and one persists by any means to attain this control of the mind, the senses, control of life; when the mind is always directed towards God for the sake of serving Him, for the sake of attaining His grace, for the sake of seeing Him, for the sake of loving Him, automatically one has control. The mind gets attached to Him, to His form, to His supreme reality. And the mind does not jump left or right when the mind is fully focused on the form of the Lord. This enables man to attain the grace of God quickly! Because of this persistence, God will run towards you.'

VERSES 36-40: HAPPINESS AND THE GUṆAS

sukhaṁ tvidānīṁ trividhaṁ śṛṇu me bharatarṣabha |
abhyāsād ramate yatra duḥkhāntaṁ ca nigacchati || 36 ||

Arjuna, there are also three kinds of happiness. Hear from Me about the happiness which is obtained after continued practise and which frees one from suffering. (36)

yat tad agre viṣam iva pariṇāme'mṛtopamam |
tat sukhaṁ sāttvikaṁ proktam ātma buddhi prasādajam || 37 ||

***Sattvic* happiness is like poison in the beginning but eventually becomes like nectar. It arises from a serene state of mind and leads to one knowing the Self. (37)**

viṣayendriya saṁyogād yat tad agre'mṛtopamam |
pariṇāme viṣam iva tat sukhaṁ rājasaṁ smṛtam || 38 ||

***Rajasic* happiness, however, is like nectar in the beginning and ends in poison. It arises from the senses contacting their sense objects. (38)**

yad agre cānubandhe ca sukhaṁ mohanam ātmanaḥ |
nidrālasya pramādotthaṁ tat tāmasam udāhṛtam || 39 ||

And *tamasic* happiness causes delusion both at the beginning and the end. It is based on sleep, laziness and foolishness. (39)

na tad asti pṛthivyāṁ vā divi deveṣu vā punaḥ |
sattvaṁ prakṛtijair muktaṁ yad ebhiḥ syāt tribhir guṇaiḥ || 40 ||

There is no being on Earth or even among the gods in heaven, who is free from the influence of these *guṇas* arising from this material nature. (40)

'Here Bhagavān says that surely, one who has this deep yearning, listening to the glory of the Lord, chanting His Name, becomes free from suffering. They have endurance, they have strength and power within. They don't cause harm to anyone, not even to an animal; they let everything take its course in life. They are fully absorbed in eternal happiness, true happiness, and once that happiness is attained, it will never leave.'

'The mind runs always towards the outside as a result of expectation, of desire: "I want a car," "I want a wife," "I want a husband." "I want money," "I want this," "I want that." When you first get these things, it's great fun, you feel great joy, happiness. How long do these feelings last? Not for too long. Only until the sense organs meet with the sense object; only for the short-term. And when these feelings subside, the mind jumps to something else. Due to this attachment to sense objects, if one fails to get something the mind desires, one goes into deep depression, one becomes aggressive, one becomes deluded.'

'In this state, one creates jealousy, one creates a state of competitiveness... So judgment arises, and when they start to judge, compare, compete, they lose all sense of happiness; they lose all their intelligence; they lose all their strength, vitality; they lose their energy, they become exhausted, drained.'

'Here Bhagavān says that you enjoy short-term happiness, but long-term suffering! This is how people with *rajasic* qualities live; enjoying, and then undergoing terrible suffering of various kinds, in numerous ways.'

'Bhagavān says, "As I am eternally present inside you, the realised soul – the one whose mind is constantly absorbed in the Lord – rises above the *guṇas*"... Who is above the *guṇas*? Only Him! No one else. The mind is not above the *guṇas*, even the consciousness is not above the *guṇas*. Here is supra consciousness. So, these realised souls are part of this world, they live their life, but...they are in constant, eternal, union with Bhagavān Nārāyaṇa, so all their qualities are transformed into only Him. It's only Nārāyaṇa-Kṛṣṇa that they perceive; wherever they look, they perceive only the Lord. They perceive only God everywhere, in each creature, each being... Their mind, intellect, senses – everything – is in God consciousness constantly. This is what is called God-realisation, this surrender to the Divine; rising above the *guṇas*; elevating to God consciousness; leaving this human plane or terrestrial plane and rising even above the celestial plane itself. So by leaving the Earth plane, leaving the celestial plane, leaving the lower planes, one attains the grace of the Lord within one's heart.'

❁ THE FOUR VARṆAS (VEDIC SOCIAL SYSTEM)

brāhmaṇa kṣatriya viśāṁ śūdrāṇāṁ ca parantapa |
karmāṇi pravibhaktāni svabhāva prabhavair guṇaiḥ || 41 ||

The duties of the *brāhmaṇas*, *kṣatriyas*, *vaiśyas* and the *śūdras*, Arjuna, are also divided according to the *guṇas* which arise from their inherent nature. (41)

śamo damas tapaḥ śaucaṁ kṣāntir ārjavam eva ca |
jñānaṁ vijñānam āstikyaṁ brahmam-karma svabhāvajam || 42 ||

Serenity and restraint, self-discipline, purity, patience, integrity, knowledge, wisdom and faith in the *Vedas* — all these constitute the qualities of the *brāhmaṇas* by which they carry out their work. (42)

śauryaṁ tejo dhṛtir dākṣyaṁ yuddhe cāpyapalāyanam |
dānam īśvara-bhāvaśca kṣātraṁ karma svabhāvajam || 43 ||

Heroism, power, determination, skill and courage in battle, generosity and leadership, are the inherent characteristics of the *kṣatriyas*. (43)

kṛṣi go-rakṣya vāṇijyaṁ vaiśya-karma svabhāvajam |
paricaryātmakaṁ karma śūdrasyāpi svabhāvajam || 44 ||

Agriculture, cattle-breeding, and trade, are the natural work of *vaiśyas*; the natural duty of the *śūdras* is labour and service to others. (44)

'Some are born into the *brāhmaṇa* caste. *Brāhmaṇas* here doesn't mean only priests, it means people who have *sattvic* qualities, who are always aware of God consciousness, always helping other people and so on. Then the *kṣatriyas* are the protectors, the ones who maintain the balance, and they have a mixture of *rajasic* and *sattvic* qualities. The *vaiśyas* the traders, are *rajasic*. And the *śūdras*, of course, people would say they are *tamasic*, but they have a mixture of *rajas* and *tamas*.'

'Here Bhagavān is not talking only about Brāhmaṇa caste as it is understood nowadays. No, He refers to a category of people who have this kind of qualities inside of them – they are *brāhmaṇas*... A *brāhmaṇa* should not have any judgment. A *brāhmaṇa* should respect everyone. No matter what colour you are, what creed you are, what faith you belong to. They don't judge anyone: this is the quality of a *brāhmaṇa*. They perceive the Lord and know that everything is by the grace of God. Bhagavān Kṛṣṇa made this very clear in this verse. This type of purity of mind, senses, body, activities, is what makes one a *brāhmaṇa*.'

'When Bhagavān Kṛṣṇa speaks here about caste, He is not suggesting that they are either higher or lower in rank. If you listen properly, this is not a caste system as nowadays people understand a caste system. Here, He talks about certain grades within society, which are required to maintain balance across society.

But as a result of pride and arrogance, the heads of these castes have corrupted everything; they have placed themselves as being superior. Bhagavān Kṛṣṇa is not talking about the superiority of anyone. He speaks about the distinction of different types of work required to create a balance. Just as the work of the hands relates to everything that the hands do; and the work of the feet is to walk. The feet can't say, "Today, I will not walk" and the hands can't say, "Okay, now I will start walking." Then when you start walking, the hands start jumping around; or your head says, "I will start walking." No, it doesn't. If this happened, then complete imbalance would result.'

VERSES 45-49: FINAL INSTRUCTIONS ABOUT KARMA-YOGA

sve sve karmaṇy-abhirataḥ saṁsiddhiṁ labhate naraḥ |
svakarma nirataḥ siddhiṁ yathā vindati tacchṛṇu || 45 ||

Through dedication to one's own duty, one attains perfection. Now listen to exactly how a person dedicated in such a way, achieves perfection. (45)

yataḥ pravṛttir bhūtānāṁ yena sarvam idaṁ tatam |
svakarmaṇā tam abhyarcya siddhiṁ vindati mānavaḥ || 46 ||

The Lord is the One from whom all beings have evolved and by whom all this is pervaded. By worshipping Him through one's own duty, one attains that perfect state. (46)

śreyān svadharmo viguṇaḥ para-dharmāt svanuṣṭhitāt |
svabhāva niyataṁ karma kurvan-nāpnoti kilbiṣam || 47 ||

Better is one's own *dharma* [1] imperfectly done, than the *dharma* of another done perfectly. When one practises the *dharma* ordained by one's own nature, one never bears any sin. (47)

sahajaṁ karma kaunteya sadoṣam api na tyajet |
sarvārambhā hi doṣeṇa dhūmenāgnir ivāvṛtāḥ || 48 ||

O Arjuna, one should not give up the work one has been born to do, even if it has faults, for all action is enveloped by some kind of fault, just as fire is covered by smoke. (48)

asakta buddhiḥ sarvatra jitātmā vigata spṛhaḥ |
naiṣkarmya siddhiṁ paramāṁ saṁnyāsenādhigacchati || 49 ||

One who is completely unattached, who is self-controlled and is free from desires, is liberated from all action. Such renunciation brings that supreme perfection. (49)

'People have to love and respect where God has put them. Whatever your work is in the outside world, that's your *dharma*. And if you do this properly, your greater *dharma* in life will come later on, when the right moment arises.'

'Only *tamasic* people believe in coincidence. People who don't believe in the Lord, they believe in coincidence. But coincidence is all a divine arrangement. He places you where you have to be.'

'When people do their work with deep gratitude and sincerity, they will attain liberation; they will attain God-realisation.'

'Bhagavān says that wherever you are, it doesn't matter what your duty is, as long as you worship Him and realise that whatever you do in life is a worship to Him, is a service to Him. If you work in a bank, you are serving the Lord. Just remove greediness and expectation from the mind, and bear in mind deeply that one is serving the Lord.

'Bhagavān doesn't say you have to change your job, no. Work there, but change your attitude, change the way you do it, change your intention! And if the intention is right, it becomes a worship. The action itself transforms into worship, into prayer. So here, Bhagavān says that God-realisation is open to all. All are born from Him, all originate from Him, and all are pervaded only by Him. So if a *kṣatriya* worships God with his qualities of valour, strength, and power, and does his duty, he will reach the same state as a *brāhmaṇa* reaches by worshipping the Lord through *mantras* and religious practices. If the mind and the senses are controlled, all practices can be dedicated to God.'

VERSES 50-53: FINAL INSTRUCTIONS ABOUT REALISED KNOWLEDGE

siddhiṁ prāpto yathā brahma tathāpnoti nibodha me |
samāsenaiva kaunteya niṣṭhā jñānasya yā parā || 50 ||

Now learn from Me briefly, Arjuna, how one who has achieved this perfection, attains Brahman, which is the highest stage of knowledge. (50)

buddhyā viśuddhayā yukto dhṛtyātmānaṁ niyamya ca |
śabdādīn viṣayāṁs-tyaktvā rāga-dveṣau vyudasya ca || 51 ||
vivikta-sevī laghvāśī yata-vāk-kāya-mānasaḥ |
dhyāna yoga paro nityaṁ vairāgyaṁ samupāśritaḥ || 52 ||
ahaṅkāraṁ balaṁ darpaṁ kāmaṁ krodhaṁ parigraham |
vimucya nirmamaḥ śānto brahma-bhūyāya kalpate || 53 ||

Using his purified intellect; subduing the mind with determination; renouncing the objects of the senses such as sound; abandoning attraction and hatred for things; living in solitude; eating little; restraining his speech, body and mind; constantly engaged in the *yoga* of meditation with a mood of dispassion; having given up all self-centred ideas along with power, arrogance, desire, anger, and material things, such a person has no sense of ownership. He remains peaceful and becomes worthy of the state of Brahman. (51-53)

'Those whose minds and intellects no longer entertain attraction towards the outside, whose minds are not longing and running towards sense pleasures, needs, wants; whose thirst for outside enjoyment has ceased; for them, there is cessation of *karma*. Their minds are subdued, controlled, free from all kinds of desires. Here Bhagavān says that such a mind, with such surrender, true discipline, and fully absorbed into *sādhana*, fully absorbed into Love, is free from the bondage of *karma*. The ones whose minds are fully absorbed in the Divine attain God consciousness. They attain the consciousness of the Lord and they start to reflect divine qualities, the divine light.'

'In whatever one does, wherever one is, one is free from personal gain, one is free from likes and dislikes, and one rises above duality.'

'When you are above duality, you don't perceive either good or bad. As I said before, when you sit in mediation, you see the Observer inside of you; this Observer doesn't feel as the mind perceives you to understand and feel. It's free. Through your *sādhana*, you are immersed, deep within the true Self. And within the true Self, one sees Nārāyaṇa.'

VERSES 54-57: REALISING PURE BHAKTI

brahma-bhūtaḥ prasannātmā na śocati na kāṅkṣati |
samaḥ sarveṣu bhūteṣu mad-bhaktiṁ labhate parām || 54 ||

Having realised the state of Brahman, and becoming full of joy, he neither grieves nor craves for anything. Being the same to all beings, he realises supreme devotion to Me. (54)

bhaktyā mām abhijānāti yāvān yaścāsmi tattvataḥ |
tato māṁ tattvato jñātvā viśate tad anantaram || 55 ||

By devotion alone, he gains the true knowledge of who and what I am. Knowing Me in this way, through this devotion, he unites with Me. (55)

sarva karmāṇyapi sadā kurvāṇo mad vyapāśrayaḥ |
mat prasādād avāpnoti śāśvataṁ padam avyayam || 56 ||

Constantly engaged in all prescribed duties, but utterly surrendered to Me, through My grace, he attains the eternal, changeless state. (56)

cetasā sarva karmāṇi mayi saṁnyasya mat paraḥ |
buddhi-yogam upāśritya mac-cittaḥ satataṁ bhava || 57 ||

Mentally dedicating all actions to Me, thinking of Me as the supreme goal, and engaged in *yoga*, focus your mind on Me. (57)

'Here Bhagavān Kṛṣṇa says that this supreme Love doesn't awaken just like that. It will never awaken in somebody whose mind is polluted, full of judgment, and criticism; who is always running towards the outside; who always sees differences and is always in competition. They will never be calm. One whose mind is always flickering around doesn't attain the state of calmness, doesn't attain the state of bliss. But whoever surrenders to Him with full devotion and love; whoever performs their daily work, knowing that whatever they do they are serving only Him; whoever is so absorbed in *bhakti* that nothing distracts them on the outside, there is no entertainment of the "I" and "mine"; they are fit to receive the supreme Love.'

'This is the connection that we all have. We are not connected outside, through the body or through the blood. Different people have come from different wombs of different mothers, but what connects us all is what we have within the heart. It's the same Lord, the Supreme Lord, seated in all hearts. And when you love, you perceive this. You are not in competition.'

'Your right hand will not compete with your left hand. Otherwise it would be dramatic, the right hand would go this way; the left hand would go that way. Your feet – imagine your two legs starting to compete with each other. It would be catastrophic! Imagine your right leg moving towards the right and the left going the other way; you will be split into two! This is what Bhagavān is saying: to realise that the whole of creation is in complete union in His cosmic body, and His Supreme Self is seated in the core of everyone's heart. One who perceives this supreme reality, with Love, will see Nārāyaṇa-Kṛṣṇa sitting in the heart of everyone.'

'When one longs for God, He Himself will come and reveal Himself, and this is God-realisation. He reveals Himself in many aspects, and the greatest of these is that He will reveal Himself in the heart of the *bhakta*. When one perceives this divine nature, the Absolute, the supreme aspect, one knows that in His *nirguṇa* aspect the Lord pervades everything. However, when He reveals His supreme aspect to the *bhakta*, it is with the *saguṇa* aspect of Himself.'

'Bhagavān is saying here that this is the highest form of *bhakti*, *parā-bhakti*. When one is fully immersed in the Lord, Bhagavān reveals Himself in one's own heart, and then one attains one's spiritual body and attains the Lord Himself.

'One will never see the outer vision of the Lord if one can't perceive the inner vision of the Lord. It is through the inner vision that Bhagavān reveals Himself, reveals His connection. It is through this inner vision that one is cleansed of all impurities. It is through this inner vision that you see His humbleness, and how much He cares for His devotees. Because the only thing He longs for is the Love of the devotee, the Love that you have. And He's waiting eagerly for you! Imagine how patient He must be. He must be very, very, very, very patient, to wait for you for so many lives! Not just one life, but until you are ready for this Love to awaken. This is how much He loves you. And this is how much you have to learn to love. You have to try your best to awaken this Love.'

VERSES 58-63: ACT AS YOU SEE FIT

mac-cittaḥ sarva durgāṇi mat-prasādāt tariṣyasi |
atha cettvam ahaṅkārān na śrosyasi vinaṅkṣyasi || 58 ||

Focusing your mind on Me, by My grace, you shall overcome all obstacles. If, however, out of pride, you do not listen to Me, you will be ruined. (58)

yad ahaṅkāram āśritya na yotsya iti manyase |
mithyaiṣa vyavasāyaste prakṛtis-tvāṁ niyokṣyati || 59 ||

If you give in to pride and think, 'I will not fight,' your resolve will be futile, for your own nature will compel you to act. (59)

svabhāvajane kaunteya nibaddhaḥ svena karmaṇā |
kartuṁ necchasi yan mohāt kariṣyasy-avaśo'pi tat || 60 ||

O Arjuna, out of illusion you do not wish to fight, but bound by the duty born from your own nature, you will be compelled to do so. (60)

īśvaraḥ sarva bhūtānāṁ hṛddeśe'rjuna tiṣṭhati |
bhrāmayan sarva-bhūtāni yantrārūḍhāni māyayā || 61 ||

The Lord abides in the heart of every being, Arjuna. By His power, He controls all their movements through life, as if they were seated on a machine. (61)

tam-eva śaraṇaṁ gaccha sarva-bhāvena bhārata |
tat prasādāt parāṁ śāntiṁ sthānaṁ prāpsyasi śāśvatam || 62 ||

O Arjuna, surrender to Him alone with your whole being. By His grace, you shall obtain supreme peace and the eternal Abode. (62)

iti te jñānam ākhyātaṁ guhyād guhyataraṁ mayā |
vimṛśyaitad aśeṣeṇa yathecchasi tathā kuru || 63 ||

And so I have taught you that knowledge which is the greatest of all mysteries. Reflecting on it thoroughly, do what you think is best. (63)

'Here, Bhagavān Kṛṣṇa, as the supreme *guru*, the *jagadguru*, is giving an order to His disciple. He says, "If you listen to Me, nothing will go wrong. But if you don't listen to Me, you are at risk." Then you do what your mind perceives you should do, and for sure you would be doomed. Then you would not have real peace. You would not have real joy in this world or the next. You would fall from your spiritual level and you will not attain Him. Here Bhagavān says if one doesn't follow what the *guru* says, wholeheartedly, and full of devotion and love, grace will not be granted. It is only through the grace of the Master, *guru-kṛpā*, that one achieves complete, ultimate success in life, and one gets the grace of the Lord Himself.'

'He is reminding not only Arjuna, He is reminding everyone, every *bhakta* on the spiritual path not to go into the fantasy of the mind. The fantasy that the mind creates can be very dangerous. That's why it is very, very important to take shelter at the Feet of the Master. Because only the Master can free one from one's self-created illusion. When one creates one's own illusion, one starts listening to one's own reason. And then the *tamasic* qualities dominate. And when the *tamasic* qualities dominate, the *bhaktas* are not fit to do their service. They pull themselves away. They will not have this Love, they will not have this feeling. And in place of having this Love and this deepness of surrender, they will develop pride and ego, and all kinds of judgment, all kinds of criticism. Here Bhagavān says to Arjuna, 'Your duty is to be obedient, and just listen to what I am saying! If you listen to Me, to what I'm telling you, you will pass safely through all difficulties, and you won't worry about anything.' But, Bhagavān also says that if there is egoism, the result will be the opposite.'

VERSES 64-65: KṚṢṆA'S ETERNAL PROMISE

sarva guhyatamaṁ bhūyaḥ śṛṇu me paramaṁ vacaḥ |
iṣṭo'si me dṛṣam iti tato vakṣyāmi te hitam || 64 ||

Once again hear My supreme teaching, the most secret of all; because you are so dear to Me, I will declare what is best for you. (64)

manmanā bhava mad-bhakto mad yājī māṁ namas kuru |
mām evaiṣyasi satyaṁ te pratijāne priyo'si me || 65 ||

Fix your mind on Me, be devoted to Me, worship Me, bow down before Me and you shall come to Me. I promise you this for certain, for you are dear to Me. (65)

'Here Bhagavān gives Arjuna assurance, because Arjuna was taken aback. The Lord gives this assurance not only to Arjuna, but to whoever is surrendered to Him: to those whose minds are continuously focused on Him; who through their *sādhana*, when they sit in meditation, are fully absorbed in Him and see Him only; who are devoted; who do all their *sādhana* in a state of serving Him, loving Him; who do their spiritual practices; who worship Him; who bow down in front of Him due to the humility in their hearts. Bhagavān says, "You shall come to Me alone." There's no other way. If you are surrendered to Him, you will achieve Him. Because if you surrender to Him fully, He will also surrender Himself fully to you. And if He surrenders fully to you, if your heart is filled with delight with the Lord, you will attain Him. He was saying, "Your job is to focus your mind, devote yourself, worship, bow down. If you do your job, I Myself will give Myself."'

'Bhagavān reminds Arjuna of His Love for him. And this is unique. He says, "Arjuna, you are Mine, and I'm yours." Bhagavān says there is no difference, "What belongs to Me, belongs to you. You are dear to Me. You have faith in Me. You have trust in Me. You are devoted to Me. You worship Me." Here Bhagavān is also saying, "Count on Me fully. Don't count on your own effort; don't count on your own strength, your own will." Somebody with pride, with ignorance, will count very much on their own effort. Here Bhagavān says that with your own effort you will reach somewhere, but if you want to reach the supreme state of surrender, if you want to achieve the goal of life, only when you surrender completely and fully to the Lord Himself will you reach this.'

VERSE 66: COMPLETE SURRENDER TO GOD

sarva dharmān parityajya mām ekaṁ śaraṇaṁ vraja |
ahaṁ tvā sarva-pāpebhyo mokṣayiṣyāmi mā śucaḥ || 66 ||

Abandoning all *dharmas*, surrender to Me alone. I will take care of all your sins; I will liberate you. Have no fear. (66)

'Bhagavān is reminding all on the spiritual path who are surrendered, all who are surrendered to the *guru*'s Feet, that they will attain the grace of the Master, the grace of the *guru*. And when one attains the grace of the *guru*, one will attain the grace of Lord Kṛṣṇa Himself. Here He says, "Abandon all *dharmas*." One who is free, one who does not hang on duality, one who does not hang onto judgment, will attain this grace. With such judgment – "I am better than this one," or "My way is better" – how would one awaken this Love? How can you love with judgment? You can't. If you love Bhagavān, you must be fully aware. You have to love Him wholeheartedly, not half-heartedly.'

'This is the main teaching of the Vaiṣṇavism: "Abandon all *dharmas* and take refuge in Me alone"... For those who are truly surrendered, whose minds are fully absorbed in surrendering to the Feet of the Master, all the rules are gone; all the regulations are gone, because that abandonment itself, the letting go of every concept and taking refuge at the Feet of the Lord, will awaken the supreme realisation.'

❁ VERSES 67-71: SPREADING THE BHAGAVAD GĪTĀ

idaṁ te nātapaskāya nābhaktāya kadācana |
na cāśuśrūṣave vācyaṁ na ca māṁ yo'bhyasūyasi || 67 ||

This teaching should never be revealed to one who is devoid of self-discipline and devotion, nor to one who has no desire to listen, and certainly not to one who is envious of Me. (67)

ya imaṁ paraṁ guhyaṁ mad bhakteṣv-abhidhāsyati |
bhaktiṁ mayi parāṁ kṛtvā mām evaiṣyaty-asaṁśayaḥ || 68 ||

But the one who gives this highest mystery to My devotees, displays the highest devotion to Me and shall come to Me, there is no doubt about this. (68)

na ca tasmān manuṣyeṣu kaścin me priya-kṛttamaḥ |
bhavitā na ca me tasmād anyaḥ priyataro bhuvi || 69 ||

There is nobody who can perform a service more pleasing to Me than this, nor shall there be another on Earth dearer to Me than he. (69)

adhyeṣyete ca ya imaṁ dharmyaṁ saṁvādam āvayoḥ |
jñāna-yajñena tenāham iṣṭaḥ syām iti me matiḥ || 70 ||

And in My opinion, whoever studies this dialogue of ours based on *dharma*, worships Me through the sacrifice of knowledge. (70)

śraddhāvān anasūyaśca śṛṇuyād api yo naraḥ |
so'pi muktaḥ śubhāṁllokān prāpnuyāt puṇya karmaṇām || 71 ||

And the one who listens to it with faith, free from envy, shall also be liberated and will attain the auspicious realms where those who have performed righteous deeds reside. (71)

'Bhagavān gives His assurance that it's not only one who studies or who meditates on it, that benefits; He says that by merely listening to the *Gītā*, one's sins are eradicated. One is cleansed from all past *karmas*.'

'Bhagavān has said that not everybody can understand this glory. Some people will just read the *Bhagavad Gītā* as a novel. They will enjoy the words, and then it will disappear. It's like throwing the seeds on the stone. They will hear it, they will read about it, but it will not make any sense. It will dry up. Some people will hear the glory of the Lord and it will make some sense to them, but they will always look at how they will use it for their own benefit. And those devotees who are surrendered they will drink this nectar; they will meditate continuously upon it and they will grow inwardly in Love and devotion.'

VERSES 72-73: ARJUNA'S DELUSION IS OVERCOME

kaccid etac chrutaṁ pārtha tvayaikāgreṇa cetasā |
kaccid ajñāna saṁmohaḥ pranaṣṭaste dhanañjaya || 72 ||

O Arjuna, have you paid attention to this teaching with a concentrated mind? Has your delusion based on ignorance, been dispelled? (72)

arjuna uvāca
naṣṭo mohaḥ smṛtir labdhā tvat prasādān mayācyuta |
sthito'smi gata sandehaḥ kariṣye vacanaṁ tava || 73 ||

Arjuna says:
My delusion has been destroyed. By Your grace, O Kṛṣṇa, I have regained my understanding. I am freed from doubts, I stand strong and will act according to Your word. (73)

Realisation is not given to everybody; it is only given when one is worthy of it. But when one is worthy of it, even by hearing the *Gītā*, one will be free, one will attain Him. You see how sweet He is? He makes it easy. Earlier He says, "If you can have devotion, if you can do this and do that…" and finally He says, "Listen! If you don't have time to do all this, don't worry. Offer one Tulsī leaf and a few drops of water with love, I will accept this." This is what Love does. For Love, He left Vaikuṇṭha. For His Love for all, He manifests several times. For the Love of His *bhaktas*, He comes to their rescue. It's due to this Love, nothing else.'

'Here Arjuna clearly, without any doubt, without any confusion, without any delusion, said, "Lord, all has been melted away. That knowledge and wisdom which You have placed inside of me, which you have revealed to me, has transformed me into a new person."'

'He understands his duty and the *dharma* that is demanded from him. He has attained mental stability. Arjuna is in this state where he can fully accept what Kṛṣṇa has taught him and he is ready to fight.'

VERSES 74-78: FINAL CONCLUSION

sañjaya uvāca
ity-ahaṁ vāsudevasya pārthasya ca mahātmanaḥ |
saṁvādam imam aśrauṣam adbhutaṁ roma-harṣaṇam || 74 ||

Sañjaya says:
Thus have I heard this astounding conversation, between Kṛṣṇa and the great-minded Arjuna, which makes my hair stand on end. (74)

vyāsa-prasādāc-chrutavān etad guhyam aham param |
yogaṁ yogeśvarāt kṛṣṇāt sākṣāt kathayataḥ svayam || 75 ||

By the grace of Vyāsa, I have heard this supreme mystery of *yoga* which has been personally declared by Kṛṣṇa, the Lord of *yoga*. (75)

rājan saṁsmṛtya saṁsmṛtya saṁvādam imam adbhutam | keśavārjunayoḥ puṇyaṁ hṛṣyāmi ca muhurmuhuḥ || 76 ||

O king, after remembering this astounding and auspicious dialogue between Śrī Kṛṣṇa and Arjuna, I rejoice again and again. (76)

tacca saṁsmṛtya saṁsmṛtya rūpam aty-adbhutaṁ hareḥ |
vismayo me mahān rājan hṛṣyāmi ca punaḥ punaḥ || 77 ||

And as I recall again that most spectacular form of Kṛṣṇa, I am filled with wonder, O king, and once more I rejoice again and again. (77)

yatra yogeśvaraḥ kṛṣṇo yatra pārtho dhanurdharaḥ |
tatra śrīrvijayo bhūtir dhruvā nītir matir mama || 78 ||

It is my firm conviction that wherever there is Śrī Kṛṣṇa, the Lord of *yoga*, and Arjuna who bears the bow, there will always be victory, wealth, success and good judgement. (78)

'What Bhagavān Kṛṣṇa speaks to Arjuna in the *Gītā* is very rich in information; it is rich with advice on how one has to love God. It's about how to love God and let go of the negative qualities. All these qualities, which Bhagavān Kṛṣṇa talks about in this chapter, are not outside; you are born with them. Some of the qualities are stronger than the others, but nevertheless if you are not aware, if you are not attentive, or if you are not conscious of them, then you let yourself be overruled by these qualities. The best of all qualities is the Love that Bhagavān has put inside your heart and that's true Love… When you anchor yourself in that Love, nothing can deviate you, nothing can move you! That's the stability of life!'

'For those who surrender to the Lord with faith and devotion, the Lord shall reside with them continuously… Only by complete surrender does one attain to the highest perfection. Only by constantly remembering of the Lord and His *līlās*, by associating yourself with the devotees of the Lord and by complete surrender and dedication to the Feet of the Master, is it possible. Nothing else.'

Chapter Eighteen Verses: Key Terms

[1] **Dharma** – in this verse, Kṛṣṇa is using the term '*dharma*' to mean the path that has been assigned to us.

LIST OF KEY TERMS

Ādityas – these are the twelve deities which take the role of the Sun. Every month these deities change, and out of them, Viṣṇu is the most radiant.

Airāvata – considered to be the best among elephants, and the vehicle of the king of the demigods (Indra).

Āśvattha tree – a sacred fig tree mentioned in various Hindu texts.

Aśvin-kumāras – twin celestial deities responsible for medicine.

Asuras – beings created by Brahmā, who are perpetually at war with their cousins, the *devas* (demigods). *Asuras* are typically associated with negative attributes. Although there are exceptions, they are generally self-centered and refuse to surrender to the Lord. The *devas* on the other hand are generally associated with positive qualities and understand their position in relation to the Lord.

ātmā – term interchanged with 'Self' and 'soul', which refers to an eternal, non-material, part of God.

Atma Kriya Yoga – given by Sri Swami Vishwananda for humanity to realise the teachings of the *Bhagavad Gītā*. It brings constant awareness of the Divine in every action and consists of a series of techniques which include meditation, *prāṇāyāma*, *āsanas*, *mudrās*, *japa*, and OM Chanting.

Bhakta – one who is devoted to God.

Bhakti-yoga – the path of loving devotion to God.

Bhāva – an intense feeling of love and self-surrender directed towards God.

Bhṛgu – one of the seven great *Sapta-ṛṣis* born from Brahmā.

Brahmā – deity born from the Supreme Lord responsible for creating within the physical universe.

Brahma-sūtra – a philosophical scripture that summarises the spiritual ideas of the *Upaniṣads*.

Brahman (Chapter 4, verse 24) – in this context, this term is used to describe the supreme reality, God or Nārāyaṇa.

Brahman (Chapter 13, verse 13) – although Brahman has been used to denote the Supreme Lord throughout the *Gītā*, here Kṛṣṇa says that Brahman is dependent on Him, which means He is referring to the all-pervasive aspect of Himself as the Supersoul.

Brahman (Chapter 14, verse 27) – this term is used here to refer to the impersonal conception of the supreme reality. Its abstract features (immortal, unchanging, eternal, blissful, etc.) have a concrete existence in the Supreme Lord.

Brāhmaṇas – one of the four classes within the *varṇa* system. *Brāhmaṇas* specialise as priests and teachers, and are responsible for preserving the sacred scriptures of Hinduism.

Bṛhaspati – deity responsible for wisdom and is the preceptor of the *devas* (demigods).

Bṛhat-sāma – a hymn which praises the Lord. The *Bṛhat-sāma* is chanted at the conclusion of auspicious *Vedic* ceremonies.

Churning of the Ocean of Milk – one of the central events in the eternal struggle between the *devas* (demigods) and *asuras*. Both groups churned the Ocean of Milk to obtain the nectar of immortality (*amṛta*).

Daityas – a clan of *asuras* who are eternally engaged in a fight with the *devas* (demigods). Prahlāda was a great king of the *asuras* and devotee of the Lord. He played a central role in the incarnation of the Nārasiṁha-avatāra.

Demigods – term interchanged with '*devas*', which refers to the limited celestial beings who occupy different heavenly realms within the material universe. Although not perfected beings, they are generally associated with positivity.

Dharma (Chapter 4, Introduction) – everything in this world is part of a natural cosmological order. As a result, each individual has a set purpose in line with this order. *Dharma* is the fulfilment of this purpose.

Dharma (Chapter 18, verse 47) – in this verse, Kṛṣṇa is using the term '*dharma*' to mean the path that has been assigned to us.

Five objects of the senses – form/colour, sound, touch sensations, flavour and aroma.

Four kinds of food – classified as being eaten, sucked, drunk or licked which leads to an increase in digestive fire. When the digestive fire is in balance with the *prāṇa* and *apāna*, the body is able to digest food properly, which has a positive impact on our mind and body.

Gandharvas – a group of celestial deities skilled in various arts such as music and dancing. Among the Gandharvas, Citraratha is said to be highly skilled in the art of singing.

Garuḍa – considered to be the best among birds, in the form of an eagle. He is the vehicle and eternal servant of Viṣṇu.

Gāyatrī-mantra – highly revered *mantra* from the *Ṛg Veda* dedicated to the Sun deity and is chanted widely by Hindus.

Guṇas – the three qualities within *prakṛti* (matter): *sattva* (purity), *rajas* (activity) and *tamas* (darkness). The different *guṇas* work together to shape and influence the experience we have in the material world.

Heaven – in the context of this verse, heaven is not the Supreme Abode of the Lord, but is considered to be the material realm of the demigods where one can temporarily enjoy celestial pleasures.

Janaka – a great king who achieved realisation through the practice of *karma-yoga*. An ideal example of one who acts in the world but is detached from his actions.

Japa – meditative repetition of a *mantra* or a Divine Name.

Jīva – the embodied Self.

Jīvātmā – term interchanged with '*jīva*', which refers to the embodied Self.

Jñāna-yoga – the path of external renunciation, where outside activity is given up in pursuit of inner enquiry.

Jñānī – the pure devotee who possesses knowledge of who the Lord truly is.

Kāmadhenu – the mother of all cows who provides her owners with whatever they desire.

Kandarpa – deity responsible for human love. Most commonly associated with Cupid in the West.

Kapila – Incarnation of the Lord and a great sage who taught His mother Devahūtī the knowledge of the Self, as mentioned in the *Śrīmad Bhāgavatam*.

Karma – any action done with the body or mind that produces further consequences.

Karma-yoga – the path by which one continues to act in the world with detachment. Such acts, therefore, do not create further consequences.

King of the demigods – also known as Indra, the leader of the *devas* (demigods) and the ruler of the heavens.

Kubera – deity responsible for material wealth, and king of the Yakṣas (nature spirits).

Kuśa grass – a type of grass considered sacred in India. It is generally used for purification or as a conduit for energy during *pūjā* and ritual ceremonies. It can also be used to construct a seat for meditation.

Līlā – when the Lord takes on limitation to uplift and interact with His devotees.

Mahā-Viṣṇu – a cosmic manifestation of the Supreme Lord Nārāyaṇa in which He classically holds the conch, discus, mace, and lotus in each of His four hands.

Manu – title given to the first man of every age (known as a *manvantara*). All humans are believed to have descended from his lineage.

Mārgaśīrṣa – the ninth month in the Hindu lunar calendar when grains from agriculture fields are collected by farmers to earn money and make their living in India.

Maruts – identified as wind deities, each with a specific function. All of them are presided over by Marīci.

Māyā – the influence of the material world that draws us away from our true relationship with God.

Meru – the sacred five-peaked mountain, considered to be the centre of the physical, metaphysical and spiritual universe. It resides in the spiritual realm and cannot be perceived with the physical eyes.

Nāgas (Ananta) – half human/half serpent beings that reside in the netherworld. Ananta is the king of the Nāgas and eternal servant of Viṣṇu. Viṣṇu is often depicted resting on Ananta.

Nārada – a great *Vedic* sage born from Brahmā and one the foremost devotees of the Lord. He wanders the universe imparting the knowledge of devotion.

Prajāpati – personification of creative power.

Prakṛti – substance from which all material creation manifests. It forms part of Kṛṣṇa's nature and is therefore under His control.

Pralaya – the periodic dissolution of the material world, in which creation is withdrawn into the body of God.

Prāṇa and apāna – vital life force connected with the breath.

Rajas – the *guṇa* relating to the quality of passion, activity, endeavour, anxiety and frustration. People predominated by this *guṇa* are impelled by their desires and live a life of intense, restless action.

Rākṣasas – a race of beings who are generally well known for their aggressive and blood thirsty nature.

Rudras – described as loyal companions of Rudra, also identified as Lord Śiva. Rudras are messengers and different aspects of Śiva and are fearsome in nature. Śaṅkara is commonly known as the ascetic form of Śiva who dwells in Mount Kailāśa.

Sādhyas – class of divine beings dwelling in the celestial planets.

Sāma Veda – one of the four *Vedas*. The *Sāma Veda* contains melodies and chants.

Saṁsāra – *karmic* cycle of repeated birth and death.

Sāṅkhya – philosophy which states that there are two realities: the Puruṣa (Self) and *prakṛti* (matter). Through an analysis of *prakṛti*, one can realise oneself as the Puruṣa, which is utterly distinct from material nature.

Satguru – there are many types of *gurus* (teachers) who help one on the spiritual path, but the *satguru* is considered to be the highest. He is the Lord Himself, who has come to guide humanity to the ultimate goal.

Sattva – quality of gentility, good conduct, enlightened understanding, purity and detachment.

Seven great seers – created by Brahmā and known as the *Sapta-ṛṣis*, they are responsible for guiding the human race during the four *yugas* (ages). They are in complete communion with the Lord at all times and work towards maintaining a balance on Earth. Before them, and also born from Brahmā, were the four Kumāras: Sanaka, Sanātana, Sanandana, Sanat-kumāra.

Skanda – born from the third eye of Śiva, he is the brother of Gaṇeśa, and leads the celestial armies against the *asuras*.

Soma juice – powerful plant extract that formed a central part of the *Vedic* ritual sacrifice.

Ten senses – the *jñānendriyas*, which are the five modes of perception (sight, hearing, touch, taste, smell), and the *karmendriyas*, which are the five organs of action (hands, feet, voice, anus, and genitals).

Three worlds – referenced in *Vedic* texts as Heaven, Earth and the netherworld.

Uccaiḥśravas – beautiful white horse produced from the Ocean of Milk and claimed by Bali, the leader of the *asuras*.

Unmanifested – the dormant state of matter not yet differentiated into the various forms of material nature.

Vajra – the main weapon of the king of the demigods (Indra) in the form of a thunderbolt.

Varṇas – the different social classes within *Vedic* culture, namely the *brāhmaṇas* (sages and priests), *kṣatriyas* (warriors and royal leaders), *vaiśyas* (merchants responsible for commerce), and *śūdras* (responsible for general labour). In order to ensure a prosperous society, these different groups were allocated different responsibilities for the welfare of everyone at large.

Varuṇa – deity responsible for the oceans.

Vāsuki – king of the serpents, who helped in the Churning of the Ocean of Milk.

Vasus – the eight elemental deities representing different aspects of nature. The element of fire is presided over by Agni.

Vāyu – deity responsible for the winads.

Vedānta – one of the six schools of Hindu philosophy. Based on *Vedic* knowledge, it focuses on describing the relationship between God, the Self, and material world.

Vedas – the earliest body of Indian scripture, consisting of the *Ṛg Veda, Sāma Veda, Yajur Veda*, and *Atharva Veda*, which lay down the fundamental principles of Hinduism.

Viśvadevas – term used to describe all the celestial deities as a whole.

Vivasvān – also referred to as the Sun-god, who was given divine knowledge by Kṛṣṇa at the beginning of the age.

Vṛṣṇi Clan – ancient *Vedic* Indian clan which Kṛṣṇa was born into. Vasudeva, who belonged to the *Vṛṣṇi* clan was the father of Kṛṣṇa.

Vyāsa – a great *Vedic* sage who organised and divided the *Vedas*. He authored many of the puranic scriptures, but is perhaps most famous for authoring the *Mahābhārata* and *Śrīmad Bhāgavatam*.

Yādava – Kṛṣṇa is a descendant of King *Yadu*, and is therefore also referred to as *Yādava*.

Yajña – this is the *Vedic* fire sacrifice. Various ritual offerings are made in an effort to appease the different gods and gain results. Throughout the *Gītā*, however, Kṛṣṇa introduces *yajña* as being more about the internal sacrifice of spiritual practice rather than just the fire ritual.

Yakṣas – class of nature spirits who serve *Kubera* (deity responsible for wealth).

Yama – the lord of death who rules the netherworld. For those bound to this material world, he delivers justice for each soul.

Yoga-māyā – the specific potency of God that conceals His true identity.

Yugas – defined as an age or epoch in Hindu cosmology. There are four distinct *yugas*: *Satya-yuga, Tretā-yuga, Dvāpara-yuga* and *Kali-yuga*, each period being shorter, darker, and less righteous than the preceding. Mankind is currently in the age of *Kali-yuga*. In this verse, Kṛṣṇa states that both a Day and a Night of *Brahmā* lasts a 'thousand *Mahā-yugas*' which is actually a thousand cycles of the four *yugas* mentioned, a period that lasts trillions of years.

TAKE THE NEXT STEP

The undeniable message of the *Bhagavad Gītā* is that our true being, and our eternal relationship to the Supreme Infinite, is obscured by our identity with the body and mind.

Kṛṣṇa tells us our goal is communion with God and the way is *bhakti*, pure devotion, which shifts us from limiting selfishness to unlimited Love. But how do we take this truth to heart and have the courage to walk into the unknown? Only by opening the heart and purifying the mind.

To help you accomplish this, Paramahamsa Vishwananda offers a holistic path of devotion that is rooted in time-honoured spiritual traditions. This *bhakti* path naturally helps you cultivate a uniquely personal, loving relationship with the Lord Himself.

Through His international Bhakti Marga organisation, you are invited to take part in a wide variety of programs and ways to learn, all of which will help you to rapidly advance on your spiritual path. Using a unique four-armed approach, Bhakti Marga helps everyone rise in love with God by strengthening faith and increasing devotion. In this way, you can grow and progress in a way that best suits you.

Bhakti Marga's four arms include:

- Philosophical Knowledge that directs the mind toward higher truths.
- Yoga & Meditation that offer a variety of meditative practices to awaken the wisdom of the soul.
- Rituals that ignite devotion, reconnecting the soul with the Divine.
- Devotional Arts that channel the natural tendency towards pleasure and expression to attain the highest happiness and loving communion with God.

Sincerely engaging in these practices over time allows you to experience the transformational power of Love inherent in the *bhakti* path. Using them consistently, the negativity of the mind dissolves, allowing faith, Love and devotion to awaken in your heart.

As you evolve on the path, ever-increasing experiences of true unconditional Love and lasting happiness become more commonplace, regardless of the circumstances. Most often, this leads to a heartfelt yearning to connect more deeply with God, and Paramahamsa Vishwananda's unconditional Love, support and guidance is available to everyone who wants to grow and evolve on this path to God-realisation.

Additional practical support is also available through online programs, courses, retreats, and a global network of like-minded communities, known as *saṅghas*.

Very naturally, as the fruits of this path blossom, you may find yourself caring more about the world around you. Such a shift leads to a growing desire to serve humanity and share the path of Divine Love with others, because, in the end, it is all about Love.

Just Love.

The greatest adventure of all.

Take the Next Step

Discover more at **bhaktimarga.org**

REFERENCES

<?> Paramahamsa Sri Swami Vishwananda (2019). *Shreemad Bhagavad Gita – The Song of Love*. Fourth Edition (p. 32). Springen: Bhakti Marga Publications.

<?> Ibid., 33.

<?> Ibid., 34.

<?> Ibid., 40.

<?> Ibid., 41.

<?> Ibid., 43.

<?> Paramahamsa Sri Swami Vishwananda (2016, August 16). *Bhagavad Gita* Course. Unpublished transcription. Bhakti Marga Archive, Springen.

<?> Ibid. 1, 47.

<?> Ibid. 1, 49.

<?> Ibid. 1, 48.

<?> Ibid. 9.

<?> Ibid. 1, 54.

<?> Ibid. 7.

<?> Ibid. 1, 56-57.

<?> Ibid. 7.

<?> Ibid. 1, 60.

<?> Ibid. 1, 61.

<?> Ibid. 1, 77.

<?> Ibid. 1, 72.

<?> Ibid. 7.

<?> Ibid. 1, 84

<?> Ibid.

<?> Ibid. 1, 96.

<?> Ibid. 7.

<?> Ibid. 1, 96-97.

<?> Ibid. 1, 100.

<?> Ibid. 1, 99.

<?> Paramahamsa Sri Swami Vishwananda (2016, August 17). *Bhagavad Gita* Course. Unpublished transcription. Bhakti Marga Archive, Springen.

<?> Ibid. 1, 100-101.

<?> Ibid. 7.

<?> Ibid.

<?> Ibid.

<?> Ibid. 1, 114.

<?> Ibid. 7.

<?> Ibid. 1, 119.

<?> Ibid. 28.

<?> Ibid. 1, 141.

<?> Ibid. 1, 132.

<?> Ibid. 28.

<?> Ibid.

<?> Ibid. 1, 160.

<?> Ibid. 1, 157.

<?> Ibid. 28.

<?> Ibid. 7.

<?> Ibid. 28.

<?> Ibid.

<?> Ibid.

<?> Ibid. 1, 164.

<?> Ibid. 1, 165.

<?> Ibid. 48.

<?> Ibid. 28.

<?> Ibid. 1, 167.

<?> Ibid. 1, 171.

<?> Ibid. 1, 167.

<?> Ibid. 28.

<?> Ibid. 1, 185.

<?> Ibid. 1, 186.

<?> Ibid. 28.

<?> Ibid. 1, 191.

<?> Ibid. 1, 188.

<?> Ibid. 1, 191.

<?> Ibid. 1, 196.

<?> Ibid. 1, 198.

<?> Ibid. 1, 200.

<?> Ibid. 1, 201.

<?> Ibid. 1, 202.

<?> Ibid. 1, 204.

<?> Ibid. 1, 205.

<?> Ibid. 1, 148.

<?> Ibid. 1, 149.

<?> Ibid. 1, 207.

<?> Ibid. 1, 209.

<?> Ibid. 28.

<?> Ibid. 1, 224.

<?> Ibid. 1, 216.

<?> Ibid. 28.

<?> Ibid. 1, 224-225.

<?> Ibid. 1, 225.

<?> Ibid. 1, 226.

<?> Ibid.

<?> Ibid. 1, 233.

<?> Ibid.

<?> Ibid. 28.

<?> Ibid.

<?> Ibid. 1, 244.

<?> Ibid. 28.

<?> Ibid. 1, 252.

<?> Ibid. 1, 257.

<?> Paramahamsa Sri Swami Vishwananda (2016, August 18). *Bhagavad Gita* Course. Unpublished transcription. Bhakti Marga Archive, Springen.

<?> Ibid. 89.

<?> Ibid. 1, 231-232.

<?> Ibid. 1, 232.

<?> Ibid. 1, 209.

<?> Ibid. 89.

<?> Ibid. 1, 279.

<?> Ibid. 1, 280.

<?> Ibid. 89.

<?> Ibid. 1, 288.

<?> Ibid. 1, 290.
<?> Ibid. 1, 292.
<?> Ibid. 1, 293.
<?> Ibid. 1, 294.
<?> Ibid.
<?> Ibid. 1, 295.
<?> Ibid. 89.
<?> Ibid.
<?> Ibid. 1, 298.
<?> Ibid. 1, 299.
<?> Ibid. 1, 302.
<?> Ibid. 1, 303.
<?> Ibid. 1, 305.
<?> Ibid. 1, 308.
<?> Ibid. 89.
<?> Ibid. 101.
<?> Ibid. 89.
<?> Ibid.
<?> Ibid.
<?> Ibid. 1, 327.
<?> Ibid. 1, 329-330.
<?> Ibid. 89.
<?> Ibid.
<?> Ibid. 1, 331.
<?> Ibid. 1, 341.
<?> Ibid. 1, 346-347.
<?> Ibid. 89.
<?> Ibid.
<?> Ibid. 1, 350-351.
<?> Ibid. 89.
<?> Ibid. 1, 372.
<?> Ibid. 1, 374.
<?> Ibid. 89.
<?> Ibid. 1, 895.
<?> Ibid. 89.
<?> Ibid. 1, 385.
<?> Ibid. 1, 386.
<?> Ibid. 1, 392.
<?> Ibid. 1, 390.
<?> Ibid. 1, 393.
<?> Ibid. 1, 394.
<?> Ibid. 1, 395.
<?> Ibid. 1, 396-397.
<?> Ibid. 1, 397.
<?> Ibid. 89.
<?> Ibid. 1, 398.
<?> Ibid. 1, 399.
<?> Ibid. 89.
<?> Ibid. 1, 403-404.
<?> Ibid. 1, 409.
<?> Ibid. 1, 414.
<?> Ibid. 1, 416.
<?> Ibid. 1, 415.
<?> Ibid. 89.
<?> Ibid. 1, 419.
<?> Ibid. 1, 427.
<?> Ibid. 1, 428-429.
<?> Ibid. 1, 429.
<?> Ibid. 1, 430.
<?> Paramahamsa Sri Swami Vishwananda (2016, August 19). *Bhagavad Gita* Course. Unpublished transcription. Bhakti Marga Archive, Springen.
<?> Ibid. 1, 432.
<?> Ibid. 1, 436.
<?> Ibid. 1, 442.
<?> Ibid. 1, 442-443.
<?> Ibid. 1, 438.
<?> Ibid. 1, 444.
<?> Ibid. 1, 448.
<?> Ibid. 1, 446.
<?> Ibid. 1, 452.
<?> Ibid. 1, 452-453.
<?> Ibid. 1, 462.
<?> Ibid. 158.
<?> Ibid. 1, 464.
<?> Ibid. 158.
<?> Ibid. 1, 465.
<?> Ibid. 1, 467.
<?> Ibid. 1, 468.
<?> Ibid. 1, 469.
<?> Ibid. 1, 471.
<?> Ibid. 158.
<?> Ibid. 1, 474.
<?> Ibid. 1, 477.
<?> Ibid. 1, 478.
<?> Ibid. 1, 480.
<?> Ibid. 1, 481.
<?> Ibid. 1, 483.
<?> Ibid. 1, 483-484.
<?> Ibid. 158.
<?> Ibid. 1, 485.
<?> Ibid. 1, 488.
<?> Ibid. 158.
<?> Ibid. 1, 492.
<?> Ibid. 158.
<?> Ibid. 1, 501-502.
<?> Ibid. 158.
<?> Ibid.
<?> Ibid. 1, 506.
<?> Ibid. 1, 514.
<?> Ibid. 1, 520.
<?> Ibid. 1, 521.
<?> Ibid. 1, 525.
<?> Paramahamsa Sri Swami Vishwananda (2016, August 20). *Bhagavad Gita* Course. Unpublished transcription. Bhakti Marga Archive, Springen.
<?> Ibid. 1, 521-522.
<?> Ibid. 1, 528.
<?> Ibid. 1, 529.
<?> Ibid. 1, 533.
<?> Ibid. 1, 537.
<?> Ibid. 1, 559.
<?> Ibid. 1, 561-562.
<?> Ibid. 1, 562.
<?> Ibid. 1, 563.
<?> Ibid. 200.
<?> Ibid. 1, 569-570.
<?> Ibid. 1, 570.
<?> Ibid. 1, 571-572.

<?> Ibid. 1, 575-576.

<?> Ibid. 1, 576-577.

<?> Ibid. 1, 580.

<?> Ibid. 1, 581.

<?> Ibid. 1, 582.

<?> Ibid. 200.

<?> Ibid. 1, 597-598.

<?> Ibid. 1, 599.

<?> Ibid. 1, 600.

<?> Ibid. 1, 581.

<?> Ibid. 1, 605-606.

<?> Ibid. 1, 606.

<?> Ibid. 1, 610.

<?> Ibid. 1, 611.

<?> Ibid. 1, 591.

<?> Ibid. 1, 615.

<?> Ibid. 200.

<?> Ibid. 1, 615.

<?> Ibid. 200.

<?> Paramahamsa Sri Swami Vishwananda (2016, August 21). *Bhagavad Gita* Course. Unpublished transcription. Bhakti Marga Archive, Springen.

<?> Ibid. 1, 621.

<?> Ibid. 1, 627.

<?> Ibid. 1, 630-631.

<?> Ibid. 233.

<?> Ibid. 1, 634-635.

<?> Ibid. 1, 637-638.

<?> Ibid. 1, 649.

<?> Ibid. 1, 640-641.

<?> Ibid. 1, 642.

<?> Ibid. 1, 644.

<?> Ibid. 1, 647.

<?> Ibid. 1, 649-650.

<?> Ibid. 233.

<?> Ibid. 233.

<?> Ibid. 1, 655-657.

<?> Ibid. 1, 665.

<?> Ibid. 1, 666.

<?> Ibid. 1, 668.

<?> Ibid. 1, 669.

<?> Ibid. 1, 674-675

<?> Ibid. 1, 677.

<?> Ibid. 1, 679.

<?> Ibid. 233.

<?> Ibid. 1, 681.

<?> Ibid. 1, 663.

<?> Ibid. 1, 684.

<?> Ibid. 1, 687.

<?> Ibid. 1, 688.

<?> Ibid. 1, 689.

<?> Ibid. 233.

<?> Ibid. 1, 700-701.

<?> Ibid. 1, 701-702.

<?> Ibid. 1, 240

<?> Ibid. 1, 716.

<?> Ibid. 233.

<?> Ibid. 1, 706.

<?> Ibid. 1, 714.

<?> Ibid. 1, 705-706.

<?> Ibid. 1, 718.

<?> Ibid. 233.

<?> Ibid. 1, 723-724.

<?> Ibid. 1, 726.

<?> Ibid. 1, 732.

<?> Ibid. 1, 739-740.

<?> Ibid. 1, 741.

<?> Ibid. 1, 742.

<?> Paramahamsa Sri Swami Vishwananda (2016, August 22). *Bhagavad Gita* Course. Unpublished transcription. Bhakti Marga Archive, Springen.

<?> Ibid. 1, 748-749.

<?> Ibid. 1, 749.

<?> Ibid. 1, 753.

<?> Ibid. 1, 755-756.

<?> Ibid. 1, 756-757.

<?> Ibid. 1, 757.

<?> Ibid. 1, 759.

<?> Ibid. 1, 768.

<?> Ibid. 1, 768-769.

<?> Ibid. 280.

<?> Ibid. 1, 776.

<?> Ibid. 1, 778.

<?> Ibid. 1, 782.

<?> Ibid. 1, 778-779.

<?> Ibid. 1, 787.

<?> Ibid. 1, 788.

<?> Ibid. 280.

<?> Ibid. 1, 789.

<?> Ibid. 1, 791.

<?> Ibid. 1, 794.

<?> Ibid. 280.

<?> Ibid. 1, 804.

<?> Ibid. 1, 805.

<?> Ibid. 280.

<?> Ibid. 1, 809.

<?> Ibid. 1, 810.

<?> Ibid. 1, 811-812.

<?> Ibid. 1, 812.

<?> Ibid. 1, 814.

<?> Ibid. 1, 815.

<?> Ibid.

<?> Ibid. 1, 818.

<?> Ibid. 1, 818-819.

<?> Ibid. 1, 820.

<?> Ibid. 1, 821.

<?> Ibid. 280.

<?> Ibid.

<?> Ibid. 1, 825

<?> Ibid. 1, 826-827.

<?> Ibid. 1, 828-829.

<?> Ibid. 1, 829.

<?> Ibid. 1, 843.

<?> Ibid. 1, 841.

<?> Ibid. 1, 845-846.

<?> Ibid. 1, 849-850.

<?> Ibid. 1, 853-854.

<?> Ibid. 1, 861.

<?> Ibid. 1, 862.

<?> Ibid. 1, 865.

<?> Ibid. 1, 870.

<?> Ibid. 1, 872-873.

<?> Paramahamsa Sri Swami Vishwananda (2016, August 23). *Bhagavad Gita* Course. Unpublished transcription. Bhakti Marga Archive, Springen.

<?> Ibid. 1, 879-880.

<?> Ibid. 1, 883.

<?> Ibid. 1, 885.

<?> Ibid. 1, 887.

<?> Ibid. 1, 888.

<?> Ibid. 1, 889.

<?> Ibid. 1, 891.

<?> Ibid. 1, 894.

<?> Ibid. 1, 895.

<?> Ibid. 1, 898.

<?> Ibid. 1, 900.

<?> Ibid. 1, 902.

<?> Ibid. 1, 903.

<?> Ibid. 1, 903-904.

<?> Ibid. 1, 906-907.

<?> Ibid. 1, 912.

<?> Ibid. 1, 913.

<?> Ibid. 1, 914.

<?> Ibid. 332.

<?> Ibid. 1, 918.

<?> Ibid. 332.

<?> Ibid. 1, 919.

<?> Ibid. 332.

<?> Ibid. 1, 834-835.

<?> Ibid. 332.

BIBLIOGRAPHY

Besant, Annie Wood. *The Bhagavad-Gita: or The Lord's Song with the text in Devanagari and an English translation.* Madras: G.A. Natesan & Co Publishers, 1922.

Giridhari: The Uplifter of Hearts. Springen: Bhakti Marga Publications, 2016.

Guru: The Rarest Life Treasure. Springen: Bhakti Marga Publications, 2017.

Sivan, Ram. "Srimad Bhagavad Gita with Gita Bhasya of Bhagavad Ramanujacarya". *Srimatham.com* January 2020. 14 February, 2020. http://www.srimatham.com/uploads/5/5/4/9/5549439/gita_bhashya.pdf

Sutton, Nicholas. *Bhagavad Gita: The Oxford Centre for Hindu Studies Guide.* CreateSpace Independent Publishing Platform, 2017.

Vishwananda, Paramahamsa. *Bhagavad Gita Course.* Unpublished transcriptions, 2016, August 16-23. Bhakti Marga Archive, Springen, Germany.

Vishwananda, Paramahamsa. *Inspiration: Timeless Stories of Divine Love.* Second edition. Springen: Bhakti Marga Publications, 2019.

Vishwananda, Paramahamsa. *Shreemad Bhagavad Gita: The Song of Love.* Fourth edition. Springen: Bhakti Marga Publications, 2019.

Vishwananda, Paramahamsa. *Sri Gopi Gita.* Springen: Bhakti Marga Publications, 2017.

Vishwananda, Paramahamsa. *Sri Hanuman Chalisa.* Springen: Bhakti Marga Publications, 2018.

Vishwananda, Paramahamsa. *The Essence of Shreemad Bhagavatam.* Springen: Bhakti Marga Publications, 2016.

Paramahamsa Vishwananda

THE ESSENCE OF EVERYTHING IS

Just Love